Beyond
Intelligent Design

God's Revelation vs. Man's Reason

– In the spirit of praise –

Mel Mulder, MD

ISBN: 978-1-932205-10-7

Library of Congress Control Number: 2002117031

Unless otherwise stated, all Scripture quotations are from:
The New International Version
Zondervan Bible Publishers
Grand Rapids, MI 49506

For interviews and seminars contact the author:
PO Box 4, Mount Hermon, CA 95041
Voice/Fax: (831) 335-5808
E-mail: muldermel@aol.com
www.muldermel.com

Cover Design by Steve Mobley

Designed and published by

Word Association Publishers
205 Fifth Avenue
Tarentum, Pennsylvania 15084

www.wordassociation.com
1.800.827.7903

DEDICATION

In the beginning was the Word, and the Word was with God, and the Word was God. He was with God in the beginning. Through him all things were made; without him nothing was made that has been made. In him was life, and that life was the light of men. The light shines in the darkness, but the darkness has not understood it (Jn. 1:1-6).

The Prophet Ezekiel saw a throne of sapphire full of fire and glowing like metal – the colors of a rainbow surrounding it. Seated on that throne was the One who had created light, yet he suffered the darkness of the womb and the blackness of the tomb for us sinners! Therefore, the redeemed shall one day sing as in *The Messiah:*

Worthy is the Lamb that was slain and hath redeemed us to God by his blood, to receive power, and riches, and wisdom, and strength, and honor, and glory, and blessing. Blessing and honor, glory and power be unto him that sitteth upon the throne, and unto the Lamb, forever and ever. Amen!

This book is dedicated to that Sovereign Lord – the Creator and Savior of the universe – who alone has the right to the praise of his creatures.

Soli Deo Gloria!

ACKNOWLEDGMENTS

The author is indebted to a new generation of bright, eager Bible-believing physicists, cosmologists, geologists, biologists, taxonomists, paleontologists, and geneticists who are forging creation-based theories to the praise of God's glory!

Equally helpful was the influence of godly parents who saw no conflict between faith and reason. Sharing their views are many who made comments and/or suggestions during the unfolding of this book:

- Physicians and dentists in the U.S. and abroad, most of whom are members of the Christian Medical/Dental Associations
- Pastors, teachers, and fellow-elders in the Christian Reformed and Orthodox Presbyterian Churches
- Friends and acquaintances in the San Francisco Bay Area – six-day creationists versed in science and theology, including the late Herman Dykstra, Ph.D. (geologist, petro-chemical engineer, and Stanford University lecturer), NASA research astrophysicist James Lemen, Ph.D. (Lockheed-Martin Corp., Palo Alto, CA.), biologist Rick Oliver, Ph.D. (Director, Mount Hermon Outdoor Science School), and Charles Watkins, M.D. (Family Practitioner, San Jose, CA.)
- Wilma Mulder (BA, English/literature/teaching), sister-in-law, who reviewed the first draft
- Sylvia Vander Linde (MA, Nursing) who commented regarding technical and Scriptural details
- Sarah Ball (BA, English) who edited the final draft
- Five children and their mates who were supportive, though sometimes muttering, "We love you, but we don't always understand you."

Of particular value was delegation to the Christian Reformed Synodical Advisory Committee on Creation and Science (1991). Though not agreeing with majority opinion, the author was exposed to a range of arguments.

Still more helpful was one who knows her Bible better than most. Qualifying for Faith's Hall of Fame, never did she waver regarding the importance of this work. Had it not been for Marge's encouragement, piety, and grace, this book could not have been written. And speaking of love, when she didn't want me underfoot she would simply ask, "Why don't you go finish it?"

But what better partner could one have than the Creator himself, in whom revelation and reason are joined? "Since the creation of the world, God's invisible qualities – his eternal power and divine nature – have been clearly seen, being understood from what has been made ..." (Ro. 1:20). What a heritage, knowing that truth is not just an intellectual exercise – and that the pen can be used for the King!

CONTENTS

AN OVERVIEW
(Chapter 1)

Anchored in Truth

Imagine being an atheist, getting up every morning and saying to yourself, "There is no God," *when in your heart you know otherwise!* As for me, I have always known that God is sovereign, that he created all things, and that he upholds them for his glory.

Having practiced surgery for most of my life, I have been filled with wonder at biological origins and the human body. Anchored in the Reformation from earliest childhood, I have been interested in *cosmology, biology, ontology* ("being" and the nature of reality), *teleology* (purpose and design), and *epistemology* (the rationale behind knowledge). My fascination with these began with the still, small voice of the Spirit by way of parents whose passion for the Lord stimulated my spiritual and mental metabolism. Like them, God gave me a burden for creation truth, but whether it has remained an interest or become an obsession is for my family to decide. Yet they, and the Spirit, spurred me along in my writing, often when I needed it most.

There are many theories concerning the early universe: some supernatural, others naturalistic, and still others merely erratic. People of science and/or religion do differ, but they have one thing in common: reflecting on the evidences, they have a *prior* faith commitment, biblical or otherwise. When writing books, their biases are evident from dust covers, endorsements, and snippets between, some being home-run hitters and others seldom hitting the ball at all. Those who do hit consistently can still strike out, but one should never disregard them, for there is also the matter of Truth!

People lose their Truth anchor because of a disregard for transcendence. Theistic evolutionists, for instance, minimize God from the outset. No matter their intent, whether because of allegiance to ordinary processes or their desire to harmonize Scripture with science, the end result is always the same: muddled science and mutated theology.

The Signature of God

Throughout history, whenever people have paused to contemplate the marvels of the universe, they have most often been filled with wonder and awe, having sensed their Creator. Psalmists and prophets, overwhelmed with God's Person and Being, have praised his handiwork in words such as these:

- The heavens declare the glory of God; the skies proclaim the work of his hands. Day after day they pour forth speech; night after night they display knowledge. There is no speech or language where their voice is not heard. Their voice goes out into all the earth; their words to the ends of the earth (Ps. 19:1-4).
- Lift your eyes and look to the heavens. Who created all these? He who brings out the starry host one by one, and calls them each by name. Because of his great power and mighty strength, not one of them is missing (Isa. 40:26).
- He gathers the waters of the sea into jars; he puts the deep into storehouses. Let all the people of the world revere him (Ps. 33:7).
- Great is our Lord and mighty in power; his understanding has no limit (Ps. 147:5).
- Do you not know? Have you not heard? […] It is he, God, who sits enthroned above the circle of the earth. He stretches out the heavens like a canopy and spreads them out like a tent to live in (Isa. 40:21-23).
- Surely the nations are like a drop in the bucket; they are regarded as dust on the scales (Isa. 40:15).
- For he views the ends of the earth and sees everything under the heavens (Job 28:24).
- Lord, our Lord, how majestic is your name in all the earth! […] When I consider the heavens, the work of your fingers, the moon and stars which you have set in place, what is man that you are mindful of him (Ps. 8:1-5)?

Some say that science and theology should never be joined. That might be true in the narrow sense, but the Bible spells out origins, so we must stop saying that the two should be separated. Human reasoning can never reach the

Almighty, so we must say with the Psalmist, "Great are the works of the Lord; they are pondered by all who delight in them. Glorious and majestic are his deeds. [...] He has caused his wonders to be remembered. [...] He has shown his people the power of his works" (Ps. 111:2-7).

To anyone who will stop, look, and listen, all Creation is a testimony – a continuing revelation of God's existence, character, and compassion. When viewed in the light of biblical truth, its imagery takes on unforgettable dimensions, pointing to the *signature of God* and his passionate love for humanity. This is why the Apostle Paul wrote in Romans 1:20, "Since the creation of the world, God's invisible qualities – his eternal power and divine nature – have been clearly seen, being understood from what has been made, so that men are without excuse."

To read the universe correctly, suppose you were assembling a barbecue in your backyard, having all the required parts except for one tiny screw. If, while planning your trip to Ace Hardware, it fell onto your patio from an overhead airplane, that would be a coincidence. Suppose now that hundreds of millions of equally incredible happenings started off the universe. *That would be a miracle!*

No matter your view of beginnings, the arguments can be stated in five general categories: 1) cosmic origins, 2) geophysical origins, 3) biological origins, 4) human origins, and 5) societal origins. The question is, do you believe in creation, or in the "evolutionary accident?"

Amongst the Ruins

To this day, an incident from my boyhood remains imprinted in my mind. One summer evening, hearing a distant siren, I raced (on my bike) to what I knew would be an accident scene. By the time I had arrived, however, the drama was over. The ambulance was now a hearse and all that remained at the railroad crossing was a train and a wrecked car. But there was something else that my keen senses detected, an odor I was to encounter frequently over the years caring for trauma victims: alcohol and blood admixed – the stench of death!

As a teenager, I had an ability never described in medical texts. With no effort at all, I could identify every automobile by make, model, and year. Confronted with this scene, however, I could only guess at the wreckage. But suddenly, there was the proof! The maker's nameplate! Chrysler!

Like that Chrysler, our world was once perfectly-crafted. But now the stench of death is everywhere! Searching the rubble, we find only grotesque remains. And there is more bad news still, for we ourselves are fallen, right from Eden. So now, like the drunk at the wheel of that Chrysler, we see our world darkly, as in a fog.

What was this world like before the Fall? Though still grand and elegant, it is no longer a paradise but only a vestige of that once glorious utopia. Today, there are fewer animal species (by far) than were originally created. Thousands are now extinct, and those still in existence are diseased and dying. What a disaster! Yet in John 1:1 we read, "In the beginning was The Word."

The Word is he who spoke all the matter and functionality of the universe into existence. So coherent is Christ's universe, even now, that it can be described in terms of the uniformity of laws and processes. That principle has operated consistently throughout time and space, governing our reliable, predictable, cause and effect universe, as in the orderliness of seasons and the synapses of the brain. Given that, and knowing certain causes, we can predict certain effects. And knowing some effects, we can say something about their causes.

Though affected by the Fall, the uniformity principle is everywhere. It is also consistent with the biblical approach to origins. However, as stated by one who took creation more seriously than most, this is an "open" universe. Said the late Francis Schaeffer, "God is outside the uniformity of natural causes". Nature, then, "is not one big cosmic machine which includes everything; rather, at a point in time the direction may be changed by God".[1] In other words, he can interpose himself anytime and in any place, superseding and countermanding his own laws, as in creation, the curse, and miracles.

As we know from observation, cause and effect produce stability in the universe, being coupled with life and death. Yet it was Christ who brought life to our planet, for "in him was life" (Jn. 1:4). He is the "Author of life" (Ac. 2:15) and there would have been no animate death at all except at Satan's instigation. Because of Satan, "the whole creation has been groaning as in the pains of childbirth even to the present time", frustrated "not by its own choice but by the will of the one who subjected it" (Ro. 8:20-22). Why all this frustration? Because of the curse of sin and the permissive will of God. Yet God remained providential, sustaining everything to this very day. Christ even gave his life "so that by his death he might destroy him who holds the power of death, that is, the devil" (Heb. 2:14) – the one "who comes only to steal and kill and destroy" (Jn. 10:10).

God could have turned his back on this entire catastrophe, but he chose instead to leave his signature, enough of it that we would be without excuse if we missed him in the rubble. As if that were not sufficient, he gave us his very own spectacles (the Word of Truth) so that we can see him as omniscient, omnipresent, omnipotent, and caring (as the Western mind would put it), and as "our Shepherd" (as the Eastern mind would say it).

"Beautiful Books"

Despite its sordid history, our world is filled with beauty: jellyfish with cellophane-like coverings; delicate orchids and rugged redwoods; strutting peacocks and soaring eagles; measureless galaxies, multicolored supernovas, etc. But how should we view their origin, nature, purpose, and destiny? Did all these amazing things evolve randomly, through natural selection? Out of necessity? Did mutational forces act on their own, or could there have been pre-existent intelligence? If so, was there a Designer and would he care about the end-product? Or, is nature its own interpreter? Who or what is authoritative in these matters, *science, theology*, or *some combination* of the two? The answer is this: The God of history who is the God of revelation revealing himself in Creation and the Bible.

As the *Belgic Confession of Faith* (1561 AD) puts it in Article 2, "We know him in two ways: First, by the creation, preservation, and government of the universe, since that universe is before our eyes like a beautiful book in which all creatures, great and small, are as letters to make us ponder the invisible things of God. Second, he makes himself known to us more openly [clearly and fully] by his holy and divine Word – as much as we need in this life for his glory and for the salvation of his own."

That being true, Creation and the Bible have been called "two elegant books". But God's works may seem at times to conflict with his words. How could this be and what can we do about it? Knowing that the two are in perfect harmony from God's perspective, any perceived disharmony is because of our fallen nature and distorted perceptions. Given such an understanding, God's two "books" are not of equal weight. Like the judge's gavel, Special Revelation rules over general revelation, the latter serving only to render the natural mind inexcusable for its suppression of the truth. Thus, we should never consider nature as *the* book of origins; nor may we say that general revelation is mediated through scientific theories alone, since these are often formulated outside the framework of biblical authority.

One who saw this clearly was Michael Faraday (1791-1867) whose crowning work was with electrical conduction. His position was simply this: "Where the scriptures speak, we speak, but where Scripture is silent, we are silent." Accordingly, when the Bible speaks it is the self-authenticating Word of God, for encouragement, instruction, warning, and reproof, which is why the Reformers insisted that Scripture is its own interpreter.

Once having determined the Bible's self-proclaiming message, it takes precedence over any rival claims, binding our minds, our consciences, and our lives – prior to outside influences, authorities, and evidences. Ultimate truth is therefore discernible only within the framework of Scripture no matter what nature might seem to be telling us to the contrary.

There is a caution here as well, however. God's words are higher than ours, so we must read them correctly. We must also approach them circumspectly, confessing that God's revelation is superior to man's reason. To illustrate this, here is a small thought. Picture a cat making its way among glass spicules. Bloody paws? Not at all. Why not? Because of respect and prudence, which is how we should approach the Bible too, recognizing its veracity, perspicuity, and authority.

A Salvation Matter?

Those confusing this may over time slight the Resurrection, bringing doubt to the Cross. Consequently one's view of origins is no less important than the analogy of Scripture, which is what the Reformation was all about.

To see this more clearly, think about the two men on the road to Emmaus. While discussing Christ's death, they were joined by the Savior himself who said, "How foolish you are, and how slow of heart to believe all that the prophets have spoken! Did not the Christ have to suffer these things and then enter his glory? And beginning with Moses and the Prophets, he explained to them what was said in the Scriptures concerning himself" (Lk. 24:25-28). Most probably, he began with Genesis 1:1, telling them about his involvement in creation. He must have spoken also about the enmity of sin (Ge. 3:15) and the Suffering Servant (Isa. 53), linking redemption with creation and the Fall. Given this relatedness, what Christ did in the past makes the future inevitable, a salvation matter indeed!

Thinking about this, I'm reminded of an experience during medical school. My anatomy partner and I were discussing the meaning of life. Said he, "So you think there's a God because it says, 'In God we trust', on this coin? Show me the soul in our cadaver and I'll believe there is one. We'll never know unless we see such a thing, right?" Though nettling me at first, his questions became deeper with time. "Do you really believe in God? And sin? Isn't everything relative anyway?" And how did he view death? Well, he saw it as part of a cycle, as natural as breathing, since spiritual things cannot be demonstrated anatomically.

My friend had rejected both the Sovereign God and his supernatural creation, his having no appreciation for either. Yet these are fundamental doctrines, and interrelated. Redemption, though of premiere importance, does not stand alone, being joined with the formative history of the universe and the fall of man.[2] Accordingly, we read in 1 Corinthians 15:22, "For as in Adam all die, so in Christ will all be made alive." Salvation is thus tied to two realities: Adam's sin and Christ's perfection. These are not isolated compartments of doctrine, or we would have no clue regarding the past, present, or future. Yet, even knowing the "who" and "why" of creation, what about the "how" and "when" of it? To see how these relate to the doctrine of salvation (soteriology), we shall have to consider *God's revelation* vs. *man's reason* (Chap. 14).

Crimson Thread

Christianity is a religion of revelation. God revealed his **hand** in Creation and his **heart** in redemption, but seeing his hand without his heart is to miss the essence of his self-revelation. Michael Horton stresses this in his book, *Putting Amazing Back into Grace*, citing these words by John the Baptist: "Behold! The Lamb of God who takes away the sin of the world" (Jn. 1:29)! "That proclamation", says Horton, "celebrates the most obvious and profound demonstration of God's love and grace, manifested in the sacrifice of Jesus Christ for our offenses." Clearly, then, the Cross is central! But Christ came not only to save sinners (1 Ti. 1:15); he came also to be "the Savior of the World" (Jn. 4:42).[3] We see then that Christ died for the sake of redeemed sinners as well as a reclaimed universe, for Paul wrote, "The creation itself will be liberated from its bondage to decay" (Ro. 8:21).

Speaking of decay, life has its moments. It can be a valley of tears and a constant death. Humans were not meant for these, which is why we live in fear of them, yet Christ suffered them for the restoration of Paradise – for which he was ridiculed and abandoned.

Still, there is a silver lining, for in Christ we are of royal blood. What a wonderful heritage! How could sinners be so privileged? The answer is this: through the gospel of the grace of the Son of God! Thus, there are historical/redemptive purposes in the Bible; not just majestic themes and moral content. Woven throughout the sixty-six books of the Canon there is a crimson thread, making death as irrelevant at the end as it was in the beginning. Christ came to destroy what he hates and reclaim what he loves, so ours is not some vast, uncaring universe but one surprisingly supportive of redemptive purposes. Missing that, everything else is pointless!

Wisdom, Clothed in Splendor

The Bible opens with a powerful declarative sentence within the comprehension of a six year old: "In the beginning God created the heavens and the earth." These are some of the most important words in the Bible, the initial lens for the remainder of Scripture (which is why many have raged over them), so we must handle them carefully (2 Ti. 2:15), employing both faith and reason.

Faith and reason are complimentary, but they sometimes clash. When that happens, truth suffers. Regrettably, those relinquishing it are often they who had believing faith to begin with, not those rejecting it from the outset. Not only is their capitulation needless, it is irrational, abandoning as it does the *Sola Scriptura* and *Sola Fide* of the Reformation.

Once we're serious about creation, God instructs us through his Spirit and Word. But doubts can still be thrown at us from every direction. Had I believed the whisperings of Satan that only the "elite" should be addressing origins, I might have been dissuaded from writing anything at all given the volumes already available on the subject. However, such misgivings are easily silenced by Moses, the Prophets, and the Gospels. To Paul God said, "My grace is sufficient for you, for my power is made perfect in weakness." Paul responded, "I will boast all the more gladly about my weaknesses, so that Christ's power may rest on me" (2 Co. 12:9). Such confidence as this is ours through Christ; not that we are competent in ourselves, but our competence comes from God (2 Co. 3:5).

You probably know that it takes faith to believe in creation. Belief in evolution requires faith too, but even more so as it turns out. We must take the texts as they present themselves in Scripture. Having the Bible as our competency, we come to it believing, though we can approach it intellectually too, presupposing a degree of interpretation. Some texts are straightforward while others require study, the problem being that even careful cross-referencing may leave us wondering, whether because of God's incomprehensibility or our human inadequacy. Even so, amateur and professional exegetes alike can see that God exists and that he cannot contradict himself in anything he says or does. But to what extent can we rely on his words? Or, on those of others?

Jesus said, "By your words you will be acquitted and by your words you will be condemned" (Mt. 12:37). To this could be added the old maxim, "Give a man enough rope and he will hang himself," ringing as true for publications like *Nature, Science,* and *National Geographic* as it does for the various theological treatises. The gurus of this world can be convincing, albeit self-condemning as well. Always seeking but seldom finding Truth, they end up contradicting themselves and each other, as in the conflicting views of astrophysicists, geologists, paleontologists, etc. And the greater their dissonance the less their credibility.

Why all this noise? Because, out of the depth of depravity and the enormity of the human predicament, people are conjuring up guesses about bygone epochs, though having only fragmentary evidences, blind eyes, and opaque spectacles. From their isolated domains they then insist on their views. But why care? Because truth is at stake, plus the validity of science and theology. And when science and theology collide, one thing is certain: they cannot both be right. The time has come then for a fresh look at the original model of *six-day creation.* For those of a different view, it needs to be supported with Scripture since scientists err and so do theologians.

Many will accept 80-90% of the Bible, but the question is this: Why not all of it? Even believing it fully, what parts of it are to be interpreted literally and how much should be taken symbolically or spiritually? Are the words to be read as poetry, symbolism, or straightforward narration? What are the rules and how should we apply them?

Theological presuppositions are necessary in our interpretation of the universe, but sometimes they get in the way. Reading correctly is crucial, for much is at stake in mishandling the text, whether veering too far toward literalism or too far toward symbolism. Both can be avoided by letting the Bible speak for itself, but that is not always easy.

Most will agree that the early writers employed figures of speech, metaphors, symbols, and even hyperbole, more often than we Westerners do. Accordlingly, we must decide whether the text demands a literal or a non-literal approach – recognizing that even non-literal language can be helpful in determining the truth. Interpretive difficulties aside, however, we must be faithful to the text, speaking to what is there and being silent when it isn't. Then too, our questions will not always be answered, needing frequently to be addressed by the Creator himself.

Why some end-run, circumventing the rules and the truth? Macro-evolution, if we use that term, doesn't seem to be happening in any meaningful way. Science doesn't support it and neither does Scripture, given the contrast between evolution and devolution, between chance and design, between randomness and purpose. Granting these differences, evolutionary ascendancy is laughable, but that is not how it plays out in the court of opinion – or even in some churches and schools. Instead, there is the mindset, "If you must express yourself, emphasize nature, not the Creator. Besides, where is your tolerance?" Given this approach, is it any wonder that so few colleges and universities have any interest in creation research? Try offering a donation for setting up such a department. Would you expect wisdom clothed in splendor, as in Scripture, or a hedged response?

Speaking the Truth in Love

Writing about origins would be a cakewalk if it weren't for the pervasive undermining of Truth by those never having accepted it. Why are some so unwilling to consider God's sovereignty? Could it be that they despise authority, even when God's hand is upon them? Speaking benevolently of such people is as difficult as countering their ideologies, and yet we must do both – for God is so big that he instructs all who come to him believing. Even among Christians there can be differences of opinion, so we must always argue for the truth, proclaiming it with conviction, which was Paul's approach when confronting the Athenians, his having both the *capacity* and the *audacity* to do so.

With that in mind, speaking the truth in love (understandably, convincingly, and winsomely) is the burden of this book. Even if some will not listen, one should not be intimidated by them, for they have generated a world of confusion. Though not singling them out as individuals, we must analyze their ideas. The question is, "Who was the "eyewitness" as the cosmos took shape during its earliest micro-seconds?" The answer is this: "the Author of history" whose work of creation was so unlike today's occurrences that it can only be called "supernatural". Given that understanding, the term "origins" is closely related to "ultimate origins", which is how it will be used in these pages.[4]

Nobody has all the answers, but Christians should at least know the basis for their assertions, scientific and/or religious. Does this suggest a literal view of beginnings? A young universe and a global flood? What would be the rationale for such a view? Obviously, it would have to come from God's Word, where we read that creation occurred during "six days", after which everything was declared "very good". Stretching these days into eons is impossible, for we are told in the genealogies that human history began rather recently. It appears, also, that no death of *nephesh* (breathing) animals occurred before the Fall. When God reacted to sin, he destroyed the world with a flood covering all the high mountains (Ge. 7:19). Should it come as any surprise, then, that the physical evidences are pointing in this direction as well?

Science is not the final answer, but properly conducted it fits the verbatim rendering of creation. This requires faith, but it is amply supported by the evidences. As most people know, during the past century there have been more scientific discoveries than in all previous centuries combined. Science now reaches into outer space, having identified also the subatomic particles, so the universe is more vast, more complex, and more intelligible than had ever been imagined. With today's thrilling flow of information, we're beginning to see the enormity of creation, which should make us all the more appreciative of our Creator. As for those harboring alternative views, we're on different paths, perhaps headed for different countries, but we should still respect each other as persons. Failing to do so we are but "sounding brass" and "clanging cymbals" (1 Co. 13:1). Truth without love, after all, is no better than love without truth.

Beyond Intelligent Design

Speaking of truth, during recent decades we have experienced an amazing revolution: the ideological demise of Marx, Freud, and Darwin, exceeded in importance only by the crucifixion of Christ. Not only has Darwin fallen, but so have the fallacies of Sagan, Dawkins, Eldredge, and Gould. Why this collapse? Partly because of the ***design arguments*** of Denton, Johnson, Wells, Dembski, Behe, Nelson, and an army of creationists. Pitting science against pseudo-science, they are dismantling naturalism, discrediting the "willfully ignorant".

Building on the best of what science has to offer, "intelligent design" is just too big to miss. Design, however, is not new. It has been with us since Paradise. What is new about it today is the increasing evidence of design as the result of ***creation*** rather than ***evolution.*** Caught in an intellectual upheaval, evolutionists are bewildered as to how to respond. More bewildering still, *theistic evolutionists* are clinging to their compromises. Though having fresh opportunities to uproot naturalism, they are strangely silent, seemingly covering their tracks and looking for exits. However, while design arguments are helpful in combating naturalism, they are neither complete nor robust, since those committed to them are not necessarily committed to Genesis, or even the Creator.

Still, what could be bigger than intelligence and design? The answer is, the God who originated them in the first place. Omitting him who transcends every imagination of the mind is inexcusable, which is the great deficiency of "ID theory." The truth is, factors beyond our reach must be re-introduced into the debate, and we must tell the whole story, reaching *beyond* intelligence and design – important though these are. The right approach is ***biblical creation***. Embracing it, we have an unusual opening for original perfection, seeing that design theory has turned the tables on myths.

In our advocacy of the biblical model, we Christians should include those in today's bastions of scholarship. What a pity to be apathetic at a time when scientists are relinquishing their evolutionary dreams, surrendering the argument when it has fallen into our laps! Also, since today's opportunity may be fleeting, we need a broader discussion immediately. Failing this, naturalism, though brain-dead, will be resurrected. Should that happen, what will replace the Berlin Wall, Freudian psychoanalysis, and *"The Origin of Species"* (by Darwin)? Will it be mysticism and materialism, or the full counsel of God? It all depends on the testimony of Christians!

Cultural Mandate

God will never be fully intelligible, but we must still reckon with him, for despite our blunted perceptions "he is there and he is not silent".[5] We humans are stewards with broad authority to carry out God's will, but this is always a struggle, since the prince of this world is stronger than we. Only through the Spirit can we fulfill such a mandate, using every gift (profound or mundane), and even then we have the problem of Creation ruling over us rather than our ruling over it.

The world is not spinning uncontrollably in space, however. It is behaving according to a divine blueprint, and it will continue in existence until Christ reclaims it. Once that happens, God's strategy will be clear, including everything related to origins. That day is marked on his calendar, and is drawing nearer every hour, yet the sobering thought is this: It is a fearful thing to fall into the hand of God. Why? Because God is a consuming fire – and the soul persists into the future.

As for the future, overpopulation, the greenhouse effect, black-holes, terrorists' attacks, nuclear annihilation – none of these will be our end. Armageddon will finish this world, but Christ will come to the rescue, ushering in the new, not with a cosmic whisper but with a loud trumpet, through the power of God's word! Accordingly, we should not be too end-oriented or too beginnings oriented, but we should be process oriented, remembering that the Alpha and Omega is in control of everything from beginning to end. Jesus himself said, "Surely I am with you always, to the very end of the age" (Mt. 28:20).

Since only *strangers* in this world will be among the redeemed, how impoverished are we when we pursue fading pleasures! Life is much more than that. We are not brutish creatures, tethered to the ages and the apes. We were created for fellowship and service, hungering and thirsting for him who made us *in* love *to* love. Human life is holy, and those in Christ can have hope and joy while illuminating and flavoring this dark and tasteless world. As recipients of grandeur, we were made for worship, as in the **Soli Deo Gloria** of the Reformation. "Oh, the depth of the riches of the wisdom and knowledge of God! How unsearchable are his judgments and his paths beyond tracing out! Who has known the mind of the Lord? Or who has been his counselor? […] For from him and through him and to him are all things" (Ro. 11:33-36).

Opus Dei

Creation was the Opus Dei (the work of God), and he got it right the first time! From eternity past there was a relationship of love among the three persons in the Trinity, spilling over into creation. The Father was the Originator (who spoke); the Son was the Agent (who molded the clay); the Spirit was the Facilitator (brooding over the waters). Given the God-head's passion for humanity, we should praise our Creator, noting also the excellence with which he clothed himself. Who but God could have generated this complexity and beauty? Beginning with color and light, creation was an outburst of God's genius, yet he wanted us to know more than *about* him; he wanted us to know *him*. More than anything else, he wanted us to be his people, in his place, under his rule, honoring his Being, his Person, and his Lordship.

One way of doing that is by studying creation, though it does call out for greater detail. The subject is broad and ever-changing, so writing about it can be a challenge. Considering also the textual and technical material at hand, if you are looking for an easy read, be forewarned. While one test of wisdom is the ability to put complex concepts into simple words, some of the discussions in these chapters may need to percolate awhile.

Another Book on Origins?

Why another book on "origins"? Because the battle for the soul is being waged on the fields of doctrine. In **Christian education** and **ministry**, therefore, people should be tools fit for the Master's use, being careful about accepting claims not found in the Bible.

This is not a book on religion, but it deals with theology, since truth is worth defending. Though not a book on science either, the geophysical evidences will be examined as well. The main objective, however, is neither theology nor science, but **apologetics**, presenting the words and wisdom of him who made heaven and earth in his own way, in his own timing, and for his own purposes. Accepting or rejecting him is critical, now and forever, so my hope is that these pages will tug at the heart, connecting with humble and sophisticated readers alike, both within and outside the community of believers, to the praise of God's glory.

Should you discover some saltiness in this book, it is because 1) many have either rejected or ignored biblical truth, and 2) some who once stood for it no longer do. James, the brother of Jesus, said, "Everyone should be quick to listen, slow to speak, and slow to become angry" (Jas. 1:19). But if salt loses its savor, of what good is it except to be thrown out (Mt. 5:13)?

The bottom line is that we can't defend creation by denying God's Word! Already in Eden there were two different worlds, the seed of the woman and the seed of the Serpent. From Eve came the Savior; from the Serpent came the frustration of Paradise. The difference is like day and night. The question is, which side are you on and to which are you committed?

While it might be a misperception to think that hardened hearts would be redirected by mere words, Springs of Living Water can soften them, convincing even the severely calcified of the truth. That is my hope for this book, for then it will ascribe to God the glory due his name (Ps. 96:8). But, first, may I ask that you look beyond this earthen vessel, focusing instead on the all-surpassing power of God (2 Co. 4:7-11)?

All things bright and beautiful, all creatures great and small,
all things wise and wonderful, the Lord God made them all.
He gave us eyes to see them all, and lips that we might tell
how great is the Almighty God, who has made all things well.

(Cecil Francis Alexander, 1818-1895)

---

[1] Francis Schaeffer, *How Should we then Live?*, F. H. Revell Co., 1976, p. 142,

[2] Regarding another view of "formative history", see Howard J. Van Till/Davis A. Young/Clarence Menninga, Science Held Hostage, Calvin Center for Christian Scholarship, InterVarsity Press, 1988, pp. 17-18.

[3] Michael Horton, *Putting Amazing Back into Grace*, Thomas Nelson Publishers, 1991, Chap. 7.

[4] The term "origins" has a number of meanings, as Dr. Van Till has pointed out.

[5] Francis Schaeffer, *He is there and he is not Silent*, Tyndale House Publishers, 1972.

WHO IS HE?
(Chapter 2)

Standing before the King

The American College of Surgeons was in session for its annual cancer symposium. Awaiting the arrival of a guest, seeing security guards positioned, I said to myself, "the diligent shall stand before kings", knowing full-well that my wife was more diligent than I, at home with our five children. I thought too about the occasion when our family had swum in the pool of a deceased king. But swimming in a dead king's pool seemed trivial compared with standing before the President of the United States, a king of sorts to me. Moments later, seeing him in person, I rose instinctively. But there were those who refused to stand. Realizing that they loathed our President, I was nevertheless astonished at their frosty reception having been taught from early on to be in subjection to rulers and authorities (Tit. 3:1).

What if this had been the Sovereign Lord, instead? Malachi wrote, "Suddenly the Lord you are seeking will come; but who can endure the day of his coming? Who will stand when he appears? For he will be like a refiner's fire" (Mal. 3:1-3). Imagine that! There is coming a time when there will be no standing at all! All who ever lived will fall down "worshiping the Creator" (Ro. 1:24). "Every knee will bow" and "all who raged against him will be put to shame" (Isa. 45:23-25). No denying creation and the Creator! Everything and everyone will be exposed, including those removing God from their equations.

Anyone Out There?

Ancient Job was asked, "Can you fathom the mysteries of God? Can you probe the limits of the Almighty" (Job 11:7)? Job faced the same question haunting all humanity: "Can you envision God, not just in theory but as he truly is?" Confronted by this, some have claimed that the universe (with its random combinations of mindless matter) is on auto-pilot. Why do they say this? Because their god is either nonexistent or very small, and all that matters to them is the material universe.

Christ said, "Whoever believes in me [...] streams of living water will flow from within him" (Jn. 7:38). Isn't this an indication that there is a God? The truth is, we come believing or we don't come at all! And only God can draw us, for he is the great initiator. His wisdom is very different from the world's, which is "foolishness in God's sight" (1 Co. 3:18-20). As Solomon put it, "The fear of the Lord is the beginning of knowledge, but fools despise wisdom" (Pr. 1:7). However, faith in God is not "believing what you know isn't true", as a child once said. It is based on the trustworthiness of Scripture, believing him who *spoke* it simply because he spoke it, and it is whispered into hearts by a voice pre-determining one's direction.

Searching for God on our own we will never find him, since we can't even imagine him. The evidences for him are convincing, but "anyone who comes to him must first believe that he exists and that he rewards those who earnestly seek him" (Heb. 11:6). Belief in God is therefore a matter of trust – i.e., "the evidence of things not seen" (Heb. 11:1). How else could we find him who is so far beyond us except by his revealing himself to trusting people? The clincher is this: In over two thousand years, not one of God's statements has been invalidated, not by any expert and not in any field!

"The path of the righteous is like the first gleam of dawn, shining brighter till the full light of day. But the way of the wicked is like deep darkness; they do not know what makes them stumble" (Pr. 4:18-20). And stumble they do, even the most scholarly. So darkening is Satan's influence that they might as well be hiding in a cave! With God's intelligence, however, wonderful things can happen. With wisdom in our hearts, truth can shine into our minds, convincing us that God exists. Not only can we know that he is *out there*, we can know that he is in us. In fact, he's everywhere!

Rock of Ages

God said to his servant Job, "Brace yourself like a man. I will question you and you shall answer me. Where were you when I laid the earth's foundation? Tell me, if you understand, who marked off its dimensions? Surely you know! Who stretched a measuring line across it? On what were its footings set, or who laid its cornerstone while the morning stars sang together and all the angels shouted for joy" (Job 38:3-8)?

Reflecting on this while observing scientists dating fossils at Grand Canyon, Mount St. Helens, Dinosaur National Monument, etc., I wondered what they might say, were I to tell them, "There is only one rock worth considering and without it your assumptions will always be wrong." Imagine their laughter! Moses, however, said, "Oh, praise the greatness of our God! He is the Rock; his works are perfect" (Dt. 32:3-4). As Peter wrote centuries later, "To us who believe, this stone is precious, but to those who do not believe, the stone the builders rejected has become a stone that causes them to stumble – a rock that makes them fall" (1 Pe. 2:4-8).

Notice again that word, "stumble"! People trip over this Rock. Paul must have had that in mind, too, when he said to Timothy, "Guard what has been entrusted to your care. Turn away from godless chatter and the opposing ideas of what is falsely called knowledge" (1 Ti. 6:20). So essential is that Rock that if we ignore him "even the stones will cry out" (Lk. 19:40) – for, unlike fossil-bearing rocks, the Rock of Ages is the "living stone".

Who is God?

Knowing that this Rock exists is one thing, but knowing him is quite another. The best descriptors are in terms of his attributes, which are of two types: 1) *incommunicable*, those belonging to God alone, and 2) *communicable*, those shared with us humans, though only partially. Here are some specifics (italics from Scripture):[1]

God is personal. He is not a thing, power, or influence. He thinks, feels, desires, and acts in ways that show him to be a living personal Being.

God is one. He says, *I am the first and the last; apart from me there is no God.* Yet God has revealed himself in a "trinity" of three Persons – the Father, Son, and Holy Spirit, each of whom is truly, fully, and equally God.

God is Spirit. He does not have a body, nor does he have any characteristics that can be defined in terms of size and shape. *"Do I not fill heaven and earth?" declares the Lord.*

God is eternal. There never was a time when he did not exist and there never will be a time when he will not exist. God describes himself as the one *who is, and who was, and who is to come.*

God is independent. Every other living being is dependent on people or things, and ultimately on God, but God is totally independent of his Creation. *He is not served by human hands, as if he needed anything.*

God is holy: The Bible says of him, *your eyes are too pure to look on evil; you cannot tolerate wrong.* And this holy God demands holiness from every one of us. His command to us today is, *Be holy, because I am holy.*

God is just. The Bible says that *the Lord is a God of justice and that righteousness and justice are the foundation of his throne.* He is also our judge, rewarding and punishing people in time and eternity with a justice that is perfect.

God is perfect: *Nothing in all creation is hidden from God's sight.* He knows everything past, present, and future including all our thoughts, words, and deeds. His wisdom is perfect and utterly beyond understanding.

God is sovereign. He is the sole and supreme ruler of the universe and nothing is outside his control. He writes all the world's history and *works out everything in conformity with the purpose of his will.*

God is omnipotent. He is all-powerful. As he said, *I am the Lord, the God of all mankind. Is anything too hard for me?*

The Westminster Confession (Ch. 2) puts it in these terms: "There is but one living and true God who is infinite in being and perfection, a most pure spirit, invisible, without body, immutable, immense, eternal, incomprehensible, almighty, holy, free, absolute, working all things according to his own righteous will for his own glory, loving, gracious, merciful, long-suffering, abundant in goodness and truth, forgiving; the rewarder of those who diligently seek him. God alone is all-sufficient, not in need of any creatures, not deriving any glory from them; only showing his own glory in, by, to, and upon them: he alone is the fountain of all beings and is sovereign over them; his knowledge is infinite, infallible, and independent of creatures. Nothing is uncertain to him. He is holy in all his counsels, works, and commands."

There is another side to God, however, for in Isaiah 34:8 we read, "The Lord has a day of vengeance, a year of retribution", as demonstrated at Babel, Sodom, and Gomorrah. Said he, "I, the Lord your God, am a jealous God" (Ex. 20:5), as displayed during Noah's days. This was also apparent in Christ's cleansing of the temple. We see then that God has a temper, though not like ours. And, like it or not, his anger has a purpose. When he flares up it is because of his justice, as well as to draw us to him.

Once, however, there was only God. No heaven, no angels, no universe, no creatures – only God. Not for a day, not for a year, not for an age, but from everlasting. As stated by Arthur Pink, "God was alone; self-contained, self-sufficient, self-satisfied; in need of nothing. He was under no constraint, no obligation, no necessity to create. That he chose to do so was a sovereign act on his part, caused by nothing outside himself, determined by nothing but his own good pleasure; for he 'works all things after the counsel of his own will' (Eph. 1:11)."[2] Had God so desired, he might have continued alone for all eternity, content within himself, showing his glory to no one. So there is a solitude to God, and it transcends the imagination. Once we understand this, "the argument from design, well meaning as it is, is limiting because it attempts to bring down the great God to the level of finite comprehension, and thereby has lost sight of his solitary excellence".[3] Who, for that matter, would *fear* such a god?

Not only did God create intelligently, he is supreme over everything he made, including demons. We know this from Christ's temptation in the wilderness. Three times he said to Satan, "It is written." No arguing the evidences! No mention of fossils or Neanderthals! No hint of human vs. divine authorship for Scripture! No reference to "poetic illustrations" or "teaching tools"! No suggestion that Genesis 1-11 might be something other than genuine history! Only, "it is written", as Jesus later reaffirmed it, claiming that the resurrection was "according to the Scriptures". What authority, and all on the strength of God's Word!

Who are We?

At home in the Santa Cruz mountains I have a detached study, my "Recovery Room". In this surrealistic setting, surrounded by redwoods, I'm filled with adoration. Here I am in harmony with my Maker, for unlike any animal I have a Spirit, rendering me capable of passion and praise. Did I acquire these traits from hopeful monsters? Not in a million years!

The truth is I was "fearfully and wonderfully made" (Ps. 139:14), for "the Lord God formed man from the dust of the ground and breathed into his nostrils the breath of life, and man became a living being" (Gen. 2:7). I am, therefore, "more than an accidental accumulation of atoms which all happen to fit together into a convenient package called 'a human being' – more than a highly developed animal or a refined ape [...] as different from other creatures as animals are from vegetables and vegetables are from minerals."[4] But I'm also different from Adam and Eve.

Our first parents were made for Paradise. Spiritual, rational, moral, and immortal beings, they reflected God's image perfectly. Obeying him gladly, they were pleased with God, and he was satisfied with them. "At that point in history, perfect people lived in a perfect environment, in a perfect relationship with each other, and in perfect harmony with God."[5] But that isn't true today. Though surrounded by spectacular scenery, people are dying in this world, myself included.

What went wrong? "Sin entered the world through one man, and death through sin" (Ro. 5:12). Though having freedom, Adam and Eve had been warned, "You must not eat from the tree of the knowledge of good and evil, for when you eat of it you will surely die" (Ge. 2:17). This was a test of man's willingness to obey simply because God required it, but Adam and Eve failed the test. "When the woman saw that the fruit of the tree was good for food and pleasing to the eye, and also desirable for gaining wisdom, she took some and ate it. She also gave some to her husband, who was with her, and he ate it" (Ge. 3:6). At that moment, sin entered the world, and defilement with it.

Adam and Eve separated themselves from God because of their disobedience. Rather than warming up to God, they were terrified. Instead of being confident and happy, they were ashamed and morose (Ge. 3:8). In one terrible moment they had cut themselves off from God, and they died spiritually. They began to die physically too, having dead souls and dying bodies – distorting their nature and that of their children. From then on, like pollution at the source of a river, sin's poison contaminated all of Adam's descendants. "In this way, death came to all men, because all sinned" (Ro. 5:12). *The Heidelberg Catechism* (LD 3) expresses it as follows:

> **Did God create man so wicked and perverse?** No, God created man good and in his own image (in true righteousness and holiness) so that he might truly know God his Creator, love him with all his heart, and live with him in eternal happiness for his praise and glory.

> **Then where does man's corrupt nature come from?** From the fall and disobedience of our first parents, Adam and Eve, in Paradise. This fall has so poisoned our nature that we are born sinners – corrupt from conception on.

> **But are we so corrupt that we are totally unable to do any good and inclined toward all evil?** Yes, unless we are born again of the Spirit of God.

Who are we, then? Creatures of clay, dead to everything spiritual. For "man without the Spirit does not accept the things that come from God; they are foolishness to him and he cannot understand them" (1 Cor. 2:14). Having "lost all our excellent gifts and retained none of them except for small traces," *The Belgic Confession* (Art. 14) says, "We are no longer able to think a single thought, except our ability is from God." Yet God calls us "saints", "joint heirs", "friends", and "co-workers", and he went even further than that, allowing us to see his *Person* in Creation, the Fall, and the Cross, for which reason we should be stunned and silenced creatures!

Heart of the Matter

The psalmist wrote, "The Lord reigns, let the nations tremble; he sits enthroned between the cherubim, let the earth shake. Great is the Lord in Zion; he is exalted over all the nations. Let them praise your great and awesome name, for he is holy" (Ps. 99:1-3). Given such transcendence, words cannot express God's exclusivity. People may see it dimly, but they will never understand it by seeing nature and God as one, joining God with the sun, the trees, the rocks, and even cows, rats, and crystals. Such a "lesser god" is not the God of the Bible, for rather than being *in* nature the Sovereign Lord is *above* what he created.

We see then that God's *Being* is not determined by reasoning alone, or by intellectual superiority. The truth is, his reality is self-proclaimed in Creation and the Word. But only through faith can we visualize this. Why the physical evidences then? So that the Sovereign Lord (the Creator and sustainer of the universe) will be plainly-seen in nature, making his Person and Being unmistakable.

Yet, no matter how much God showed of himself in the world, he has more in store for us in his Word – and God's Word is never contrary to his works! Nor could he deny his perfection in creation. Even Satan will admit this, knowing both *that* God is and *who* God is.

So where is God most clearly evident? In his Son, Jesus Christ! Knowing him, wouldn't you want to sing his praises? And that is what the redeemed will do throughout eternity, as in these words:

Holy, holy, holy! Lord God Almighty!
All Thy works shall praise Thy name in earth and sky and sea;
Holy, holy, holy! Merciful and mighty!
God in three Persons, blessed Trinity!

Holy, holy, holy! though the darkness hide Thee,
Though the eye of sinful man Thy glory may not see;
Only Thou art holy – there is none beside Thee,
Perfect in pow'r, in love and purity.

Reginald Heber (1783-1826)

---

[1] Excepted from John Blanchard's devotional, *Ultimate Questions*, Evangelical Press, Darlington, Co.Durham, England, 1997, pp. 1-11.
[2] Arthur W. Pink, *The Attributes of God*, Baker Book House, Grand Rapids, MI, 1998, pp. 10 & 11.
[3] Ibid, p. 12
[4] John Blanchard, *Ultimate Questions*, Evangelical Press, Darlingon, Co.Durham, England, 1997, p. 12
[5] Ibid, p. 13

THE BIG BANG AND THE PAST

BIG BANG	GENESIS 1
1. Light, light elements	Earth and water (Day 1)
2. Stars	Light
3. Heavy elements, water	Firmament, oceans (Day 2)
4. Sun, moon, earth	Dry land (Day 3)
5. Dry land	Vegetation
6. Oceans	Sun, moon, stars (Day 4)
7. Marine life	Marine life (Day 5)
8. Vegetation	Birds
9. Animals (reptiles)	Animals (Day 6)
10. Birds	Man
11. Animals (mammals)	Woman
12. Fruit trees, grasses	
13. Sub-humans and man	

(Adapted from *God and Cosmos*, John Byle, The Banner of Truth Trust, 2001, p. 183)

GLUON AND EONS
(Chapter 3)

Early Stirrings and an Eerie End

My life's calling was inspired by two things, poliomyelitis and chemistry. When illness threatened my earthly substance (while in high school), I felt a tug toward medicine. But the intellectual hook was exposure to atoms and molecules.

Prior to the linear accelerator, the smallest particles of matter were supposedly protons, neutrons, and electrons, forming the atoms for every element in the periodic table. However, when particle physicists collided protons (at high speeds) with other protons and electrons, they discovered subatomic particles. They then divided these into two groups, leptons and hadrons. The best known lepton, or "light" particle, is the electron. To account for the emission of electrons from nuclei, neutrinos (essentially massless and neutral particles) were postulated. Muons and taus, both more massive than electrons, comprise the rest of the lepton family.

Hadrons are divided into two groups, mesons and baryons, each consisting of smaller particles, called quarks. Quarks were named by Cal Tech physicist Murray Gell-Mann, who won the Nobel prize for his work in 1969. A number of varieties (flavors) of them exist, held together by a strong nuclear force, "gluon". There are in fact six different quarks: up, down, charmed, strange, top, and bottom. Each comes in three different colors: red, blue, and green (having nothing to do with appearance). Baryons are composed of three quarks; mesons of a quark and an antiquark.

According to the *uncertainty principle*, one could measure the position and motion of sub-particles, but not both simultaneously. Behaving as waves with electrical energies, these may or may not be *the* elementary particles from which everything was fashioned since they themselves may consist of smaller particles. True or not, "we may be at or near those basic particles", says Hawking. Putting it whimsically, God must have had fun designing these things, though explaining them can be difficult!

Whether discussing initial stirrings or some bizarre end, scientists view the universe in terms of two partial theories, *relativity* and *quantum mechanics.* Relativity describes the forces and effects of gravity acting on the large-scale universe – from a few miles to billions of miles distant. Quantum mechanics deals with phenomena and particles on extremely small scales, such as a millionth of a millionth of an inch.[1]

In both cases, cosmologists are studying time, space, and matter, or some combination of them (like space-time), hoping to explain their origin. According to Hawking, these are the greatest intellectual achievements of the first half of the twentieth century, but they are inconsistent with each other. Hawking says they cannot both be right, so one of the main endeavors in physics today is the search for a new "Grand/Unified Theory" that will incorporate them both.[2]

All over the world people are asking, "Did the universe have a beginning?" If so, what started it off? Is it limitless, or does it have boundaries? What is its purpose and how will it end? Wheelchair-bound by Lou Gehrig's disease, Hawking tried to answer these questions in his *A Brief History of Time* (recently revised), surveying the broad sweep of history from the Big Bang to black holes. In the forward to that book, reflecting on Hawking, the late Carl Sagan (Cornell astronomer and Pulitzer Prize winning co-author of the *Cosmos* television series) commented, "Hawking embarks on a quest to answer Einstein's famous question about whether God had any choice in creating the universe, as he explicitly states, to understand the mind of God. This makes all the more unexpected the conclusion of the effort – a universe with no edge in space, no beginning or end in time, and nothing for a Creator to do."

Equally oblivious to the Creator/God, referring to space-time's rippled fabric ending one-hundred-thousandth of a second after the universe began expanding, best-selling writer John Gribbin claims, "It produced so much matter in the universe that the gravity of everything it contains is strong enough to one day halt and reverse the cosmic expansion into a cosmic collapse; the space between galaxies will shrink [...] and everything will be compressed back into a super-dense fireball; a mirror-image of the Big Bang."[3]

Says Gribbin, our universe is located somewhere within a black hole. However, "black holes do not necessarily represent a one-way journey to nowhere. [...] A black hole can be a one-way journey to somewhere – to a new expanding universe in its own set of dimensions. Instead of a black hole singularity [the point where the laws of physics break down completely] 'bouncing' to become an exploding outpouring of energy, blasting back into our universe, it is shunted sideways in space-time. The dramatic implication is that many – perhaps all – of the black holes that form in our universe may be the seeds of new universes. And of course our own universe may have been born in this way out of a black hole in another universe."[4]

What could be the meaning of such an ill-fated universe? Nothing really! Just nature and its ordinary laws and processes. This is far from the truth, however, for the purpose of creation is God's praise and glory! Disallowing these, why not just forget about the equations?

Naturalistic Chronology of Origins

Using sophisticated mathematical tools, theoretical physicists suggest that the universe began fifteen to twenty billion years ago. Before that, say they, there was nothing but a tiny lump of matter, no larger than a walnut and perhaps much smaller. Yet within that nugget was the potential for every molecule of the universe – producing stars, planets, earth, sea, animals, people, and even the far-flung galaxies. Its particles are believed to have reacted, collided, and expanded, creating great celestial clusters, the solar system, and Planet Earth. Incidentally, time did not exist before the cosmic egg; nor did space.

As for the origin of life, many see it beginning in primeval oceans. Oceanic compounds became a rich pre-biotic soup by means of tide-pooling and electrical discharges. Amino acids were then synthesized into proteins, the building blocks for life. Next came DNA, the doubly-helical molecule (on the cover of this book) serving as the nucleotide in chromosomes – providing instructions for the development of single-celled organisms which later became multi-celled. Cold-blooded animals became warm-blooded, invertebrates became vertebrates, and higher animals became rational, moral, and perhaps even spiritual. In this scenario, man (the ultimate beast) is at the pinnacle of the evolutionary pyramid, and there is every hope for further progress, even for humans.

What about the fossils? Paleontologists point to vast geologic strata deposited by local flooding, erosion, silting, and glaciation. Using isotopic chronometers, they postulate lower life forms in the older/deeper strata and higher forms in the younger/superficial strata. Coupling these "findings" with the "evolving features" of fish, birds, and land animals, evolutionists are offering their theories as "fact" in written volumes, television documentaries, video series, etc.

One such presentation, *"A Brief Summary of Current Scientific Views of Origins"*, was appended to a special report to the 1991 Synod of the Christian Reformed Church in North America.[5] Written by that Synod's Committee on Creation and Science, this report and its addendum arose because of conflicts between scientific views and what had been understood (traditionally) as the biblical view of origins. Though dated, this report is still useful as a springboard for discussion, keeping in mind that the Appendix was added for completeness, "attributing no particular validity or adequacy to the expressed views".

Quoting from the report, "Key to the scientific approach to origins is the concept that the underlying physical laws of our universe are the same everywhere and *have not changed over time* [an assumption, of course]. If what is known now about some process is correct, then from this knowledge one can deduce something about what happened in the past and make reasonable predictions about the future." Said the authors, "The existence of these underlying physical laws may be seen as evidence for design of the highest order and subtlety in the structure of the universe at its most fundamental level, the natural inference being that design of such brilliance and profundity requires a Master Designer." In other words, mathematics appears to be the language of the Creator!

According to the Appendix, the universe seems to be constantly changing and has a history which has been going on for a very long time [another assumption]. To describe it, we must use numbers on the order of millions and billions of years. Even simple chronologies of key events would fill a very large library. For convenience and simplification, therefore, whatever may have happened in the various evolutionary epochs is listed with an approximation of the presumed chronological times in history. When something "appears", it is because the historical record indicates that it was present at that time, not before. Here then is that chronology from the report's Appendix:

20 to 10 Billion years ago: Our entire universe was concentrated in a very small volume and it would be generally described as very hot and very dense. The conditions were so extreme that ordinary matter as we know it did not then exist, and space and time were, at least initially, strongly distorted. "Quantum fields" were in very "highly excited states" at this time. Such an initially hot and compressed universe might be expected to expand and cool. This expansion, popularly known as the Big Bang, should be governed by Einstein's general relativity equations for the geometry of space-time. The Big Bang is often taken to be synonymous with the beginning of our universe, but it might be that prior events led up to it.

1 millionth of 1 millionth second later: Our universe has expanded and cooled to the point where the quantum fields later are less excited, and consequently their state can be more nearly described in terms of "ordinary matter" as we know it. That is, there are quarks, electrons, positrons, neutrinos, photons (light, x-rays, gamma rays), and other such particles which are all familiar to present day high-energy physicists.

1 millionth second later: Our universe has expanded and cooled further to the point where quarks bind together in groups of three to make protons and neutrons. This process continues until all free quarks are used up.

3 minutes later: Further expansion and cooling has occurred so that protons and neutrons can combine to form helium nuclei. The amount of helium nuclei relative to the number of protons (hydrogen nuclei) that should be formed can be predicted (based on the current knowledge of nuclear physics), and it agrees with experimental measurements of the present-day helium/hydrogen abundances in our universe. Heavier elements are not formed. At this time our universe consists of photons, electrons, positrons, neutrinos, protons, and helium nuclei.

700,000 years later: Further expansion and cooling have occurred so that electrons can combine with protons and helium nuclei to form neutral hydrogen gas and neutral helium gas. This process uses up all the free electrons and protons and helium nuclei. Prior to this time, all positrons have been destroyed by colliding with electrons to form photons. Consequently, there are now no free charged particles. Our universe now consists of photons, neutrinos, and neutral hydrogen and helium gas. Now that the constituents of our universe are electrically neutral, it follows that the photons will no longer interact with the hydrogen and helium. That is, the contents of our universe are now essentially transparent to photons that were present 700,000 years after the Big Bang. The only difference is that they should now have much longer wavelengths, since they have continued to cool off as our universe has continued to expand. Indeed, based on known laws of physics, they should now be largely microwaves with a temperature of about 3 degrees Celsius above absolute zero. Such microwaves, with exactly these properties, have been observed in exquisite detail by specially designed instruments aboard the COBE (Cosmic Background Explorer) satellite launched by NASA.

10 through 6 billion years ago: Our universe continues to expand and cool to the point where gravitational forces can begin to play a role. Gravity causes the hydrogen and helium gas to form billions of large clumps. In turn, billions of smaller clumps of matter (hydrogen and helium) form within the larger clumps. The smaller clumps are raised to locally high temperatures as they fall into each other under gravity. Eventually the temperature and density of the smaller clumps reach the conditions at which thermonuclear fusion takes place and the smaller clumps become stars. The larger clumps, consisting now of billions of stars, are what we call galaxies. Thus there are now billions of galaxies, and each contains billions of stars. In some of the larger galaxies, the material in the center continues to fall together to form black holes (as predicted by Einstein's general relativity equations for the geometry of space-time). This in-falling material is heated to enormous temperatures and emits copious quantities of light. These galaxies are the quasars.

At this point it is worth remarking that if our universe is in fact expanding then the galaxies should be moving farther apart. In particular the galaxies which are moving the fastest should be those that are the farthest away. This is indeed observed to be the case. In fact, the time of the Bang is obtained by extrapolating the observed galactic expansion backward in time to estimate how long ago our universe was concentrated within a very small volume.

The scope of the chronology now narrows to only the continued history of our own galaxy, the Milky Way.

10 through 6 billion years ago: The first-formed stars in our galaxy convert the hydrogen and helium out of which they were originally formed into heavier elements (lithium, carbon, nitrogen, oxygen ... all the way in the periodic table up to iron) by the process of nuclear fusion. Elements heavier than iron are formed by collisions with neutrons. These reactions take place in the biggest stars, and these stars soon (on stellar time scales) use up all their fuel. When a large star uses up all its fuel, it first collapses to a very dense state and then violently explodes to produce a supernova. In this dense state and subsequent explosion, more heavy elements are formed. Moreover, in this explosion all the elements that have been made in the star are spewed back into interstellar space. Thus, after some time, our galaxy contains some heavier elements as well as the remaining initial hydrogen and helium. With the current knowledge of nuclear physics, it is possible to predict how much of each element should be formed by these processes. It is found that these predictions agree with the experimentally measured abundances of all the various elements in our galaxy.

5 billion years ago: Some of the hydrogen and helium gas in our galaxy, along with some of the heavy elements formed in earlier stars, again clump under the action of gravity to form a star. This star is our sun. Thus our sun is a second-generation star, since it is made in part out of material that has been formed in previous stars. Indeed, some of the material in our sun may have gone through several star-formation to star-dissolution (by supernova explosion) cycles.

4.7 billion years ago: Some of the material in the vicinity of our sun clumps together (again under the action of gravity) to form the planets which comprise our solar system. These planets are also made both out of helium and hydrogen and the heavier elements produced in earlier stars. The inner planets (Mercury, Venus, our Earth, and Mars) are made mostly of heavier elements and are solid. The outer planets are made mostly of lighter elements and are gaseous. Considerable material remains between the planets.

4.6 billion years ago: The planets sweep up the debris surrounding them to bring the solar system to its present form. The surface of the Earth at this time is much like that of our present-day moon: rocky, without atmosphere, and without water.

The scope of the chronology now narrows further to only the continued history of our own planet, Earth:

4.5 through 4.4 billion years ago: The Earth melts because of heat from the radio-active decay of some of the radio-active elements in its composition. The heavier elements (mostly iron) flow to the center of the earth to form a heavy molten core. The surface of the Earth cools to form a thin solid crust.

4.4 through 4 billion years ago: Hotter molten material from below flows upward by convection to produce volcanoes. These volcanoes spew out (in addition to lava) nitrogen, carbon dioxide, and water vapor. Water and carbon compounds also arrive from meteor and comet bombardment. The earth now has an atmosphere of nitrogen, carbon dioxide, and water vapor. There is less oxygen in the atmosphere than at present (The oldest rocks on Earth, dated at 3.8 billion years, show no sign of rust). Rocks were presumably formed even earlier on Earth but subsequently were destroyed by remelting). However, the exact amount of oxygen that is present at this time has not yet been firmly established. Most of the water vapor condenses and rains fall. Oceans, seas, lakes, and streams are now produced, and the hydrological cycle begins.

4 through 3.5 billion years ago: Period of "chemical evolution"? (This entry in the chronology is followed by a question mark because there is presently little evidence concerning chemical evolution). It is presumed that during this period – starting with water, carbon dioxide, and nitrogen – ever more and more complex organic molecules are formed as a result of various competing chemical reactions and chains and cycles of chemical reactions.

3.5 billion years ago: Simple single-celled life forms (organisms having the capability for metabolism and reproduction) appear, and microfossils of these cells, some of which seem to resemble bacteria, are formed. There is still less oxygen in the atmosphere than at present.

2.8 through 2.2 billion years ago: Rocks formed though this period begin to show signs of rust, thus indicating that oxygen is now present in the atmosphere in substantial amounts. Presumably, blue-green algae-type cells have produced this oxygen by photosynthesis. Oxygen is poisonous to most of the newly existing life forms, and these life forms become extinct.

2.2 billion years ago: From this time on, single-cell marine life becomes abundant.

1.4 billion years ago: Complex cells appear. These cells have compartments for a nucleus, mitochondria, and chloroplasts.

850 to 570 million years ago: Simple multi-cellular life forms appear, such as jelly fish, sea pens, and segmented worms. The oldest fossils of invertebrates are 675 million years old.

410 to 345 million years ago: Ferns and club mosses appear as the first green plants on dry land. Centipedes and millipedes also appear on dry land. Fish begin to appear in the water.

345 to 280 million years ago: Insects appear on dry land. Amphibians appear, going between the water and the land.

280 to 225 million years ago: Reptiles appear on land. Coniferous forests also appear.

195 to 136 million years ago: Mammals first begin to appear. Dinosaurs flourish.

136 to 67 million years ago: Flowering plants (plants with seeds) first appear. Birds also appear. Dinosaurs become extinct.

67 million year ago: First primates appear.

3.5 million years ago: Bipedal hominids leave footprints similar to human footprints in soft volcanic ash.

2 million years ago: Homo habilis appears and makes stone tools.

1.6 million to 500 thousand years ago: Homo erectus appears and spreads throughout the Old World.

100 thousand years ago: Early Homo sapiens and Neanderthals appear. They use fire. They bury their dead.

30 thousand years ago: Modern Homo sapiens is found in all parts of the world except the Americas. Earliest art appears.

12 thousand years ago: Modern Homo sapiens appears in Americas

10 thousand years ago: First farming and animal husbandry begin.

5 thousand years ago: Technology for making and working bronze is discovered. Sumerian civilization flourishes in Ur

4 thousand years ago: Abraham leaves Ur

According to this chronology, the universe is *finely tuned.* Its fundamental constants have exactly what is required for it to have the magnificently beautiful structure and variety that exists. Correspondingly, if all physical laws and processes are derivable from one grand mathematical principle, then only one set of constants is allowable. In this case, the universe is a profound mathematical creation requiring a Master Mathematician of incredibly great intellect.

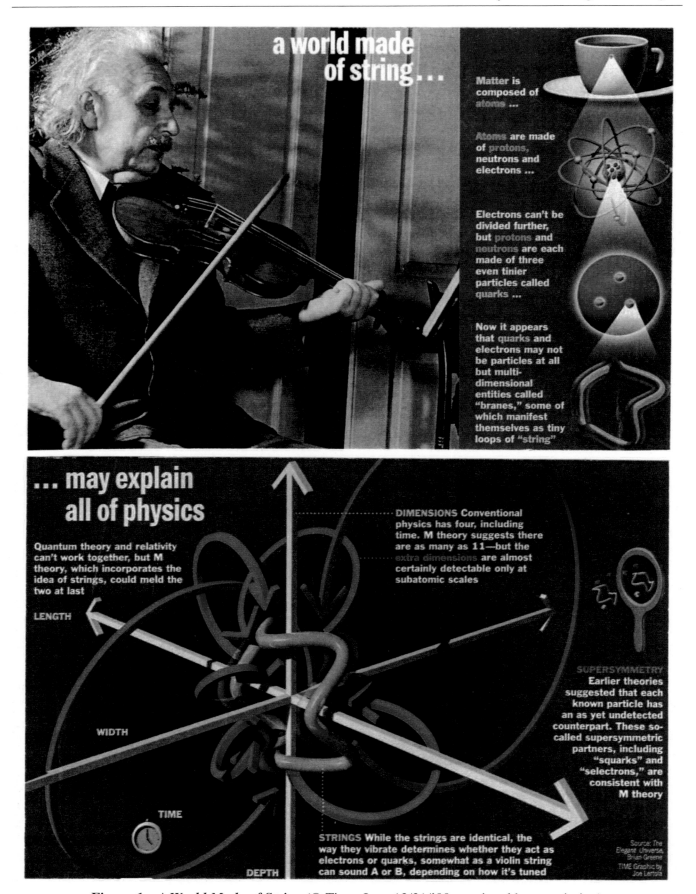

Figure 1: *A World Made of String* (© Time, Inc., 12/31/'99, reprinted by permission)

Weighing the Evidences

During the late 1960's *"string theory"* arose in an effort to describe nuclear forces as waves rather than particles. It ran into trouble, though, because it required what nobody wanted, a massless particle with two units of spin plus ten or even eleven-dimensional space-time. This led to the newer concept of "super-symmetry" which then became the generic feature of *"superstrings."*

In 1985, a series of discoveries convinced many that superstrings might lead to a grand/unified theory. By 1994, the first superstring theory yielded to the second since theoretical physicists were discussing multidimensional space-time on mini- to maxi- scales, all the way from subatomic particles to orbits, planets, nebulae, and galaxies. Today there are at least five such theories, each requiring nine dimensions of space and one of time.

In the euphoria following the superstring revolution the phrase *"theory of everything"* was coined, though it was misleading for several reasons. For starters, even if one mastered quantum dynamics, such theorizing could never characterize initial conditions. Even were they known there would still be much about the universe that couldn't be explained. Existence itself is unknowable, given God's creativity and sovereignty. Were it not so, supernatural causation would be understandable too, lessening God's divinity – which is why these all-encompassing models are becoming more elusive with time.

All along, physicists had doubts about early conditions, though hoping that science would uncover the facts. One could dismiss their ideas as fancy, but we shall try to analyze them in coming chapters with a patient, analytical mind. Understand, however, it is difficult to reason with those claiming to know how the universe began (self-governing and eons ago) when they supposedly "know" also how it will end, based on today's laws of physics. As Cornelius Van Til characterized their reasoning, "Non-Christian thought can give no answer to the fundamental problems. [...] All non-Christian philosophy is essentially a covert attempt to flee from the living God, the ontological Trinity who makes himself known to all people."[6]

Echoing Van Til, Francis Schaeffer spoke of the need for presupposing the existence of God, since denying him is to dismiss all factuality and meaning. It follows that the Bible must be brought into the debate, for even without knowing how the universe was built, we can know him who sees the past and future simultaneously. The Creator/God spelled out history so precisely that only his calendar is determinative. Timing aside though, wouldn't it be thrilling to know how he assembled the pieces?

Left with boundless reaches of space and time, scientists wobble between certainty and guesses, placing the evidences where they seem to "fit" best. Moses, however, knew the truth all along. Though lacking modern methodologies, he spoke definitively. Admittedly, Moses' words may mean dismissing certain evidences entirely, but Blocher insisted, "The place of the sciences in our reading of the scriptures is this: they can have neither authority, nor even a substantial ministerial role within the actual interpretation."[7]

In plain English, God's Word is never to be overshadowed by theorizing since God is subservient to no other authority – and on this there can be no compromise. Having said this, we might be deterred from further inquiry, but we should have more curiosity than that. With God's mandate as our motivation and the Bible as our guide, we can weigh the evidences objectively, recalling also that Jesus said, "I am the way and *the truth* and the life" (Jn. 14:6) and that God never made anything contradicting, denying, or rescinding his attributes.

The bottom line is this: We can be excited about new information as viewed through the *eyes of science,* but we must focus it through the *spectacles of Scripture* (see Chapters 4 and 5). The path is free then (and our calling clear) to receive Genesis 1 as definitive, consistent with the remainder of Scripture and its language.[8] Understand, though, that there are principles for biblical interpretation.

As for various positions on origins, there are two major approaches, the *presuppositional* and the *evidentiary*.

Both require faith, not only in philosophical/religious terms but also in terms of the realities of the universe. How naïve to think otherwise – i.e., that the evidentiary approach would be totally free of bias! The question is, where do our faith constructs begin and end? If we accept only *naturalism* as true and substantive, we end up slighting God (since ultimate truth is spiritually discerned), but if we embrace the *supernatural*, we glorify him, which was his objective from the beginning.

As a corollary, the physical evidences (however important) cannot enlighten us sufficiently. Some are satisfied with them alone, but there is also the question of *life*. What is its meaning, purpose, and essence? Can we explain rationality and the human soul at the molecular level? Are these attributable to time and chance alone, or is there another dimension involving presuppositions?

The Christian's presupposition assumes an authoritative, sovereign, self-revealing God, based on the Bible's infallibility. Knowing that nature is bound by *God's* nature, we need not fear or ignore the evidences. Doing so would be to discard a major portion of God's Creation, that dimension which is other-worldly, and to deny *that* is to be strictly evidentiary.

For those of such a mindset, life has always been elusive, from particles to people – from gluon to glory. As a scientist from yesteryear lamented, "The meaning of life will probably never be grasped as a pure, crystalline gem of truth. It is just not likely to be that simple." Said Albert Szent-Gyorgi in his personal reminiscences:

> In my hunt for the secret of "life", I started my research in histology. Unsatisfied by the information that cellular morphology could give me about "life", I turned to physiology. Finding physiology too complex, I took up pharmacology. Still finding the situation too complicated, I turned to bacteriology. But bacteria were even too complex, so I descended to the molecular level, studying chemistry and physical chemistry. After twenty years' work, I was led to conclude that to understand "life" we have to descend to the electronic level; to the world of wave mechanics. But electrons are just electrons, and have no life at all. Evidently on the way I lost "life". It had run between my fingers.[9]

[1] Stephen A. Hawking, *A Brief History of Time*, Doubleday Dell Publishing Group, 1988, pp. 65-67, 72, 73

[2] Ibid, pp. 11,12

[3] John Gribbin, *In The Beginning*, Little, Brown, & Co., 1993, p. 157

[4] Ibid, pp. 244 & 245 – bracketed words added for clarification of "singularity".

[5] Committee on Creation and Science to the Synod of the Christian Reformed Church in North America, *A Brief Summary of Current Scientific Views of Origins*, Christian Reformed Publications, Grand Rapids, MI, 1991, pp. 414-420

[6] Bruce Milne, *Know the Truth*, InterVarsity Press, Downers Grove, IL, 1998, p. 72

[7] Henri Blocher, *In the Beginning*, InterVarsity Press, Leicester, England/Downers Grove, IL, 1984, p. 27

[8] Ibid, p. 27

[9] Robert A Wallace, *Biology, The World of Life*, Scott, Foresman and Company, London, England, 1990, p. 45

THE EYES OF SCIENCE
(Chapter 4)

Divine Revelations

Why bother with origins when we already have the answer? Don't we have a completed Canon of Truth in the Bible? The trouble is, we have only a divided world. Even Christians, though clutching their Bibles, have little agreement amongst themselves, lacking a doctrine of creation. We may be united about Christ as Redeemer, but we can't agree on beginnings, except that God is the causative agent.

Some think it essential that God not upset the laws of the universe; others say that divine intervention is pivotal. Jesus himself said, "I am the light of the world. Whoever follows me will never walk in darkness". The Pharisees challenged him, saying, "Here you are, appearing as your own witness; your testimony is not valid." Jesus answered them, "Even if I testify on my own behalf, my testimony is valid, for I know where I came from and where I am going" (Jn. 8:12-14).

What a remarkable affirmation of Christ's authority, by way of *Special Revelation*! Creation itself is a testimony, pointing to God's works by way of his *general revelation.* All chronologies must therefore be placed within these two revelations, though interpreting them can be arduous.

Right Framework

During my surgical residency, cardiac transplantation was pioneered at Stanford University, but the issues and concerns at that time were different from today's. Heart transplantation is now of age; though still formidable, it is performed almost routinely. For transplants to succeed there must be a knowledge base: anatomic, physiologic, pathologic, and therapeutic. There are also some principles related to antisepsis, healing, and tissue compatibility. Tools are equally important, including defibrillators, oxygenators, and monitors. Then there are the techniques: tissue typing, harvesting, bypass, and implantation. When these are all combined with the right attitudes and approaches, things usually go smoothly, providing there is cooperation and communication all along.

Knowledge, principles, tools, and techniques; orchestration, approaches, and attitudes; these are related to a centuries-old approach involving the "trivium" of grammar, logic, and rhetoric, co-dependent methods of learning.[1] In this method, "grammar" refers to factual knowledge; "logic" to the ability to process ideas, examine concepts, raise questions, and draw conclusions; "rhetoric" to the ability to express oneself in convincing and persuasive ways. These are routine in the surgical setting, being restatements of knowledge, wisdom, and understanding, as in the Proverbs of Solomon.

Such equipage is useful also in the study of origins, for "the fear of the Lord is the beginning of knowledge" (Pr. 1:7). Without that, assembling facts into a cohesive whole is impossible. Empiricists, for example, may search for the truth, but they merely swerve in and out of it. On their own, they can neither achieve nor sustain it because the physical evidences alone are insufficient.

The fool says in his heart, "There is no God" (Ps. 14:1), so we must reject "the foolishness of the wise". But first we must ask *why* we disagree with it. We might ask too why we Christians so frequently disagree with each other. One answer is that when rubbing two flints together, we're bound to get sparks, as we do when rubbing one sinner against another. Wouldn't it be wonderful if that didn't happen among believers? But it does! Why? Because we're sinners!

Christians don't agree on every detail, but we should be of one mind biblically (Php. 4:2,7). With that as the launch-point, believers can be yoked together, knowing that "as iron sharpens iron, so one man sharpens another"

(Pr. 27:17). Note also that "disagreements are not necessarily a sign of something gone wrong". They can be signs of life! Some things do seem to point simultaneously in different directions, and we may not be able to put them together. Even our differences can provide opportunities for growth, and "sometimes both sides end up being better, having had the disagreement".[2]

The truth is, we're confronting darkness; not just theories, and for this we need the mind of Christ (Php. 2:5), remembering also that "he who wins souls is wise" (Pr. 11:30). Particularly when addressing **believers**, we are to be "humble and gentle – patient – bearing with one another in love, making every effort to keep the unity of the Spirit through the bond of peace" (Eph. 4:2-3). For, as C.S. Lewis said, "When all is said about the divisions in Christendom, there remains by God's mercy an enormous common ground."[3] So, yes, we may attack an idea, but not the one holding it. In other words when our principles are solid, there can be oneness of mind, but when they are at odds there is little hope for unity, intellectual or otherwise.

Even having the right framework, can we really face the world on the basis of our having searched the scriptures? Have we "attained to the whole measure of the fullness of Christ," not as "infants, tossed back and forth" (Eph. 4:13-14)? To arrive at that point, we must hold firmly to God's Word, "encouraging others by sound doctrine and refuting those who oppose it" (Tit. 1:9).

Contemplating Origins

The subject of origins is important because Jesus thought it so. To the Pharisees he said, "Haven't you read that at the beginning the Creator made them male and female" (Mt. 19:4-5)? He was referring here to a **genuine beginning** for the human race, giving the lie to animal forebears. Doubting this, we're unlikely to trust the remainder of Scripture, and what we think of **it** will affect our entire belief system, including our views of morality and ethics.

But isn't the information too technical? No, it need not be, since most of us can understand at least the essentials. Also, God's people have a responsibility to robust science and responsible hermeneutics (biblical interpretation), so we should think deeply about creation, rather than too little about it. Can we think *too much* about beginnings? Yes we can, for even if our purpose is to see God's perspective, these matters can become all-consuming and distracting. We can also become so focused on the universe that we lose the blessings to be gained from it. There is, after all, a spiritual dimension to the universe, so creation should impact the soul, not just the mind. Moreover, we should occupy ourselves with things of greater substance than just models and alternatives, keeping in mind creation's *purpose*. Seeing God's glory everywhere, shouldn't we be hushed by his presence?

Worth of Science

These are exciting and controversial times, for scientists and Bible students alike. But can science actually tell us that we share our ancestry with gorillas? Did life begin as a shell game, or have we come further than that? Parking our minds will not do, so how should we view science and its worth? This is where grammar, logic, and rhetoric come into play, as do knowledge, wisdom, and understanding. As Augustine commented regarding science, "To investigate the motions of heavenly bodies – to determine their positions, measure their distances, and ascertain their properties – demands skill and careful examination. And where these are so employed that the providence of God is thereby more fully unfolded, it is reasonable to suppose that the mind takes a loftier flight and obtains a better view of God's glory" (*Astrologia Magnum Religiosis Argumentum*).

Reflecting on the science of his day, Calvin said, "None who have the use of their eyes can be ignorant of the skill manifested so conspicuously in the endless variety, yet distinct and well-ordered array of the heavenly hosts. But herein appears the ingratitude of man who, finding God a hundred times both in his body and soul, makes his excellence in this respect a pretext for denying that there is a God. He will not say that chance has made him different from brutes, but substituting nature as the architect of the universe, he suppresses the name of God" (*Institutes of the Christian Religion, I,1,5*).

Augustine and Calvin saw stirrings of the mind as rooted in God. Science can augment one's understanding of the universe, but are its theories bringing us to the nirvana of enlightenment? Do its laws apply to primeval events, or are there factors beyond quantification? The answers may elude us to an extent, but that should not deter us from looking into the questions. After all, the understanding of the universe has only begun. Science is thus a legitimate sphere of endeavor for anyone committed to the Bible. Besides that, we are instruments for the truth, and the task of inquiring was given us by our Maker. But how one *interprets* the data is at the heart of the debate!

Skirmishes over Beginnings

Christians wrestle with non-Christians and even amongst themselves. The question is, "What can science say to the Bible and what can the Bible say to science?" Given such dissimilar sources, how should one interpret them and what are their boundaries? These questions arose when Galileo invented the telescope in the 1600s, invalidating Aristotle's geocentric model while confirming Copernicus' heliocentric solar system. This brought Galileo into conflict with the church, since his ideas were considered a threat to infallibility.

The church was wrong, however, and science was right. In Schaeffer's opinion, "The conflict was not because Galileo's teaching contained anything contrary to the Bible. Church authorities thought it did, but that was because Aristotelian elements had become part of church orthodoxy, and Galileo's notions conflicted with them."[4] Reading the Bible, we need to understand that truth is often framed according to human perception. Furthermore, the terms, "sunrise" and "sunset" do not preclude the earth's revolving around the sun, since Scripture is merely using common terminology here.

The discussions of Galileo's day did have a positive side, since they ushered in the Scientific Revolution, and that movement was rooted in the biblical world view. Said Schaeffer, "The rise of modern science did not conflict with what the Bible teaches; indeed, at a crucial point the Scientific Revolution *rested upon* what the Bible teaches."[5] The notion that science was born out of Christianity was also held by Whitehead and Oppenheimer. Whitehead (1861-1947) was a mathematician and Oppenheimer (1904-1967) was famous in the field of atomic energy. Neither claimed to be a Christian, yet both admitted that science developed out of the Christian view.

As for the Galileo clash, some compare it with today's young-earth/old-earth controversies, but that isn't a valid comparison. Galileo was studying observable bodies behaving predictably in current space-time, while modern cosmogony deals with laws and processes not necessarily operative now. Such comparisons (and the clashes they occasion) do, however, focus our attention on the nature of science, the relationship of science to religion, the autonomy of each, traditional vs. contemporary science, whether or not the Bible is scientific, and the contribution each brings to the discussion.

Nature of Science

Isaac Newton (1687) provided the knock-out punch for the Copernican doctrine. Newtonian physics was based on the *inductive   method*, requiring empirical data from the outset. Scientists sometimes muster such a preponderance of evidence inductively that a general statement can emerge without any preconceived goal or premise. In the *deductive method*, on the other hand, theories are proposed, requiring subsequent experimentation to prove or disprove them.

Scientists rely heavily on inductive reasoning, though most would prefer a combination of both methods. When formulating their proposals, if mini-theories suggest a general theory *inductively*, maxi-theories can be developed *deductively*, and tested. When all the sub-theories support some maxi-theory, the idea becomes tenable. So what is science, then? It is based on three approaches: the empirical, the objective, and the rational. These are key to the scientific method, but much is argued over what they are, how they are exemplified within science, and whether or not all of them can be seen in the workings of science and scientists.[6]

When a scientist has a premise, it is at first merely an idea requiring testing, defined as an "hypothesis". Without testing, it remains provisional, but if careful research supports that hypothesis, it gains the status of a "theory". Theories are usually considered "scientific" after being checked by experimentation against observable, repeatable phenomena. With this rationale, atomic theory and germ theory are considered scientific, but theories which can never be validated are simply guesses.

A fully-documented theory can become a "law of nature," but to achieve any real status in the scientific community its supporting hypotheses must have been corroborated. Stated differently, events in nature (e.g., star formation) may tell scientists something, but speculation alone doesn't carry the weight of experimental proof. Hypotheses must still be confirmed, meaning that they must be able to be confirmed, or falsified. Also, no matter how vigorously one might structure an argument, there are limitations to the scientific method, and these may be quite severe, considering the singularities of the universe.

Some models will never be testable, so there is no way of knowing whether or not they describe something useful. There is also the requirement of *fit* amongst the various fields of knowledge. The subsets of any theory should coalesce into a unified *(concordant)* assemblage. *"Life"* and *"Earth"* sciences, for example, can be conflicting disciplines when assumptions are brought to bear, harmonizing little with each other and sometimes less with their *cosmological cousins.* Holding to the integration of parallel data streams, these should unite into a single *body of truth,* but all too frequently we find biological theories agreeing poorly with geological ones and cosmological theories moving in another direction still, fitting poorly amongst themselves and even less with Scripture.

In the real world, all the data sets and models should be coherent, fitting with God and nature (not just as it *is* but as it once *was*). Nature began with harmony and balance, not happenstance and confusion, and it still has cohesion, albeit different from its original. Scientists seldom consider this, however, ill-equipped as they are to deal with original perfection. Lacking genuine history, why wouldn't they slip into absurdity? Even when everything seems congruent (believable), they should be skeptics, claiming no more certainty than actually exists. This explains the need for scientific literature and the community of peers, both of which are useful checks, as was demonstrated when scientists repudiated cold fusion. Reviewers, however, are no better than their biases.

People make educated guesses, but these are not science. At singularities, "we can put these guesses together and call them a theory, but we can never verify the link between past causes and present effects."[7] The problem is that science is limited, mutable, subjective, and trendy. It is also easily intermingled with prejudice. It then changes into *faith*, whether holding to fantasy or to God's Word. Momentum builds, supporting a certain model, and though not fully tested (or testable) people proclaim it as "fact", in which case objectivity takes wing, particularly when the Bible is either buried or banned.

Recognizing the requirements put upon science by faith, many are suspicious of both science and religion, saying that they must be assigned separate niches (given the conflicts surrounding faith tenets within science). Nevertheless, most continue to combine their beliefs, good or bad, with their theories, partial and whole. The result is a "theology of origins" which is suitable, given the right framework, but pseudoscientific when naturalistic presuppositions alone are entertained.

This brings us to biblical vs. secular science, each with its distinctive features. Of course there can be some commonality between them, but there are obvious differences between seeing God's handiwork as *supernatural* vs. seeing it as *"one of those things that sometimes happen"*. Given these, "we may hear all the notes of science, but without the theistic context and perspective we will not hear the song."[8] And, even hearing it, we might not be able to interpret it on our own.

Science and Religion

Dr. Brigitte Boisslier, trained in physical and biological chemistry at the University of Dijon, France, is a "Raelian," one of an estimated 25,000 members in a sect whose religion is science. Her silver pendant resembles the Star of David, with added swirls representing the "eternality of time and matter", indicating her belief that humans came from extra-terrestrials and that immortality can be achieved through cloning.

Because science and religion are so easily intermingled and adulterated, Howard Van Till (in his *Science Held Hostage*) proposes a significant separation between the physical sciences and one's religious views, suggesting that science conduct its work separately. Says he, "Science held hostage by any ideology or belief system, whether naturalistic or theistic, can no longer function effectively to gain knowledge of the physical universe. [...] Each needs to learn from the other what lies outside its own domain."[9]

According to Van Till, the way to understand beginnings is to see Scripture as culturally-conditioned, specific to the time in which it was written. Says he, "The Bible's historical literature is authentic to its ancient Near Eastern cultural and religious context – a setting quite different from our modern Western world." He then advises everyone, whether committed to Christianity or not, to "exercise great care and caution in making statements about biblical data and its relevance to contemporary scientific theorizing."

Van Till suggest dividing created reality into *"internal affairs"* (the domain of the natural sciences) and *"external relationships"* (the domains of philosophy, theology, and ultimately of scriptural authority). For Van Till, "Scientific knowledge is inherently intelligible and equally accessible to all," whereas "religious faith and supernatural matters are in the realm of the transcendent". Theories of supernatural creation are therefore "theistic" and outside the domain of science.

Those favoring this approach prefer that any consideration of the ***supernatural*** be separated from origins, but this suggests a dichotomy between faith and reason, as well as between God's general and Special revelations. Now, this might be acceptable for pulmonary physiology, but it cannot work for origins. In fact, it creates more problems than it solves! Such a ***dualistic approach*** negates the view of the Reformation which held that, because of the mutual interdependence of God's revelations, all knowledge (including faith-knowledge) is of ***one piece***, resulting in the integration of ***faith*** with ***reason.***

To get a grip on this, look again at God's two revelations. ***General revelation*** describes God's work in nature by which his grandeur is manifested, moving us to adore him. ***Special Revelation*** is reserved for the broad sweep of redemptive history occasioned by sin's entrance into the world – a history coming from the Word, through the Spirit, into our hearts.

Regarding these revelations, Calvin said in his Institutes that the knowledge of God, even as Creator, is through the "more clear light" shed on it by the written Word. *The Belgic Confession* also subordinates general to Special Revelation, prohibiting any attempt to know God and his world "apart from the clear and sufficient revelation in the written Word". However, the Bible reigns over all spheres, including science. There is also a vast difference between what people discover (or think they discover) and what God has revealed. So, when Moses describes supernatural events (creation and miracles), science has no choice but to incorporate them into its thinking.

The inference that the study of origins (to be scientific) will have to proceed without a supernatural belief system, detouring by way of the antiquity and ambiguity of Scripture, conveys the impression that God reveals himself along two separate authoritative tracks which cannot be harmonized. Leading expositors like Calvin and the "Divines" saw the argument differently. Rather than science vs. religion, they spoke of general and Special Revelation ***together*** making their contribution to knowledge, but ***not coequally***.

When the Bible tells us about extraordinary happenings, it alone has the authority, so we have no right to explain the supernatural away, whether through science, religion, or some corruption of the two. Referring to those *not* sharing this view, T. Plantinga and C. Venema wrote, "By Special Revelation they mean the Bible and by general revelation they mean nature, perhaps supplemented by history and culture. Yet, although such people talk about nature as a revelation, in effect they wind up accepting science (a body of writings about nature) as revealing God to us. They maintain that when we study science, we pick up additional knowledge of God along the way."[10]

Returning to those "beautiful books," this terminology has its usefulness, but we should not press it too far. After all, nature is not a book that somehow governs God's Word. As Berkhof wrote in his *Manual of Christian Doctrine*, "The element of corruption entered God's beautiful handiwork and obscured, though it did not altogether obliterate the handwriting of God. Nature still has the earmarks of its divine origin, but it is now full of imperfections and a prey to destructive forces. It has ceased to be the perspicuous revelation of God which it once was."[11] Though still a mirror of God's virtues, nature is decidedly curved, making things look different from what they are. While we can still see in it the essence and will of the Maker in terms of his power, divinity, and wisdom, it is no longer decisive for Truth.

Were it not for Scripture, scientists would dismiss the supernatural altogether, so science cannot be assigned its own authority, which would give it a blank check. The bottom line is that God does things so foreign to our thinking that we're not at liberty to interpret them on our own. Religion and science are only man's declarations, not God's. Furthermore, there is neither inherent authority nor neutrality in nature; nor are there isolated domains of intelligence in it.

As Berkhof said in his *Summary of Christian Doctrine*, "The Bible gives us the only reliable account of the origin of religion. Moreover, it comes to us with the assurance that God, whom man could never discover with his natural powers, revealed himself in nature and, more especially, in his divine Word. Finally, it teaches us that God created man, endowing him with the capacity to understand this revelation."[12] By God's providence, thousands of students in Christian schools are being taught just that!

Autonomy of Science

Science involves systematic research, collecting information and advancing knowledge according to generally accepted methods. This differentiates what scientists can do autonomously from the more restricted activity of synthesis which reflects judgment, prejudice, and belief. Assembling evidences into a coherent theory, and then proving or disproving that theory, is the work of scientists; not historians, musicians, artists, and theologians – and scientists must have autonomy to carry out their work within the scope of what pure science is. But science can vary, and there is often a provisional aspect to it, so the freedom of scientists will have to be tempered.

What then is science's authority in origins? We could begin by asking, "What is the relative weight of science compared with other spheres of learning?" As C.S. Lewis explained, "It is widely believed that scientific thought puts us in touch with reality, whereas moral or metaphysical (supernatural) thought does not, but the distinction thus made between scientific and non-scientific thought will not easily bear the weight we are attempting to put on it. [...] If popular thought feels 'science' to be different from all other kinds of knowledge because it is experimentally verifiable, popular thought is mistaken and one should abandon the distinction."[13]

What is Lewis saying here? I think he is pointing out that there are insights which, though not purely scientific, can be brought to the discussion. These can be as pertinent as scientific research itself. Examples are the narratives of Moses, the prophets, and the Gospels, all mentioning real occurrences with a weight of their own, requiring no vindication of any kind.

What else might affect the autonomy of science? Judgments such as value, worth, and benefit. Since God himself decreed morality and ethics, science must be coupled with these. There is also the integration of science beyond its borders into one's world view. When scientists engage in this, they embrace both faith and religion, which is acceptable as long as their science is differentiated from that which masquerades *as* science.

When biases enter into the equation, science moves into a ***confluence of thought.*** This is permissible given the right faith construct, as when biblical knowledge is combined with empirical investigation, but we end up with conditional autonomy, variably applied, depending on the project and the extent to which faith plays a role in it. Synthesizing aspirin, for example, is different from cloning humans or unraveling cosmic history, so the scale of autonomy will have to vary from total to none at all.

Scientists may desire unlimited freedom, insisting on their objectivity, but this is naiveté in light of him who claims everything as his own, including the presumed autonomy of science. Were science neutral, there would be little need for a Christian approach to it, but scientists seldom remain at the level of objectivity. Though desiring neutrality, they blend their "findings" into progressively larger segments of "knowledge". Though starting out with innocence and wonder, they then end up seeking influence and power, and the blessings of science become a curse, science having surrendered itself to another agenda.

Contemporary Science

We live in an age when people are passionate about science, though defining it on their own. Too often, they cobble together what they ***call*** science, but is merely a distortion of it. As a result, science has come under fire from many directions. No longer does it command the near universal respect it once held. As Dr. Ratzsch, Professor of Philosophy at Calvin College, comments, "From the right has come a fresh attack on Darwinism and arguments for intelligent design. From the left, postmodernists have attacked the very notion of objective truth claims – scientific or otherwise."[14]

Galileo himself was a traditionalist, realizing that "science cannot be done in the absence of presuppositions about the uniformity of nature, the consistent operation of causal mechanisms, and so on."[15] Today, however, some are rejecting the idea of consistency, forcing the issue of traditional vs. contemporary science. This drives all kinds of questions. Should science still be tethered to empiricality? Must we insist that it be rational and objective? Should it always be so? Why couldn't science be competent on its own? As Ratzsch posits for discussion purposes, "Why can't we learn about the universe by purely contemplative means, as we sit in our recliners?"

Pondering these questions, we must look at the other side of the equation as well. "Are there ever situations in which we *ought* to reject the deliverances of science, even though they seem rationally impeccable?" "Just how should Christians incorporate science into their world?"[16] And what about the supernatural? If science isn't permitted in that area, must we remain ignorant about it?

Confronted by these questions, Karl Popper (1902-1994) argued (as did Lewis) that metaphysical, philosophical, and other non-empirical principles could be brought to science. This raises the question of what exactly *are* the criteria for real science. "Popper concluded that *falsification* was the only approach left to science which was both data-based and logically rigorous. So how then should science proceed? As Popper saw it, scientists should propose empirically testable, falsifiable theories, and test them as stringently as possible."[17] This was his answer to what differentiates ***science*** from ***non-science.***

Popperian falsification created a stir. According to Popper, research data should be able to contradict any proposed theory, and if this couldn't occur the theory itself might be in jeopardy. "But the most serious challenge to traditional conceptions of science came in part from a different direction. That challenge was so serious that some believe the traditional picture of science is now only a historical curiosity."[18] Scientists saw that some of the principles of science are themselves suspect, which led to the postempiricist philosophy of Thomas Kuhn, based on his 1962 essay, *The Structure of Scientific Revolutions.*[19] The most significant component in Kuhn's view of science is the notion of a ***paradigm.*** Kuhn argued that "science had to be defined in terms of paradigms and that in the absence of paradigms there was no such thing as science."

Paradigms are faith-constructs consisting of several elements, including symbolic generalizations, metaphysical commitments, values, and exemplars (models). As such, paradigms can be useful – and/or totally scary! Note carefully that paradigms add something new to science: the introduction of metaphysical and value principles. Kuhnian science is thus different from evidentiary science.

Building on Kuhn's ideas, some have adopted frankly mystical positions fitting in with "New Age" mentality. When science uses its persuasive power in this way, building on shifting sand, it moves outside empiricality into an arena where Truth itself is suspect. If the focus is on this, not merely verifying or falsifying theories, what are scientists doing in their research? Kuhn would argue that they are "trying to account for various phenomena and observations in terms and categories dictated by the paradigm."[20] Any result contrary to the paradigm-generated expectation would be an "anomaly". And what do scientists do with anomalies? Says Ratzsch, "Sometimes they do not even seem to notice the anomaly, and sometimes when they do, they simply ignore it."

In Kuhnian ideology, "an anomaly may involve something so central to the paradigm that it cannot be ignored. Sometimes the sheer number of anomalies becomes alarming." There are times when anomalies resist solutions so consistently that the paradigm itself is in jeopardy. When that happens, confidence in the paradigm disappears and it must be replaced by another theory. Note as well that "the apparently cavalier attitude toward anomalies is seriously at odds with a literal reading of the hypothetico-deductive method."[21]

Kuhn was on to something, albeit in a twisted sense! Lacking Scripture, the only access we have to truth is through perception, and perceptions are paradigm-colored.[22] This was known long before Kuhn, but he placed it at the core of science – not in terms of biblical faith but in terms of subjectivity. The problem is, when science is manipulated in this way, values are determined humanly. There are then no rules for rationality, leaving little room for the Creator but a wide opening for postmodernism and superstition.

What is postmodernism? Says Ratzsch, it is "too diverse to be given a simple definition. Postmodernists share a nonnegotiable hostility to what they take to be the defining views of *modernity*, the conceptual and cultural structures associated with the scientific and social revolutions of the sixteenth through eighteenth centuries [based on Christian principles]. Views from that time included the idea that there is an independent and objective reality; that there is thus only one objective Truth (one correct, global, all-encompassing story),"[23] just as in the Book of Genesis!

What about theorizing in general? Traditionally, science has held that maxi-theories are valid only when their bolstering arguments make sense, but with today's paradigm this is not always enforced (or even desired). Given such whimsy, how could any scientist keep another honest? Who determines truth when objectivity is jettisoned, and who will decide the degree to which mini-theories need to support maxi-theories before they can become law? Is science a law unto itself?

Given science's vagaries, the study of origins follows few hard and fast rules. As Dembski remarked, "The philosopher of science, Paul Feyerabend (with the history of science to back him up) went even so far as to deny that there is a scientific method."[24] And what has postmodernism offered in its place? The equal legitimacy of all perspectives based on the absence of Truth! But why would this be considered scientific, let alone rational? Totally at odds with Scripture, this should be repudiated by everyone embracing creation. Yet there is growing receptivity toward this lunacy, and if people accept that, who is to say but what the entire scientific community may have been sucked into a black hole?

Left with only a fuzzy consensus as to what science is, there is an even deeper concern. Claiming the privileged position where it alone defines truth, science stumbles at celestial things too. Having no use for them, it scoffs at extraordinary occurrences of any kind, as did the Sadducees of old, denying angels, spirits, and the resurrection

(Ac. 23:8). With such a casual dismissal of the truth, "not only can we not get any 'correct' general picture of history and reality; there may not even be any such all-encompassing truth."[25] What we're left with is subjectivism, irrationality, and relativism. And, an impotent god, if he even exists!

These ideas have not yet won the day, however. Because of the reawakening of design theory, objectivity and empiricality are making a comeback, and even maxi-theories can be dislodged when they are erroneous. But, while critiques of Darwinism may raise the spirit, they are not sufficient in themselves. Christians should therefore be developing a biblically-based model showing how science fits with the truth. Truth, after all, can die if Christians are lethargic. We do not always choose evil consciously; we simply allow the good to slip away.

Is the Bible Scientific?

Oxford biologist, Richard Dawkins, said that if superior creatures from space visit Planet Earth, the first question they will ask is this: "Have they discovered evolution yet?" Claiming evolutionary ideology as the mark of an advanced society, Dawkins continued, "It is absolutely safe to say that if you meet someone who claims not to believe in evolution, that person is ignorant, stupid, or insane" – thereby revealing much about evolutionists!

Having made a commitment, evolutionists can be as dogmatic about it as the most narrow-minded person in the world, religious or otherwise. Bertrand Russell, a brilliant mathematician/philosopher, said, "there is no God". Freud, Marx, and Sagan all alleged the same. Though geniuses in some ways, they were nonetheless foolish, for the psalmist said, "The fool says in his heart, 'there is no God' (Ps. 14:1)". To think that scientists are always open-minded, following the evidences wherever they may lead, is a serious mistake. Many have prejudices, so we can be freed from the myth of their objectivity! And, the notion that Scripture is unenlightened.

Though written millennia ago, the Bible needs no revision. Its truths are settled for all time. It is also unique in content, dealing as it does with every subject under heaven. When it speaks about astronomy, history, geology, etc., it comes with the same infallible authority as when it speaks about spiritual matters and salvation. Truth is, the Bible is the final authority on everything with which it deals, making it the most reliable book ever written!

Is the Bible a book of science, then? Of course not. Nor was it intended to be, since it is not strictly human in authorship or intent. Neither is the Bible a textbook of psychology, mathematics, or any other human endeavor, since it says little about research and even less about science as conducted by humans. Not only is the Bible different from science, it yields different answers, superseding what all other sources are telling us. Yet, when it touches on any area of science, it is totally accurate. Above all else, the Bible is covenantal. Unlike any book of science, it addresses God's dealings with his people, from creation to re-creation.

Reigning Paradigms

When we take our stand in the center of God's Word, we are safe intellectually and spiritually. But how can we get a better handle on it? With more data, like that from COBE's microwaves, Hubble's photos, and Chandra's x-rays? How about the "Boomerang Project," mapping cosmic microwaves with a balloon-borne telescope circumnavigating Antarctica? Or, the "Sophia Project," the telescope aboard a Boeing 747? People applaud these experiments and others like them, including ice-core sampling, CT imaging of dinosaurs' hearts, chromosome mapping, etc. Ever admiring of science, they interpret the "evidences" through what is already in their minds. But, though perhaps beginning with God, they yield to the data of man, preferring human paradigms over God's.

How did humans end up in this lofty position? By skewing the facts and caving in to mutable models. Thus, the paradigm of the world was born, admitting all views *except those of the Bible*. According to the world's paradigm, chemical evolution began four billion years ago producing animals of immense size (though they died out 67 million years ago). This is the requirement placed on Truth, though nobody can imagine what a billion years would look like. Or, what might or might not have happened during those eons of time!

Unlike secular science, Genesis tells us that the world is different from what it was. Early on, animals and people were bigger, stronger, healthier, older, and more intelligent (by far) than they are today. Having a reliable book to tell us about these things, we can avoid nodding our heads in habitual agreement with what science congers up. Yet, this is where the conflict is raging, and it isn't just a battle of people vs. people. It's a battle for the mind involving the "powers of this dark world" (Eph. 6:12), and that battle is over one basic issue: ***Truth vs. non-Truth – biblical ideology vs. non-biblical ideology.***

Swayed by the world, people put themselves on the throne, thinking they can do better without God, so we have a wasteland as far as the eye can see, playing out in people's attitudes, approaches, and interactions. Unlike divine wisdom, theirs is "madness and folly", a mere "chasing after the wind" (Ecc. 10:17), so perhaps we should recall that Solomon wrote, "If the ax is dull and its edge unsharpened, more strength is needed" (Ecc. 10:10).

For that kind of strength, we need more than science; we need spectacles! Putting them on, one should never read Scripture as contrary to itself, which is the rule overriding all the machinations of the mind. Otherwise science would end up in a dominant position every time, given its desire for autonomy. As for the contributions of science, here is a reminder:

In the beginning was the Word, and the Word was with God, and the Word was God. He was with God in the beginning. Through him all things were made; without him nothing was made that has been made. In him was life, and that life was the light of men. The light shines in the darkness, but the darkness has not understood it (Jn. 1:1-5).

[1] See, Dorothy Sayers, *The Lost Tools of Learning*, reprinted as an Appendix in Recovering the Lost Tools of Learning, by Douglas Wilson, Crossway Books, Wheaton, IL, 1991
[2] Del Ratzsch, *Science and its Limits*, InterVarsity Press, Downers Grove, IL, 2000, p. 169
[3] C.S. Lewis, *Christian Reflections*, Wm. Eerdmans Publishing Co., Grand Rapids, MI, 1987, Preface (vii)
[4] Francis A. Schaeffer, *How Should We Then Live?*, F. H. Revell Co., 1976, p.131
[5] Ibid, PP. 132,133
[6] Del Ratzsch, *Science and its Limits*, InterVarsity Press, Downers Grove, IL, 2000, p. 14
[7] Family Radio School of the Bible, *In the Beginning*, Family Stations, Inc., Oakland, CA, p.35
[8] Del Ratzsh, *Science and its Limits*, InterVarsity Press, Downers Grove, IL, 2000, p. 159
[9] Howard J. Van Till/ Davis A. Young Clarence Menninga, *Science Held Hostage*, by the Calvin Center for Christian Scholarship, InterVarsity Press, 1988, pp 41-43
[10] Theodore Plantinga & Cornelis P. Venema, *Evolution, Original Sin, and our Creeds*, The Outlook, Journal of Reformed Fellowship, Byron Center, MI, Feb., 1991, pp. 5,6
[11] L. Berkhof, *Manual of Christian Doctrine*, pp. 27,28
[12] L. Berkhof, *Summary of Christian Doctrine*, The Banner of Truth Trust, Tenth Impression, Carlisle, Penn., 2000, pp. 7-9
[13] C.S. Lewis, *Christian Reflections*, Wm. Eerdmans Publishing Co., Grand Rapids, MI, 1987, pp. 61,62
[14] Del Ratzsch, *Science and its Limits,* InterVarsity Press, Downers Grove, IL, 2000, back cover page.
[15] Ibid, p. 19
[16] Ibid, p. 16
[17] Ibid, p. 35
[18] Ibid, p. 37
[19] Ibid, p. 41
[20] Ibid, pp. 42,43
[21] Ibid, p. 44
[22] Ibid, p. 46
[23] Ibid, p. 54
[24] William A Dembski, *Intelligent Design*, InterVarsity Press, Downers Grove, IL, 1999, p. 258
[25] Del Ratzsch, *Science and its Limits*, InterVarsity Press, Downers Grove, IL, 2000, p. 55

THE SPECTACLES OF SCRIPTURE
(Chapter 5)

Believing Faith

Sooner or later, every physician father will be asked, "Daddy, are you a *real* doctor?" When my daughter asked this, she wanted mainly to confirm what she already knew, though conditionally. Months later, following a bicycle accident, she needed no convincing at all! While suturing her lacerated lip, I knew that my credentials had become palpable – even to an eight year old skeptic. Now, however, the tables are turned, and I ask occasionally, "Are you a real nurse?"

Like my daughter, we humans seldom accept things on the basis of their claims alone. We want proof, experience, evidence, etc. When we come to the Bible, however, we come to it **believing** or we don't come at all. How strange! Doesn't this verge on the bizarre? Yes, it does. True faith is so unnatural that it is other-worldly, or Spirit-breathed. And once having received it, we are to be governed by it, not by intellect and reasoning alone.

Accepting this without doubt, the author of Hebrews wrote, "In the past God spoke to our forefathers through the prophets at many times and in various ways, but in these last days he has spoken to us by his Son, whom he appointed heir of all things, and through whom he made the universe. The Son is the radiance of God's glory and the exact representation of his being, sustaining all things by his **powerful word**" (Heb. 1:1-4). Thus, "faith is the sure knowledge and conviction that everything God reveals in his **Word** is true" (*Heidelberg Catechism*, L.D. 7). "Without faith", in fact, "it is impossible to please God" (Heb. 11:6).

We read in the NIV, "Now faith is being sure of what we hope for and certain of what we do not see" (Heb. 11:1). Or, as in the King James, "the substance of things hoped for; the evidence of things not seen". "By faith we understand that the universe was formed at God's command, so that what is seen was not made of what was visible" (Heb. 11:3). But how about demanding the evidence, as Thomas did? The problem with such faith is that it is *conditional*. Thomas believed only when presented with the facts, yet once having witnessed the wounds of the cross, he exclaimed: "My Lord and my God", as we all would! Jesus then replied, "Because you have seen me, you have believed; blessed are those who have not seen and yet have believed" (Jn. 20:29).

Considering how Thomas came to believe, let me suggest two unusual words; two separate ways for coming to the truth: **axiopistic** and **autopistic**. "Pistic" is derived from the Greek for "faith". "Axio" is from "worth" and "Auto" from "self". The *axio* approach stands or falls on the strength of one's having examined all the evidences and found them worthy or convincing, as Thomas did. The *auto* approach stands on its own self-declaring veracity. Applying these words to Christ's resurrection, here is the question. Shall I gather all the evidence saying, "I will believe, but not until the facts are in," as in the axiopistic method? Or, should I say, "There is within the self-revelation of God's Word all the evidence and all the certainty that I could ever need, so I need no further substantiation," as in the autopistic method?

Given these approaches, faith is of two types: *general* and *believing*. General faith is the axiopistic confidence of knowing that my car will start when I turn the key based on past experiences which I understand, though not without prior evidence. Believing faith, however, does not rest on the physical evidences alone, at least not ultimately. Thus, the evidences themselves are not always deciding or conclusive. Why? Because believing faith is autopistic, flowing as it does from a conviction which the natural mind cannot comprehend. However, it isn't merely an abstract assumption. Rather, it is the trust we have in him whose highest revelation of himself is in his works of creation and redemption. Believing faith is thus the absolute certainty that believers have, not in the scientific evidences themselves, or in fancies of the mind, but in God himself.

Applying these concepts to origins, we would be without excuse if we saw the biblical account of creation as less than sufficient in itself, though the physical evidences can be convincing to an extent. Those seeing it otherwise are axiopistic skeptics, refusing the Bible's claims. But shouldn't we be saying, "Show me the evidence?" Didn't Thomas end up in the right place? What could be so wrong about intellectualizing things?

The problem is that the evidentiary information can provide only a *psychological* certitude. Basing everything on physical evidence alone, how could you make up your mind having only partial evidence? To illustrate this, may I ask you a question? Would you have a coronary artery bypass knowing that you had a 100% likelihood of a good result? Of course you would, providing you needed the operation. Now let's change the odds. How about 50%? Or 20%?

You might say, "I'm convinced that DNA arrived over millions of years", but how about the *real* probability, which is more like zero minus infinity or the square root of minus one, contrasted with the certitude of Genesis? And what will you do when the evidences change or seem to be pointing in opposite directions? Will you fabricate something like Gould did with his "punctuated equilibrium", or will you come up with yet another end-run around natural days and supernatural creation?

Our conclusions may be supported by evidence, but the evidence itself is not always conclusive. Unbelievers ridicule this, as they do the confession that Christ is Lord and that God raised him from the dead (Ro. 10:10), but Truth is written within them as well (in their conscience), though they deliberately suppress it. Nevertheless, their disbelief does not make believing faith any less a requirement for knowledge, for "all men are like grass and all their glory is like the flowers of the field; the grass withers and the flowers fall, but the Word of the Lord stands forever" (1 Pe. 1:24).

But how can we get a better handle on it? Here is a suggestion. Take a good look at the Artist! When Rembrandt painted a portrait, it was not a Picasso. How do we know that? By evidences within the work itself: tiny stroke-marks and shades of light. Not being an artist, I would probably miss these, but there are those who identify the master by them. Yet even among the experts mistakes are made, so what then? Well, were the artist living, she or he could identify the work immediately, even on a bad day!

So it is with the portraiture of God. There are evidences in his artistry indicating both his authorship and character. Unlike Rembrandt, however, the Creator is alive. Better still, the Alpha and Omega of the universe left us with two revelations, although the evidences and markings in the physical universe are less distinct than those in the Bible. Reading both revelations, Christians have the advantage, having the Spirit and the Word to clear up the smudges.

When people refuse Genesis on its own merits, the deficiency is not in the Bible but in them. In fact, they are blurring the picture even further, as if one or both of God's revelations didn't exist. But doesn't the autopistic view indicate a lack of regard for the evidences? Not at all. Christians should have as much interest in the physical findings as anyone in the world, especially seeing them misread and manipulated. But, while the evidences can give us a deeper appreciation for the Creator, and while it might be nice to have them, we really need none of them at all, seeing that we have the answer already in the shades and strokes of the Master. To interpret these we must view the evidences through a prior faith construct. And that's the core of the argument, Truth being from the Author's Word – not that of some "expert".

Does this mean that I have a built-in prejudice regarding creation? Most certainly so! My bias is that of taking God at his Word. If the Author said "yes", who am I to say "no"? Fact is, I don't need more evidence, since it has been provided already in vivid color and bold print in the shades of God's portraiture and the strokes of his pen.

Since the beginning of the world, "God's invisible qualities – his eternal power and divine nature – have been clearly seen, being understood from what has been made, so that men are without excuse" (Ro. 1:19-21). But how can something invisible be seen or understood? The answer is that God is so plainly evident everywhere we look that there is not a man, woman, or child who cannot grasp his attributes simply by viewing his workmanship.

God has made himself *very* evident in nature, and we should be jumping for joy because of that! But he has shown himself even more clearly in his Word, and if we fail to see *that*, the deficiency is in *us*, not in his revelations, for it is *we* who haven't gotten the message. However, flesh and blood cannot reveal it to us, for only the Creator can give us that kind of finality. Wondrously, he made himself so visible in his handwriting and handiwork that we should be shouting it from everywhere!

Donning the Spectacles

Jesus rebuked those who wouldn't trust him unless he performed signs and wonders for them. The problem was their lack of faith since he had already proven his divinity by his declarations. Even lacking evidentiary signs, people should have believed him, which was true as well of the Israelites of old. The Apostle Paul wrote, "Faith comes from hearing the message, and the message is heard through the Word" (Ro. 10:17-19). Didn't these people hear the message? Of course they did! All day long God held out his hands to these disobedient and obstinate people, but they would not listen (Ro. 10:21). Though hearing his words, they refused to accept "Springs of Living Water".

How could anyone be so foolish? God's self-manifestation is the access to his stockpile of truth! But most haven't a clue as to what Truth is. Though possessing Creation and the Bible, it's as if these are closed books to them. Given the hardness of their hearts and the blindness of their eyes, maybe we should work harder at convincing them. But this requires donning the spectacles. What's more, we must put on the full armor of God, standing firmly with the shield of faith, the sword of the Spirit, and the belt of truth (Eph. 6:14-16).

Faith in faith isn't *faith*, however, so fidelity to Scripture should never be equated with a refusal to think. Fact is, there is logic to faith, so the physical evidences can be useful too. Don't expect the Spirit's guidance while embracing the world's sophistry, however, for the Spirit isn't at rest with shallow thinking. Rather than that, wouldn't you want the credibility of God's Word? If so, take it – it's yours! Once having received it, though, you will need to take a stand, since having the armor means taking it up from time to time. After all, some things are so important that we must be willing to fight for them.

Is this being a religious crack-pot, or might it be a new perspective? Return with me, if you will, to Rembrandt. Seeing him in his art, one would have to believe that he once existed. Why then would it be different with God? Unlike Rembrandt, however, God no more relinquished his work than a mother would abandon her child, never to return. Nor is he on break from his duties, having little to do with his universe. What an absurd distortion of God's providence!

In Proverbs 1:22 we read, "How long will mockers delight in mockery and fools hate knowledge?" Isn't this an indication that some are missing the truth? Why are they so myopic? Because anyone who comes to God must first believe that he exists and that he rewards those who earnestly seek him (Heb. 11:6).

Have you stopped to think that it *is* possible to discover him who created the universe? Without faith, though, we cannot even perceive of him. Left to ourselves, we have only doubt and darkness, both of which are ugly intruders into the world. We need not be joined with them, however, not when we can be joined with God – meaning that we must be Scriptural to the core, following the Bible wherever it leads us.

Reformed Hermeneutics

Those tracing their roots to the Reformation treasure the progenitors of the faith and their exegetical principles. People of that stripe take God seriously, knowing that "from him and through him and to him are all things" (Ro. 11:36). Calvinism is based on the conviction that the Bible is God's Word, that it is reliable, and that we must interpret it correctly. What a contrast between that hermeneutic and all lesser formulations! Many evangelicals are not deeply invested in the Bible's self-interpretation. Though they are brothers and sisters in Christ, and people do subscribe to their thinking, theirs is not the best approach to the Bible.

Here is the crux of the matter. There are rules for interpretation, holding that where Scripture is clear we must follow it all the way – rather than going our own way – although we do have our conscience to guide us if Scripture isn't clear. Apart from these principles, and the direction of the Holy Spirit, God's words are easily misread. Concerning the requirements for responsible hermeneutics, R.C. Sproul wrote:

> The Bible is not to be interpreted arbitrarily. Certain fundamental rules of interpretation must be followed to avoid subjectivistic or fanciful interpretation; rules developed by the science of hermeneutics. […] What is unclear or obscure in one place may be clarified in another. We are to interpret the obscure in light of the clear, the implicit in light of the explicit, and narrative in light of the didactic.

> At a technical level the science of hermeneutics becomes quite complex. The biblical scholar must learn to recognize different forms of literature within the Scripture (genre analysis). For example, some parts of the Bible are in the form of historical narrative, while others are in the form of poetry. The interpretation of poetry differs from the interpretation of narrative. The Bible uses metaphor, simile, proverb, parable, hyperbole, parallelism, and many other literary devices that must be recognized in any serious work of interpretation.

> One of the Reformation's chief accomplishments is the principle of the literal interpretation of Scripture [which is not to say that all Scripture is to be taken literally]. The actual principle, called *sensus literalis*, is that the Bible must be interpreted according to the manner in which it is written. *Literal* refers to the literary form of Scripture. […] *Sensus literalis* was designed to seek the plain sense of the Scripture and to focus on one meaning. Though a text may have a multitude of applications, it has only one correct meaning.

> The principle of the *sensus literalis* is closely related to the *grammatico-historical* method of interpretation. This method focuses on the historical setting in which Scripture was written and pays close attention to the grammatical structure of the biblical text. In a broad sense, this method means simply that the Bible is to be interpreted like any other book.[1]

One great legacy of the Reformation is the principle of "private interpretation", and with it comes the responsibility for handling the Bible responsibly. John Bunyan (born in 1628) was from a poor family and had limited educational opportunities. Imprisoned for preaching, he wrote *The Pilgrim's Progress,* which Spurgeon called the most important book in his life, its having been read and translated more often than any other book except the Bible. "So much truth can be learned from it", said Spurgeon, that "if a person will prick Bunyan, he will bleed the Bible."

Spiritual giants have fed on Bunyan, seeing in him the marks of an accomplished theologian. So doing, they were affirming the rule of private interpretation – by a man of rudimentary schooling no less. How might this fit with the verse, "Above all, you must understand that no prophecy of Scripture came about by the prophet's own interpretation"? Kistemaker answered this in his *New Testament Commentary*. "The difference centers on the word, 'own', one meaning being that a person has no freedom to interpret Scripture; the other that Scripture does not originate from the interpretation of a prophet, but from God. […] The first translation stresses the use of Scripture; the second its origin."[2] The second is of course the better interpretation.

Mindful of that, the Reformers held that believers are free to interpret the Bible, keeping in mind that it testifies to its own veracity. That is not to say that teachers and commentaries are unnecessary, or that we can simply disregard ecclesiastical regulation, for as Sproul said, "God has not gifted teachers for his church in vain."

With this as the backdrop, when we set out to unravel God's Word we find that it begins with heaven and earth, darkness and light, seas and skies, land and vegetation, stars and planets, animals and humans, sin and redemption. We find also that many of the themes from the first three chapters of Genesis are reflected in the last three of Revelation,[3] exhibiting remarkable continuity from creation to de-creation to re-creation. Note also that there is neither randomness nor chance in the Bible, although there may be obscurities.

Regarding these, E.J. Young said, "There are no such complexities or obscurities of meaning in the early chapters of Genesis that we should be dissuaded from speaking plainly and forcibly on the truths conveyed in them. Some have maintained that these early chapters are poetry or myth, not to be taken as straightforward accounts, hoping to remove interpretive difficulties in this way. [...] To adopt such a view, they say, removes all troubles with modern science. But the truth is, if you accept such beliefs and methods you are abandoning the Christian faith."[4]

Quoting Luther on the same subject, Young wrote, "We must everywhere adhere to the simple, pure, and natural meaning of the words, avoiding as the most deadly poison all figurative language which Scripture itself does not force us to find in the passage." The fact is, God is the plainest writer and speaker ever, so his words can have no more than one meaning or sense (and that the most obvious), which is what theologians call the *literal* or *natural* sense of Scripture.[5]

Keeping in mind these rules of grammar and speech, what can we say about the historicity of Genesis? Young offered this: "There are poetic accounts of creation in the Bible – Psalm 104 and certain chapters in Job – and they differ completely from the first chapter of Genesis. Hebrew poetry had certain characteristics and they are *not found* in the first chapter of Genesis."[6] Does this mean that these are verbatim accounts – i.e., literalistic truth? To answer that, we shall have to look at the language, along with the context and intent of the verses.

In Genesis 1, the words are simple, direct, and condensed, denoting almost a reticence in their portrayal of creation. Even so, what they convey is miraculous and timeless. "Behind the words are vast movements, separations, and gatherings, all of them vivid, majestic, and mysterious! Had Moses written these words as a mere man, imagine how many erroneous deductions (current in his day) he might have included in his accounts. Yet one is taken with the accuracy of the record, as well as its majesty and simplicity."[7]

As A. Wetherell Johnson taught in her *Bible Study Fellowship*, "Even when seen against the background of the still limited science of our own day, there is no statement which can be disproved. At the same time, many statements are now discovered to be far in advance of their time – so profound that each progress of scientific knowledge gives new meaning to this ancient description of the beginning of our earth."

Today we can appreciate Moses' words even better than did the ancients, but the tools of science do go hand in hand with those of hermeneutics. Using them properly, the evidences support the literal view of creation, for although Moses had none of our models or methods, he had something infinitely more reliable handed him: The words of Almighty God!

Veracity of Scripture

The surprising thing is not how well science agrees with Genesis, but how far people have gotten away from both science and the Bible. A guide in a nearby redwood park, an elder in his church, is on the verge of cashing in his faith. Wherever he goes, he talks about billions of years. People listen quietly, whether accepting his explanations or playing the tolerance card, but the proof is in the Bible, not in his head.

God's Word is "a lamp to our feet and the light upon our path" (Ps. 119:105). But the Bible didn't drop out of heaven, nicely formatted and bound as a completed book. Under the Spirit's power, holy men of old wrote in their own words and styles, producing an end-product free of defect and totally believable. The Reformers insisted that Scripture is infallible in its utterances, that it speaks authoritatively, and that it needs no verification of any kind. Why were they so unbending about this? Because "prophecy never had its origin in the will of man, but men spoke from God as they were carried along by the Holy Spirit" (2 Pe. 1:20-21).

Like a precious jewel, the Bible is lustrous and pure – genuine, honest, and dependable – with a veracity of its own. Were it a mixture of truth and error, it would be of no value at all! The psalmist wrote, "The commands of the Lord are radiant, giving light to the eyes." The analogy is to that of a faultless gem, unmixed with any conflicting material, having value beyond measure (Ps. 19:8). Not only is the Bible infallible, it is inerrant, providing we understand what inerrancy means as it relates to the original documents. During translation there may have been some minor inaccuracies, but God's Word has been divinely preserved, and its declarations are true. Therefore, the Bible has primacy over every square millimeter of the universe, including the halls of science.

Authority of Scripture

When my grandson was only a few years old, I asked him to do something for me. Hours later, seeing he hadn't begun it, I asked, "What were you doing all this time?" Innocently or otherwise, he replied, "Thinking about God." The question is, was he being impish or profound? "What were you doing all this time?" cannot be asked of God, however, since there was no *time* in *eternity*. We know this because God said, "I make known the end from the beginning; from ancient times, what is still to come" (Is. 46:9,10), meaning that pre-historic and future events simply *are* in God's scheme of things.

Time-bound as we humans are, our perspectives are very different from God's. There is more to creation than time, of course, and we can learn about it from the entire Bible; not just a few passages here and there. The most detailed descriptions are in the early chapters of Genesis where we find unequivocal statements about nights and days, work and rest, good and evil, etc. As well, there are references elsewhere in Scripture, detailing God's nature and works. Whether in plain narrative, poetry, metaphor, simile, or parable, they all refer to creation as factual and historical:

- **Pointing to creation as a fundamental work of God:**
  Isa. 45:18: He who created the heavens, he is God; he who fashioned and made the earth, he founded it; he did not create it to be empty, but formed it to be inhabited.
  Col. 1:16: For by him all things were created: things in heaven and on earth, visible and invisible, whether thrones or powers or rulers or authorities; all things were created by him and for him.
  Rev. 4:11: You are worthy, our Lord and God, to receive glory and honor and power, for you created all things and by your will they were created and have their being.
- **Describing God's sovereignty and purpose in nature:**
  Isa. 43:6-7: I will say to the north, 'Give them up!' and to the south, 'Do not hold them back'[…] everyone who is called by my name, I created for my glory.
  Ro. 1:25: They exchanged the truth for a lie, and worshiped and served created things rather than the Creator.
- **Stressing the Omnipotence of God in his creative works:**
  Isa. 40:26: Lift your eyes and look to the heavens: Who created all these? He who brings out the starry host one by one and calls them each by name.
  Am. 4:13: He who forms the mountains, creates the wind, and reveals his thoughts to man – the Lord God Almighty is his name.
- **Confirming God's infinity over nature:**
  Ps. 90:2: Before the mountains were born or you brought forth the earth […] from everlasting […] you are God.
  Ac. 17:24: The God who made the world and everything in it is the Lord of heaven and earth.
- **Referring to the wisdom of God in his creation:**
  Jer. 10:12: He founded the world by his wisdom and stretched out the heavens by his understanding.
  Jn. 1:3: Through him all things were made; without him nothing was made that has been made.

With these verses in hand, people should have no difficulty deciding whether the early creation narratives are real or imaginary. And yet they do, some holding that long periods of time elapsed between various epochs of creation, others that the days themselves were periods of time. The question is, where can we go for the real story? Do the words in their historical setting refer to *literal happenings* and *actual timetables*, or should they be read differently?

Howard Van Till, in his "vehicle model", maintains that we must distinguish between *vehicle* (literary genre), *packaging* (symbols, stories, etc.), and *content* (God's message to us), separating vehicle and packaging from the content as one would do in removing the wrapper from candy. "Vehicle" and "genre" are inseparable to him, and "packaging" (says he) must take into account "symbolism and cultural patterns forming the context."[8]

With this method, there is considerable separation between what is said and how it is said, and that should be of concern to faithful expositors. This dichotomy between "errant husk" and "inerrant kernel" opens the way for *theistic evolution*, an obvious distortion of the creation account. Given that methodology, who is to distinguish packaging from content? Separating the two has ruinous ramifications when applied to the totality of Scripture, as in the virgin birth and the resurrection of Christ! Note also that this form/content hermeneutic was the dominant method in the liberal tradition of the 19th and 20th centuries, and by now it has been thoroughly discredited!

During the Reformation of the 16th century, faithful believers came to the scriptures submissively – accepting God as the writer and man as the reader. Risking their lives, they approached the Bible *from below* (with believing minds), asking "What does the text say?"

The contrasting approach is "higher criticism", where the reader sits *above* the text as its critic, viewing it as any other historical document – the assumption being that the Bible is a collection of human writings by ancient men, addressed to remote and specific audiences. It is left to the reader to determine the author's intent, but that is a thoroughly humanistic approach viewing Scripture as time-conditioned and variable in meaning.

Still another method is that of the charismatics. Seeing the Bible as true but not final, they claim that God speaks through visions, dreams, tongues, and other revelations, even today. To them, truth is revelatory but also experiential, continuing, and changeable. When this approach is combined with higher criticism, yet another hermeneutic evolves: a hybrid asserting correctly that the Bible is God's Word but wrongly that God provided a second book of nature to be understood through the "eyes of science".

Given these approaches, how does creation tie in with history? Quite obviously, any interpretation questioning the event/character (factuality) of the first and fundamental chapters of the Bible cannot be spiritually derived, since the Spirit never leads one to believe something in addition to (or contravening) the words of Scripture. Nor may we view the early chapters of the Bible as merely God's "accommodation to the human situation by way of highly-stylized accounts", as Van Till suggests.

Putting it positively, we are to trust *God's authority over man's majority*, reading all pre-Abrahamic chronology as genuine and historical, including its timetables and genealogies. Reasons for this are many, but basic to them all is the principle that *Scripture is self-authenticating*. While extra-biblical perspectives (linguistics, archaeology, natural science, history, etc.) may illuminate the text to an extent, they have no authority for calling into question the *event/character of the account*. How do we know this? By comparing Scripture with Scripture, allowing the Bible to speak for itself. Also, by contextual analysis of the many New Testament texts corroborating Old Testament narratives. Here are a few of them:

- **Concerning the "goodness" of Creation:** For everything God created is good (1 Ti. 4:4).
- **Describing Adam as created from non-living material:** The first man, Adam, became a living being [...] of the dust of the earth (1 Co. 15:45-47).
- **Regarding the order of creation:** For Adam was formed first, then Eve (1 Ti. 2:13).
- **Contrasting Christ with Adam:** For as in Adam all die, so in Christ all will be made alive (1 Co. 15:22).
- **Comparing Noah's Flood with Sodom's judgment:** It was the same in the days of Lot. People were eating and drinking, buying and selling, planting and building. But the day Lot left Sodom, fire and sulfur rained down (Lk. 17: 28,29).
- **Comparing the Flood with Christ's second coming:** For in the days before the flood, people were eating and drinking, marrying and giving in marriage, up to the day Noah entered the ark [...] That is how it will be at the coming of the Son of Man (Mt. 24:38-40).
- **Illustrating the Old Testament "heroes of the faith":** By faith, Abel [...] By faith, Noah [...] By faith, Abraham, etc. (Heb. 11:4-8).
- **Presenting the genealogy of Jesus:** see the record of Christ's lineage from Joseph, to Adam, to God the Father (Lk. 3:23-37).
- **Identifying the Flood and baptism (as covenantal signs):** Only a few people, eight in all, were saved through water, and this water symbolizes baptism that now saves you also (I Pe. 3:20-22).

As the saying goes, "The New is in the Old contained; the Old is by the New explained." New Testament accounts corroborate earlier events, chronologies, and genealogies, so there is nothing illusory about them. Not only did all the NT writers see these as real; they accepted them *literally*, just as Jesus did. As Boice wrote in his *Genesis, An Expository Comment*, "A special aspect of the attitude of Scripture to Genesis is the teaching of Jesus Christ. This obviously carries special weight. [...] Did Jesus consider the accounts of Genesis historical? Indeed he did! He quoted them as fact."[9] Seeing that he viewed them as such, they are not symbolic illustrations or parabolic portrayals!

Others have said it even more forcefully. Referring to the high regard we must have for literal truth, M.R. DeHaan wrote, "If we can repudiate or disprove the authenticity of the Pentateuch, we have destroyed the very foundation on which all of Scripture rests. But there is a more serious implication: a clever, subtle attack upon the authority not only of Moses, but upon the authority and veracity of Jesus Christ. Jesus quoted more often from the writings of Moses than from any other part of the Old Testament. Jesus believed, taught, and asserted that the books of Moses were authentic, binding, and as genuine as he himself was."[10]

There is no question, of course, that portions of Genesis are treated as **types** in the New Testament. The first Adam, for instance, is a contrasting type of the second. But types are not doctrinal statements, except when writers make applications from them such that they become doctrinal assertions, and even then whatever value such illustrations have is from the historicity of the events themselves.

Finally, the Bible is a completed canon, a closed body of truth. Nothing new is being added, nor does God contradict or supersede what he has written in it. Given that degree of finality, and the remarkable continuity throughout the Canon, the Bible speaks its truths to all generations.

Still, there can be problems with interpretation since Scripture doesn't come with identifying headers telling us that certain parts of it are literally true and others not. Nor does it tell us how the original authors and their audiences understood the message. Faithful interpreters have always examined syntax, grammar, and word usage as well as the purpose of the text in the context of redemption. In this way, the Bible interprets itself, as in the grammatico-historical method. Deciphering it, we needn't be experts in languages, antiquities, or science, but we must submit to the text and handle it carefully.

Regarding the usefulness of the Bible, it is authoritative in every area of life, whether we see that or not, and when we advocate something contrary to Scripture (literalistically or otherwise), we make it harder for people to take it seriously. Also, we may never declare the Bible figurative simply because certain evidences seem to be pointing in that direction. The evidence notwithstanding, when Scripture teaches something plainly, we must accept that as factual. Science, for example, leaves little room for miracles, but God's Word is filled with them, so the evidences must be tested by Scripture – never the reverse. And yes, there *is* literalism in the Bible.

Perspicuity and Sufficiency of Scripture

In Eden God talked with Adam in the clearest of language, telling him some wonderful truths. The question does arise as to how he told Adam about his supernatural deeds, but whatever Adam heard was sufficient for him. Later in history, Moses was handed a record in stone: "In six days the Lord made the heavens and the earth, the sea and all that is in them" (Ex. 20:11). God must have told him more than that, also, but we must be content with what is written since the Bible is sufficient for all our needs.

We call this the perspicuity and sufficiency of Scripture, meaning that it is intelligible and adequate. Though perhaps unfathomable to an extent, its doctrines are so clearly presented that even the unlearned can grasp them. And yet, there is a distance between God and man, for he is infinite and we are bound by nature. Human knowledge is therefore limited, for knowing God fully would mean participating in his attribute of infinity.

Given human deficiency and unbelief, many say that the Bible is obscure, that it cannot be taken as factual, and that its vagary is in the very areas where we need answers (gender diversity, church leadership, termination of life, the singularities of the cosmos, etc.). This supposed fogginess of Scripture has been used to "free" humanity from restraint, which is a huge threat to the Christian faith, begging questions like these: Are the early chapters of Genesis to be read as true history? Does it really matter what Jesus said about them? Aren't these stories rather ill-defined, anyway? How do they relate to modern man, and who cares, really?

Adjusting the Spectacles

One of my surgical colleagues, committed to an aged cosmos, said to me, "If I can tolerate your creation 'days', why can't you tolerate mine?" The answer is obvious, isn't it? But to see it we must adjust the spectacles or the truth will always be blurred.

When Joshua and Caleb spied out Canaan, they demonstrated for all time that there is a difference between truth and opinion. Opinion is not always reliable, nor is truth variable, as if it were mutable. There is also a distinction to be made between truth and tolerance. Truth is *unity, unity, unity*, coming as it does from the Spirit. While there may be commonality among people, *unity* is from God, and the most natural reading of his Word! *Your* opinion and *mine* are therefore irrelevant except when properly grounded.

Sin has so darkened the mind that we have trouble letting God speak for himself. This is especially problematic combined with a smattering of knowledge, making us garble the facts. But couldn't we solve this by saying that *Scripture trumps science*? Actually, faulty interpretations trump nothing; faulty views have no commanding authority at all, so if we say that Special Revelation trumps general revelation we must mind our hermeneutics. Having done that, however, wouldn't "days" be *days* unless there is compelling biblical evidence to the contrary? Wouldn't that be true for the Bible's chronologies, sequences, and genealogies, as well? In fact, shouldn't all our views match God's declarations?

People have trouble with this, and "Reformed thinking" is not always a sure remedy. Why not? Because some are only "culturally Reformed", having never themselves embraced the scriptures. Whether because of their creativity or congeniality, even "giants of the faith" have stumbled, so their arguments are not always valid.

Why do people stray so far from sound hermeneutics? Because they see science and Scripture as *coequal*, albeit a misapplication of the principles. Remember, wrong views stem from faulty *presuppositions* (authority claims) and faulty *epistemologies* (views of truth), influencing people's *apologetics* and *methods*. There is room for presuppositions, epistemologies, apologetics, and methods, to be sure, but these must yield to him whose thoughts and words are higher than ours. Believers should thus be wary of all human spins, and this is where many stumble, even within the Reformed camp. Could it be that they have forgotten the Reformation?

The Holy Spirit both authored the Bible and guides us in our understanding of it, but even possessing the full measure of faith, we Christians can have trouble with the scriptures, and with each other. Therefore, we must measure our thoughts with those of fellow believers, especially regarding God's two revelations. As J. I. Packer put it, "Understanding does not usually, and certainly not fully, occur outside the fellowship of faith", which is why Paul wrote, "Let the word of Christ dwell in you richly as you teach and admonish one another with all wisdom" (Col. 3:16). So remember, though God enlightens us through his Word and Spirit, he does so also through the Christian community.

As demonstrated over the centuries, the insight of fellow-believers can be helpful, but we must look also into our hearts, being sure that we aren't interpreting things after our own fancy. Furthermore, we must never elevate human teachings above God's Word, as if they were idols. Nor may we ride hobby horses, since truth involves balance. We can be passionate about our views, but they must fit with Truth, and an accurate representation of that implies more than a casual acquaintance with the Bible.

Mindful of Scripture and each other, we can better evaluate the models connected with origins. Whether this leads in a literalistic or a non-literalistic direction, the Bible must make that clear as its own interpreter. It will do just that, serving as our spectacles, providing we have the *eyes of faith* and the *lens of the Spirit*.

Concerning the intellect, God says, "The battle is mine; I will never leave nor forsake you."

God moves in a mysterious way his wonders to perform.
He plants his footsteps in the sea and rides upon the storm.

Deep in unfathomable mines of never-failing skill,
he treasures up his bright designs and works his sovereign will.

Blind unbelief is sure to err and scan his work in vain.
God is his own interpreter, and he will make it plain.

(William Cowper, 1774)

RESPONSIBLE HERMENEUTICS

> The analogy of Scripture: The Bible is its own interpreter.
> Exegesis, not isogesis: Being true to the text, not reading into it.
> The text can have only one correct interpretation. It may have some specific application, but that must be from Scripture itself.
> Individual texts are to be understood within the overall context (verse, chapter, book, and the Bible itself).
> The obscure is elucidated (made plain) by the more obvious.
> The Bible should be read according to its most obvious meaning and its literary sense (*Sensus literalis*).
> The authority of Scripture is not to be subordinated to external evidences, influences, & authorities.
> General revelation is interpreted in light of the clear teaching of Scripture.
> Genre is important. Eastern and Western minds can differ, so the Bible is to be read according to how it was written, minding its grammar, syntax, setting, etc.
> The historico-grammatical method is tied to real history with its factual events, specific times, actual places, & genuine people.

– The N.T. is in the Old contained; the O.T. is by the New explained –

[1] R.C. Sproul, *The Heart of Reformed Theology,* Baker Books, Grand Rapids, MI, 1987, pp. 61,62
[2] Simon J. Kistemaker, *New Testament Commentary*, Baker Books, Grand Rapids, MI, 1996, p. 271-272
[3] NIV Study Bible, *Introduction to Genesis,* Zondervan Bible Publishers, Grand Rapids, MI, p.4
[4] E.J. Young, *In The Beginning,* The Banner of Truth Trust, Carlisle, PA, 1984, pp. 12,13
[5] R.C. Sproul, commenting on *"What Luther Says"*, *The Heart of Reformed Theology,* Baker Books, Grand Rapids, MI, 1997, pp. 56,57
[6] Ibid, p. 18
[7] A. Wetherell Johnson, *Overview of the Book of Genesis,* Zondervan Bible Publishers, Grand Rapids, MI, 1984
[8] Howard J Van Till, *The Fourth Day,* Wm. B. Eerdmans Publishing Co., Grand Rapids, MI, 1989, pp. 14-19
[9] James Montgomery Boice, *Genesis, An Expositional Commentary, Vol. 1.,* Zondervan Publishing House, Grand Rapids, MI, 1982, p 21
[10] M.R. DeHaan, *Genesis and Evolution,* Zondervan Publishing Co., Grand Rapids, MI, 1962, pp. 40-43

THIS IS MY FATHER'S WORLD
(Chapter 6)

Miracle of Knowledge

The psalmist wrote, "Your works are wonderful. I know that full well. My frame was not hidden from you when I was made in the secret place. When I was woven together in the depths of the earth, your eyes saw my unformed body. All the days ordained for me were written in your book before one of them came to be" (Ps. 139:14-17). Isn't it amazing that God knew us so long ago and that he himself initiated our friendship? More surprising still, he knew all along that his Son would descend down the stairway of the stars, taking on our flesh.

Paul said that someone might give his life for a good person, but he marveled that Christ would show *sinners* such love (Ro. 5:8). From eternity past, God had selected those whom he would call his sons and daughters, for as John wrote later, "How great is the love the Father has lavished on us, that we should be called children of God! And that is what we are! The reason the world does not know us is that it did not know him. Dear friends, now we are children of God, and what we will be has not yet been made known. But we know that when he appears we shall be like him, for we shall see him as he is" (1 Jn. 3:1). How marvelous! Could this be why we shall one day cast our crowns at Jesus' feet?

We earthlings are not deserving of Heaven! Paul wrote to Timothy, "This grace was given us in Christ Jesus before the beginning of time, but it has now been revealed through the appearing of our Savior, Christ Jesus, who has destroyed death and has brought life and immortality to light through the gospel" (2 Ti. 1:10). Regarding this, we are told in Revelation, "The inhabitants of the earth whose names have **not** been written in the book of life from the creation of the world will be astonished" (Rev. 17:8). Their fall, like that of all humanity, came as no surprise to God. As Horton put it, "Things don't just happen – God is always in charge! Just when it looks like the tragic end of a short play, the curtain rises, the orchestra flourishes, and the drama of redemption begins. The opening act of this redemptive play takes place in the royal court of heaven, in eternity past."[1]

In that court God appointed Christ the **primary agent of creation** and the heir of all things. We believe this so that we know and we know it because we believe. How strange! Can we really base our thinking on such reasoning and still be scientific? Some think not, having only hearts of stone, but others have this handed them directly, as in the words of this song: "I will pour water on him that is thirsty; I will pour floods upon the dry ground. Open your heart for the gift I am bringing; while you are seeking me, I will be found" (Lucy J. Rider). Receiving this on the strength of God's Word, believers have the advantage, for their faith knowledge convinces them of three things: 1) *that* God is, 2) *who* he is, and 3) that he can be *found*. This comes to them from an intelligence source outside the usual realm of thought, so believers see what others cannot imagine.

Were knowledge only the reasoning of the mind, and were we to rely on it alone, we would be rationalists (not believers), but true knowledge implies faith and reason, and the two can be in perfect harmony. When they clash, as they sometimes do, it is usually reason that is at fault. But that doesn't consign it to the wastebasket. Faith fits the evidences, so we should be willing to dig for the detail, but the Spirit must first enter into our hearts, mysterious though that might be.

Two ancient church fathers, Augustine and Anselm, saw this clearly; they held that faith knowledge is in accord with intellectual knowledge. They went on to say that faith precedes intelligence *(fides precedit intellectum)*. Intelligence is thus anchored in faith, but that doesn't mean that Christians are imbeciles. Believers are convinced of certain realities because of the evidences **and** by faith, but this is easily confused since faith is not primarily a function of the mind. The sinner is *dead*, after all, so something has to be done about that. Someone must give us insight, or there will never **be** intellectual knowledge, and that Someone is the Spirit of the Living God. Not one iota of wisdom is from our own doing, or it wouldn't be a gift! How peculiar and how extraordinary!

Knowledge of Miracles

Everyone has *faith* based on some prior commitment. Either we allow the Divine through the door or we don't, and if we deny him it's like cross-threading a bolt: the more we force it, the harder it becomes. Whether believing in God or dismissing him entirely, it is our starting point that shapes our thinking. Knowing this, believers have had the benefit all along having experienced answered prayer, sometimes miraculously. Why not look beyond the cosmos, then, since God is a God of miracles?

But what are miracles, and what is their cause? Miracles are from a first cause, God's power, absent any secondary causes like the laws of the universe and/or human intervention. Miracles are distinctive because, as in everything related to creation, God departs from his usual order and produces something extraordinary through the power of his will. These actions are so filled with wonder and so very unusual that they evoke in us feelings of awe. Lockyer defined miracles as "work wrought by a divine power for a divine purpose by means beyond the reach of man – events or efforts in the physical world deviating from the known laws of nature and transcending our knowledge of these laws – extraordinary, anomalous, or abnormal events brought about by a super-human agency, out of the usual secondary causes and effects which cannot be accounted for by the ordinary operation of those causes."[2] Why should there be any question then as to why miracles have stirred humans to adoration and praise?

Real and mind-boggling though miracles are, one should be selective in the use of the term as it pertains to creation, the Fall, and the Flood. Unlike other miraculous happenings, these were epochal events, without parallel in history – sentinel events that never happened before or afterward, involving incredible feats, great upheavals, and whole populations of people and animals. Though miraculous in nature, they are better described as one-time, supernatural occurrences exhibiting a reversal of nature's laws at special times and for specific purposes. Deviating from known processes, they demonstrate that God is more than a maker of laws, since he is sovereign, dealing with the universe as he sees fit – whenever and wherever, according to his own will and purposes.

Miracles are mentioned in the Bible as real and historical, so our faith would be lacking if we set them aside. "Those denying them", said Lockyer, "are 'like the poor' – always with us." Matthew Arnold dismissed them airily. Said he, "They simply do not happen." Huxley ("Darwin's bulldog") said sacrilegiously, "Evolutionary man can no longer take refuge from his loneliness by creeping for shelter into the arms of a divinized father figure whom he has himself created." Little wonder that the psalmist wrote, "The one enthroned in heaven laughs at them. The Lord scoffs at them. Then he rebukes them in his anger and terrifies them in his wrath, saying [...] *I will proclaim the decree of the Lord*" (Ps. 2: 4-7).

The delusion of our day is that the universe could have come from something *other than* extraordinary activity. Were one to limit everything to secondary, explainable causes (undirected at that), science could never investigate supernatural causes. Lockyer said it well: "Nature is not the 'straight jacket' from which God cannot escape"[3], for if we deny God the power to create uniquely, he is no longer the God of freedom, above and independent of nature. Having said that, is there still room for a supernatural God in a naturalistic world? Well, how could one answer that, having no such world? There are more flaws in that question than there are words!

The Bible describes a complex array of creative activity where supernatural agency was everywhere! It tells us also about the confusion of tongues, the sun's reversal, the plagues of Egypt, the turning of water into wine, the dead rising, and the immaculate conception of him who (later) arose from the grave. Nothing naturalistic here! These are all supernaturalism on display, demonstrating processes which we cannot in principle explain! In fact, it would be arrogant to think otherwise – that one could grasp God's speaking the cosmos into being, with all its functioning parts. As recorded in Psalm 19:1-2, "The heavens declare the glory of God; the skies proclaim the work of his hands. Day after day they pour forth speech; night after night they display knowledge." Such knowledge comes easily to the wise, but the mocker seeks wisdom and finds none (Pr. 14:6). The problem is, the natural mind is at enmity with God, hostile toward him from the outset, due to unseen forces of evil.

Heavenly Hosts

My wife and I served for several years in a Native-American hospital where we encountered some colorful surnames: "Sees the Bear", "Pretends Eagle", "Callous Leg", "Came Running", "Kills Pretty Enemy", etc. While on the reservation, we were distressed by the "demon in the bottle". Demons are of course not confined to bottles. Believers know that demons are everywhere, and as real as angels of light. *The Belgic Confession* (Art. 12) refers to angels as follows: "He also created the angels good, to be his messengers and to serve his elect, some of whom are fallen from that excellency in which God created them into everlasting perdition; and the others have by the grace of God remained steadfast and continued in their first state."

People of all religions believe in a spiritual world, but they may not know where it originated. The truth is, God made that world, "for by him all things were created; things in heaven and on earth, visible and invisible, whether thrones or powers or rulers or authorities" (Col. 1:16). As to when these hosts were created, the time cannot be fixed. Berkof wrote in his *Systematic Theology*, "The opinion of some (based on Job 38:7) that as 'morning stars' they were created before all other things, really finds no support in Scripture. The only safe statement seems to be that they were created before the seventh day."[4]

Billy Graham said the important question is not, "When were angels created?" but "When did they fall?" It is hard to imagine their fall occurring before God placed Adam and Eve in the Garden, since God rested after he pronounced everything good. "By implication, up to this time even the angelic realm was good. We might ask, then, 'How long were Adam and Eve in the Garden before the angels fell and before Satan tempted the first man and woman?' Regrettably, this question must remain unanswered."[5]

The Bible does mention two kinds of angels, those remaining true to God and those rebelling against him. Lucifer declared war on God, and that battle has been raging since shortly after the dawn of history. Of him, Berkhof wrote, "He appears in Scripture as the recognized head of fallen angels. He was originally, it would seem, one of the mightiest princes of the angelic world, and became the leader of those that revolted and fell away from God. The name 'Satan' points to him as 'the Adversary', not in the first place of man, but of God. He attacks Adam as the crown of God's handiwork – and us today."[6]

Good or bad, angels have superhuman powers varying according to their regard for the Creator. Though invisible, they have taken on visible forms, both animate and inanimate. They are also multitudinous, for in Deuteronomy we read, "The Lord came from Sinai […] from myriads of holy ones" (Dt. 33:2). In Revelation we read, "I looked and heard the voice of many angels, numbering thousands upon thousands, and ten thousand times ten thousand" (Rev. 5:11). Taken literally, there would be at least 100 million of them. None can ever experience the joy of salvation, however, so there are things that angels clearly do *not* do. They are not born and they do not marry; they do not tire and they are not afflicted with illness or death. They do have capabilities, ranks, and positions; they also have intelligence and responsibilities, and they are rational, moral, and immortal in character.

As an aside, what do you suppose would have happened had Christ called out for help from the Cross? The legions would have sprung into action immediately had he but asked! After all, who made them? But wouldn't Satan have come out the winner in this scenario? And what then? Knowing the Devil's inability to manage anything of value, the universe would have collapsed! Rest assured, though, that none of this could have happened without violating God's consistency. Never was there any doubt about this, for Christ had set his face like flint and would cry out only in agony. How thankful I am that he chose instead to bear my sins!

Heaven's hosts do presuppose the heavens themselves, but how many are there and how do they differ? Whitcomb mentions three, only one of which was designed for celestial beings. Says he, "For convenience of human thought and expression, the Bible refers to three heavens. The third heaven is that glorious place surrounding the immediate presence of God, to which Paul was carried in a transcendent vision early in his Christian experience (2 Co. 12:1-4). The second heaven seems to be equivalent to what we call 'outer space'; while the first heaven consists of the atmospheric blanket surrounding the earth, in which clouds move and the birds fly."[7] Given this explanation, it is the third heaven which is populated with faithful angelic beings.

What do angels and demons have in common? They appear in the Bible and must answer to their Maker. Unbelievers have no comprehension of them at all but only of magic and wizardry. To them, the legions of heaven are metaphysical abstractions as unreal as heaven itself. But that does not remove them from the universe. Though not to be found by the scientific method, they are genuinely present and active for good and for evil. We might not be able to see that now, but we shall see it when the Son of Man comes in his Father's glory with his angels (Mt. 16:27). On that day, we may be surprised to learn the number of times angels interceded in our lives, assisting, protecting, and delivering us – and the number of times we knowingly or unknowingly served demons. But some things will be seen only after the heart stops beating.

In the Beginning

Angels aside, what can we say about beginnings? The fact *that* God made the universe is unmistakable, but *how* he made it is another question, for we have never seen anything like it! He simply spoke things into existence, *ex nihilo* (out of nothing), by his divine *fiat* (proclamation, or decree). From the language itself, we see that God spoke these words rather recently compared with the naturalistic framework.

All the material and information in the universe appeared during a week of ordinary length, in a state of completed perfection, in all its splendor, diversity, and complexity. And whenever God made something new, it emerged fully functional and whole. God then crowned his creation week by making Adam and Eve, forming them with his own hands, Adam from dust and Eve from Adam's rib. Afterward, nothing new was added: no new matter, no new energy, no new "kinds" – though sin did *change* things later on.

The word "Genesis" means "origins". Chapters 1-11 of Genesis are primeval (primitive) history, and the remainder of Genesis is the history of the patriarchs. Genesis is a superb introduction to creation as well as to the whole of Scripture. It starts majestically, "In the beginning, God created the heavens and the earth." With disarming understatement and in the clearest of language, Moses is describing the origin of time, energy, space, and matter.

Although everything takes place supernaturally, we're told about it in the most natural of terms, highlighting the fact that apart from God there is no explanation for beginnings. However, to appreciate this we must admit that there was a *beginning*, which is inconceivable to those saying, "In the beginning there was matter."

Ten times in the first chapter of Genesis we read, "and God said." Each time, by the power of his Word he created something new and magnificent, demonstrating his omnipotence. The first thing striking the reader is that when God spoke, things happened! Everything bowed to his decree, including the laws of the universe. Not only that, but the creatures God made were functionally developed from the very outset, or how could he have commanded them to reproduce?

Unable to evolve, decay, or die, they were later inundated by water, destroying all breathing animals except for those in the Ark. That this is genuinely historical is central to the Christian faith, for either we accept Moses, the Prophets, and the Gospels or we sit in judgment on them. To be blunt about it, there is no alternative. Either we receive the Bible as written, or we reject it totally, thus losing our claim to salvation.

Genesis is the tap-root for everything else in Scripture. If God is not who he says he is in Genesis, then perhaps he is not our Redeemer either. If he didn't create the universe as he said he did, then perhaps he will not recreate it either. If we reject Genesis, we reject the Canon, and if we reject *it* we reject the Savior – in which case we are lost as to the past, present, and future. Once having accepted Genesis without watering it down, we can have assurance about many things, but we don't have the liberty to tamper with it, for God says what he means and means what he says!

Acts of Creation

Time didn't exist until God spoke it into existence. Neither did space, energy, and matter. These all came at his command, and the heavens and earth appeared on Day 1, not over eons. It was time in particular that provided the framework for everything else. So specific was it that nothing arrived outside its parameters, called "days". Within them were the following acts of creation:

Day 1: Light and darkness – day and night
Day 2: Earth's atmosphere – the firmament
Day 3: Dry land and seas; plants and trees
Day 4: Sun, moon and stars – for seasons, days, and years
Day 5: Sea creatures and birds
Day 6: Land animals, creeping things, and man

Eons were invented by humans, but God needed only days. Though ordinary in length, they were extraordinary in creativity. But why would God have created things in the first place? Because he wanted creatures with whom he could *commune*. To them he would reveal his wisdom, power, and grace, from the Garden to the Cross, from the Cross to the Banquet! In return, humanity was to glorify him forever.

Each day after making something new God called it "good", but after making Adam and Eve in his own image and likeness he looked again, calling what he had made, "very good" (Ge. 1:31). What a profound demonstration of unaffected prose! Here was perfection on display, matching God's "good" with his goodness! How could this have been said by one who merely wound up the universe and abandoned it? How could a *deistic* god (one who is not supernatural) be eternally caring? Could God have said "good" over some lengthy process of death and decay without tarnishing his image? Flawed things could have come only from a *dualistic* god (mixing bad with good). But aren't these the brush marks of Satan? Reflect on this as we focus on the adventures of each day.

On Day One, God's Spirit was hovering over the deep. The earth was without shape or habitation – formless, dark, and empty – the very antithesis of harmony and order. Everything was "waste and void", as in the rhythmic reinforcement of two Hebrew words, *"tohu"* and *"bohu"*. Day One was also different from those following it, since matter existed before time as we know it (i.e., before the creation of light). As to how long the earth was in this timeless state, that is irrelevant, not because the Bible's chronology is speculative but because Exodus 20:11 tells us, *"in six days* the Lord made the heavens and the earth, the sea, and all that is in them, but he rested on the seventh day."

Once the darkness was lit, "there was evening and there was morning, the first day" (Ge. 1:5). Thereafter, God's acts followed an explicit formula reflecting the Jewish custom that each new day begins at dusk and ends at dawn. Think about that as you rotate a globe on its axis. Lighting it from any fixed position such as yourself, turn it slowly away for a single rotation. The point nearest the light source will move into darkness and again into the light, completing a full circle like that of the first day.

Now, picture the world from God's perspective, with him holding the light. Could this be the explanation for our reading *nowhere* in Scripture that "days" were years or years were "eons"? In terms of the earth's rotation, eons make no sense at all, which is why we read only about days like our own, transitioning from evening to morning. With this interpretation, the Jewish Sabbath is easily understood, as are the days of creation.

As to where the first light originated, we haven't the answer, but we do know that God didn't need the sun's rays, since he has the capacity to create how and when he wishes, whether making the light of antiquity or that of today. The initial light could have been transitory, becoming bound on the fourth day to the luminaries, but how about its speed? Did the light of yesteryear travel like today's? Many insist that it would have traveled no faster initially than now, but God isn't bound by laws or photons. The first rays could in fact have been a reflection of God's glory, as Moses reflected it in his face. But how presumptuous to think that we would have all the answers!

God himself said, "Have you ever given orders to the morning, or shown the dawn its place" (Job 38:12)? Said the Lord, "What is the way to the abode of light? And where does darkness reside? Can you take them to their places? Do you know the paths to their dwellings" (Job 38:19,20)? "Will the one who contends with the Almighty correct him" (Job 40:2)? "*I* form the light and create darkness" (Is. 45:7). "Woe to him who quarrels with his Maker" (Is. 45:9).

On Day Two, God rearranged the environment. Creating an expanse between the waters, he called it "sky", separating the waters below from those above. But here is the question: Could there have been a vapor canopy blocking solar radiation and enhancing organic growth? Such a firmament would have been advantageous, although it might also have raised temperatures and pressures to ruinous levels. Had it existed, it could have obscured the celestial bodies to the extent that they would not have been visible for signs and seasons on the fourth day. Moses doesn't explain this, but the movement of water from below to above must have been momentous! Yet God managed it so effectively that no harm occurred, whether such a canopy once existed or not.

On Day Three, God separated the earth from the water. As Peter wrote centuries later (referring to Earth's pre- and post-flood status), "the earth was formed out of water and by water" (2 Pe. 3:5). God called the dry ground, "land", and the gathered waters, "seas". Isn't it amazing that he reached down to the very details of human language specifying the words "land" and "seas"? God also caused the land to produce vegetation, "seed-bearing plants and trees bearing fruit, according to their kinds". But thorns and thistles were not mentioned until after the Fall.

When did the rains arrive? Probably not before the Flood, for we are told in Genesis 2:6 that "streams came up from the earth and watered the whole surface of the ground", but "no shrub of the earth and no plant of the field had yet sprung up, for God had not sent rain on the earth and there was no man to work the ground" (Ge. 2:5). How very different from rain-drops splattering the shales, long before Adam's appearance, as held by *geologic uniformitarianism.*

On Day Four, God made the sun, moon, and stars to govern the day and the night, and to separate the light from the darkness. The question is, how does this fit with the light of Day One? Once again, we don't have the answer, though we do know that light existed before light-bearers. It would seem also that if day five was a solar day, the earlier days would have been similar in length, seeing that they were fixed by the earth's rotation and the words of Moses.

There is also the question of an inflationary bang. Could one theorize such an event even if the Bible doesn't mention it? Perhaps so, but only on God's terms. The Bible doesn't reject a bang, but it doesn't affirm it either; neither does Moses mention billions of years for the unfolding of the universe, or stars appearing before the earth. We should have no trouble with expansion, though, for we read in Psalm 104:2, "You wrap yourself in light as with a garment; you stretch out the heavens like a tent."

The problem with cosmic expansion is the naturalistic explanation of it. Scientists offer expansion on the basis of *inflation theory*, but they haven't proven "The Bang", no matter the research or expense. But why try, seeing that starlight reached this planet on the *fourth* day for signs and seasons, just as in Genesis 1? Lesser cosmogonies may reach for the stars, but they never seem to grasp them. And yet there are those who see these wonders as "cosmic coincidences".

Think about the One who made the stars almost as an afterthought, as in the phrase, "he made the stars also!" How could anyone fathom him who said, "My own hands stretched out the heavens; I marshaled their starry hosts" (Is. 45:12)? Who but the God of the Universe could have stretched out over 100 billion galaxies in a single day, red-shifted or otherwise? Yet all these billions of galaxies and zillions of stars were individually named!

On Day Five, God made the birds and sea creatures. Birds didn't mutate from reptiles, and sea creatures didn't evolve from the slime. Fish didn't arrive before birds, and insects didn't precede birds either. What about the great sea monsters? Those of Job's day must have been awesome indeed, but (though extinct) they didn't die out eons ago. These are all myths, unknown to Scripture. The fact is, God spoke these creatures into existence during a day of ordinary length, and not through cosmic seeding or lengthy processes. He gave them reproductive capacities too, confounding evolutionists. But where could the **"nephesh chaya"** (breath of life) have come from, except from the Almighty?

On Day Six, God created land creatures, each "kind" with its fixed genetic code. Scientists tell us that a gram of DNA contains enough information to fill a trillion compact discs and that the calculations made by a living cell during one second would require a year's computation by a person. Obviously, cells are supercomputers, though less so (by far) than whole organisms! The supreme example of complexity, however, was Adam. In creating him, God changed his fiat declaration from "let there be" to "let us make man in our image and in our likeness." Having said this, he made them male and female, ready for service.

But isn't something missing here? Where are the micro-cephalic, hunch-backed, carnivorous, and cannibalistic intermediates? Not only are they *missing* but their crouching and grunting would have been foreign to Paradise. So enormous is that chasm between animals and humans that Adam couldn't have arrived except by God's personal fashioning. This is that aspect of mankind unexplained by unbelieving anthropologists and their hominids.

Like strobe-lights on a police cruiser, Adam reflected God perfectly! Here was God on parade! No other creature could have so mirrored the Creator; nor could any animal relate so personally to God. Unlike apes, Adam stood erect before his Maker, his spine attached to the base of his skull. So special was this first Adam that the second would have a body like his! Here was a creature with rationality, awareness, and purpose – one with whom God could communicate and fellowship.

Consider for a moment how remarkable we are, which is why we do the things we do. Gifted for higher things, some of us can sing while others listen; some paint while others admire; some bear children while others transplant hearts. Though touched by sin and tainted by it, we have the glory of God within us!

Could others but see that in us, they might be more inclined toward their Maker. As Paul wrote, "If I have the gift of prophesy and can fathom all mysteries and all knowledge, and if I have a faith that can move mountains, but have not love, I am nothing. If I give all I possess to the poor and surrender my body to the flames, but have not love, I gain nothing. [...] Now we see but a poor reflection as in a mirror; then we shall see face to face; then I shall know fully, even as I am fully known. And now these three remain: faith, hope, and love. But the greatest of these is love" (1 Co. 13). The question is, can people see that in you? If so, they are looking at your Creator, albeit only a reflection.

Oh that my unbelieving friends could see that too! Though having their doctorates and their Chairs, few know God or have an appreciation for Adam. Like Darwin and Sagan, they end up foolish and deceived. Believers need not be like them, however, "for he chose us in him before the creation of the world to be holy and blameless in his sight" (Eph. 1:4).

No Place Like Home

A bumper sticker tells it like it is: Good planets are hard to find! "People have been finding more planets every year, but Planet Earth seems to be more exceptional than ever. Yet we take this all for granted." So said Robert Craddock, geologist at the Smithsonian Center for Earth and Planetary Studies. Summarizing his comments:

> Our blue seas, green hills, snow-covered mountains, rivers and plains (photographed from the moon by Apollo astronauts over 30 years ago) remain unrivaled in their adornment and advocacy for life. Nothing like our planet has been found anywhere in the solar system, or among the 20+ alien planets detected around other stars. Earth's size, location, physics, and chemistry are all exactly suited for people, trees, rabbits, whales, birds, bacteria, etc. Here we have the right recipe, right size, right distance, right spin, and right ingredients.

Our air is composed of 78 percent nitrogen, 21 percent oxygen, 0.03 percent carbon dioxide, and traces of other gases, all in the right proportion to sustain life and block ultraviolet radiation (which might otherwise sterilize our planet). Orbiting comfortably 93 million miles from the sun, our planet has moderate temperatures allowing water to be mostly liquid, a precondition for life. Even in Antarctica, summer melts allow algae, bacteria, and worms to survive. And we're protected by a magnetic field, generated by the rotating Earth's core of iron, shielding us from solar winds like those stripping oxygen away from Mars.

Planet Earth is different from all the inhospitable planets. Unlike Venus and Mercury, our world is not too close to the sun. Unlike Mars, Uranus, and Neptune, we're not too far away from it either. Venus is too hot for life, registering at 900 degrees Fahrenheit. It also has an atmosphere too thick for life. Mars has one too thin with too little gravity to retain its atmosphere. Jupiter, 13 times more massive than Earth, captures passing comets like the one smashing into it in 1994. Our planet is different, as well, from the gas giants whirling around stars, all of them inhospitable to life.

Why is everything so cooperative, so agreeable, and so enjoyable on Earth? Why all this fine-tuning? Is it because the universe is on *auto-pilot*, needing no outside input at all? Or, was it *tailor-made*, without which we wouldn't be here?

For astrophysicist Hugh Ross, the ever-lengthening list of cosmic occurrences didn't just happen. As a believer, he considers them evidence for creation, since there are just too many godsends to call them "coincidences". As a uniformitarian, however, he sees them as proofs for the Bang. But isn't that irrational exuberance, given the plain meaning of Scripture and the weaknesses of Bang theory itself?

Providence of God

Seeing yuccas in full bloom in the desert, I'm aware that God determined the boundaries of my habitation. How do I know that? Because "from one man he made every nation of men, that they should inhabit the whole earth; he determined the times set for them and the exact places where they should live. He did this so that men would seek him and perhaps reach out for him and find him [...] for in him we live and move and have our being" (Ac. 17:26-28).

Marveling at God's providence, the psalmist wrote, "How many are your works, Oh Lord! In wisdom you made them all. The earth is full of your creatures. [...] These all look to you to give them their food at the proper time. When you give it to them, they gather it up; when you open your hand, they are satisfied with good things; when you hide your face, they are terrified. When you take away their breath, they die and return to the dust. When you send your Spirit, they are created, and you renew the earth. May the glory of the Lord endure forever. May the Lord rejoice in his works" (Ps. 104:24-32).

I'm reminded of this daily as California Quail descend from the chaparral near our home. God feeds them with my birdseed – not sparingly, but lavishly! His care for quail is different, however, from his care for us humans, for as Horton said, "we were created with class." Never before had God made a creature with such intimate ties to his own character; so much did he love humans that he gave his only Son, "that whoever believes in him shall not perish but have eternal life" (Jn. 3:16). This aspect of God's providence is so special that we call it "saving grace". Receiving it, we "cast our burdens upon him" and "he will sustain us" (Ps. 55:22). There is also the promise that "the eyes of the Lord are on the righteous and his ears are attentive to their prayer" (1 Pe. 3:12).

Quail don't share in our redemption, so what does providence mean for them? According to Berkhof, "Divine providence is that work of God by which he preserves all creatures, is active in all that transpires in the world, and directs all things to their appointed end."[8] This implies 1) divine preservation, by which God upholds all things, 2) divine concurrence by which he cooperates with all creatures, making them act as they do, and 3) divine governance by which he rules all things so that they answer to the purpose of their existence.

Here is what *The Belgic Confession* (Art. 13) says regarding God's providence: "We believe that this good God, after he created all things, did not forsake them or give them up to chance or fortune but leads and governs them according to his holy will, in such a way that nothing happens in this world without his orderly arrangement. [...] This doctrine gives us unspeakable comfort since it teaches us that nothing can happen to us by chance but only by the arrangement of our gracious heavenly Father. He watches over us with fatherly care, keeping all creatures under his control, so that not one of the hairs on our heads (for they are all numbered), nor even a little bird can fall to the ground without the will of our Father."

The Heidelberg Catechism (L.D. 10) expresses it similarly: "Providence is the almighty and ever present power of God by which he upholds, as with his hand, heaven and earth and all creatures, and so rules them that leaf and blade, rain and drought, fruitful and lean years, food and drink, health and sickness, prosperity and poverty – all things, in fact – come to us not by chance but from his fatherly hand. Therefore, we can be patient when things go against us, thankful when things go well, and for the future we can have good confidence in our faithful God and Father that nothing will separate us from his love. All creatures are so completely in his hand that without his will they can neither move nor be moved."

So it is also with the forces of nature. Although we can upset the balance, God is in control of the environment. He provides rain or withholds it; nurtures crops or withers them; blesses humans or curses them. Though bringing great calamities (floods, winds, earthquakes, and pestilences), in none of these is he sitting idly by, looking leisurely at a pre-programmed world. As Calvin said, "God holds the helm and rules all events." His providence is also mysterious, for "from him and through him and to him are all things" (Ro. 11:36).

God's ways are deep and past finding out, and they are not our ways. Unlike ours, his ways are always right. He provides for all things, great and small, everywhere and always, and his care is universal and all-inclusive. His providence is so pervasive that it extends to embryos and atoms. Even the sub-particles of the universe obey his voice, since everything is preserved for his glory. At his command, flies, frogs, locusts, and lice once filled Egypt, but avoided the Camp of Israel.

Luke wrote, "Are not five sparrows sold for two pennies? Yet not one of them is forgotten by God" (Lk. 12:6-7). Does this surprise you, the fact that God's *sovereignty* is so absolute that nothing is outside his control? Then rest assured that he upholds all things by the power of his Word (Heb. 1:3), for in him all things consist and hold together (Co. 1:17). It follows that there is no such thing as happenstance or luck, for we read, "The lot is cast into the lap, but its every decision is from the Lord" (Pr. 16:33). What might *appear* as chance or randomness is thus always under God's governance.

Hendriksen wrote in his *New Testament Commentary on Colossians*, "The world is not a chaos but a cosmos; an orderly system. This to be sure does not always appear on the surface. Nature seems to be 'raw in tooth and claw', without harmony and order. Yet, a closer look soon indicates a basic plan. [...] Certain plants need certain definite insects. These insects are present, and so wondrously constructed that they can perform their function. The polar bear is able to live where there is ice and snow. It is kept from slipping on the ice by having fur even on the soles of its feet. The yucca plant can live in the hot, dry desert because not only does it have roots reaching down deeply into the soil for water but also leaves so formed that evaporation is very slow. Our lungs are adapted to the air we breathe, and our eyes to the light by which we see. Everywhere there is *coherence*."[9]

Coherence is *not* coincidence, however! It is *covenantal*. To Noah God promised, "I will establish my covenant with you and with your descendants after you. [...] Never again will all life be cut off by the waters of the flood" (Ge. 9:9-12). But is this still meaningful today? Of course it is! We depend on God's care for our very survival, as in the predictability of orbits, the regularity of tides, and the seasonality of climates. Why is God so caring? Because he wants us to love him. To Moses he described himself as "compassionate and gracious, slow to anger, abounding in love and faithfulness – maintaining love to thousands, and forgiving wickedness, rebellion, and sin" (Ex. 34:6,7). Even midst Satan's prowling, God is never capricious. "Whoever is wise, therefore, let him heed these things and consider the great love of the Lord" (Ps. 107:43).

Butterfly Wings and Tornadoes[10]

Can a butterfly's wings in Brazil set off a tornado in Texas? This was asked by MIT meteorologist Edward Lorenz. One would think that a butterfly couldn't cause a tornado, since its wings can make only tiny changes in the air. But what if small changes led to larger ones? Could it be that eventually, thousands of miles away, a tornado might result which wouldn't have occurred except for the butterfly's flapping? The butterfly effect is an example of *chaos theory*, which holds that tiny changes in initial conditions can lead to major differences in outcomes. These could be so small initially that they can't be measured, but they can make such a huge difference down the line that one couldn't predict certain outcomes in advance.

What prompted Lorenz to suspect that tiny changes could make such a huge difference? Running weather simulations one day, he studied one sequence more carefully, but rather than starting from scratch, he took a shortcut, duplicating the numbers from a prior printout. The new run should have reproduced the original, but it differed incrementally until the simulated weather had nothing in common with what it had been. Lorenz was puzzled, thinking his computer had failed, but then he realized that the problem was in the numbers entered from the original sequence.

Assuming that a difference of less than one in a thousand wouldn't matter, Lorenz had entered rounded numbers. This made all the difference in the world, and the more he looked into it the more convinced he became that the tiniest variations in initial conditions can produce very different outcomes over time, including chaos.

Dictionaries define chaos as "disorder" or "confusion", so when people hear about chaos theory they think it negates order in the universe. Some even twist it to support irrationality, like worshipping nature, but their notions have little in common with Lorenz, who realized that specific laws are involved in nature, random events being anything but random since patterns evolve after awhile. Humans don't have that kind of specificity, but the Creator does. He knows every butterfly and every molecule of air. He knows also the temperature of every drop of water, the location of every speck of dust, and the path of every falling leaf. In fact, he knows everything that has ever happened and ever will. All eventualities are factored into his plan, whether by his ordinary laws or special intervention. Yet some see everything as random and purposeless. And that is chaotic indeed!

Chaos theory has value, but the label can be misleading. Rather than seeing everything as disorderly, it stresses the underlying orderliness in complex, nonlinear, dynamic systems. Some causes may be so minute as to be undetectable initially, but the resultant outcomes may be quite different from the expected. This means that to know much about the past or future, one would need to be infallible to the tiniest detail, knowing the laws of the universe without error as in the *"law of uniformity"*.

Laws of the Universe

Uniformity is so embedded in people's thinking that many have forgotten who instituted it. It can give surgeons confidence, based on predictability, but nature's laws are at God's command! He rules and overrules everything, both the ordinary and extraordinary, through acts of his will. Those seeing it otherwise end up either denying or downgrading God's *sovereignty* since they view nature as an iron-clad system of laws and processes. Though perhaps invoking God as governor, they confine him to a closed system of causes and effects (supposedly ever present and always functioning).

There *are* of course predictable laws and processes, but they don't function independently. Rather than answering to nature, they answer to their Creator, as H. Morris wrote in his monumental book, *The Biblical Basis for Modern Science*.

> Nature is reliable and can be studied and described effectively by means of the scientific method. This very fact, of course, is a witness to the power and wisdom of God and makes meaningful and reasonable God's command to man to "subdue the earth" and "have dominion over it" (Ge. 1:28).

> The prevailing uniformity in the present cosmos is thus quite biblical. All processes operate within the framework of the first and second laws of thermodynamics. According to the first law, *nothing in the physical realm is now being created or destroyed* – even though it is continually changing in form. According to the second law, *all things tend to decay and die*, a situation that evidently dates from the imposition of God's curse on the earth.
>
> The two laws of thermodynamics are the laws of conservation and decay. 'Mass-energy' must always be conserved and 'entropy' must always increase. These two entities are the basic concepts common to all phenomena occurring in our space-time universe, and the two laws constitute the constraining framework within which all such processes apparently function.[11]

Lacking outside energy, nature exhibits increasing disorder, posing a real problem for those seeing life as upwardly mobile. In any closed system entropy always increases to maximal value, corresponding to equilibrium, or chaos. Everything drifts from higher to lower levels of organization, like the log that turns to rubble even when undisturbed. Yes, there are degrees of openness (isolated systems having neither mass nor energy flowing in or out), but vertical progression could have come only from supernatural activity.

Summing up the laws of thermodynamics, the first relates to the *conservation of quantity*; the second to the *decay of quality*. There are other laws also, associated with the speed of light, gravitational pull, electromagnetic fields, erosion, hydraulics, radioactive decay, biological processes, etc., but cobbling them into some man-made maxi-theory introduces the error of *compounded assumptions*.

The prime example is the **Cosmic Bang**, hinging as it does on relativity, quantum mechanics, strings, singularities, curvatures, gravitational lensing, etc. Calling *that* science is to endorse any number of rickety theories (much as in the **Biological Bang**). Yet this is the formula labeling our universe "ancient", and it is warmly endorsed by Ross, who writes:

> Because light travels at a fixed, finite velocity, we see and measure the conditions of astronomical objects as they were when the objects began radiating light toward us. When we look at the sun, for example, we see its conditions eight minutes ago, when the visible light and radiation we now detect left the sun. When we map the Orion Nebula, we see it as it was 1,200 years ago. When we examine the center of our galaxy, we discover what was happening there 30,000 years ago. When we study the Andromeda Galaxy, we observe what took place 2 million years ago. [...]
>
> To see how the creation was taking shape a number of years ago, we need only focus our instruments on objects the appropriate distance away. With recent technological advances, we can actually see all the way back to a split second after the cosmic explosion in which all the universe's time, space, matter, and energy began. [...] Astronomers are now observing the maturation of galaxies from infancy to middle age [...] like a photo-album of our life from babyhood until today. One of the latest sets of photo images shows us an epoch before galaxies existed, like a photo of your parents just before you were born. Only the building blocks – small clumps of hot young stars – of galaxies are visible in these shots. Such images of the pre-histories and life histories of various galaxies give the most visually convincing testimony yet that the cosmos arose from a powerful creation event.[12]

Ross invokes God in this process, but Hawking isn't so sure. Hawking is certain about two other things, however: 1) The known laws of physics do not apply during the earliest micro-milli-seconds, and 2) we are not yet at a grand unified theory of everything.[13] To understand how things started out, Hawking says we would need laws holding true at singularities, but he is unable to formulate them since nobody knows what might or might not have happened at such "badly behaved points" in history. Hawking does at least admit that classic theory can no longer explain the cosmos, saying we would need more exotic theories to describe its initial stages. But isn't he proposing something so absurd as to have no merit at all, allowing only *explainable* laws and processes?

The concern is this: whether embracing the supernatural (as Ross does) or rejecting it (as Hawking does), both are approaching the evidences **conditionally** through their uniformitarian grid – expecting God to pass through it as well. This is a net allowing only the **ordinary** and **explainable** through it, as if nature could account for its own laws and processes, which is a mechanistic construct, based on an elaborately tuned world, all too reminiscent of an exquisite clock designed by a "blind watchmaker."

As described by Dr. Norman DeJong, such a world would be ***atomistic***, "based on natural laws immutably embedded in nature, as proposed by those who not only changed our conception of nature but also our conception of nature's God. He then ends up a 'cosmic legislator, a grand governor, a deific designer, and a sustainer of the clockwork image', but no longer is he 'the righteous and angry Creator who, in his fury, upset the world with a cataclysmic flood'. No longer is he 'The Emanuel who intervened in nature for the sake of his people'. No longer is he 'our Father'. He merely designed natural laws and set them in motion."[14]

With only such a lesser god, everything is nonsensical. Why? Because, absent the Sovereign Lord, there is no sphere within which intelligence can function. Reformed theology doesn't permit that, holding as it does not just to an ***ordinary God*** but a ***Sovereign God***. Deny the God of the Bible (whose ***works*** match his ***words***) and you will deny the foundation of knowledge! Deny ***that*** and you will make sense out of nothing! People may ridicule this, but this is my Father's world, after all!

Evolution vs. Devolution

Solomon said, "There is nothing new under the sun", implying that everything was present when first created, at least potentially. Atoms can be converted into energy, motion, heat, and new life (as in eating a sandwich, or in the birth of a baby), but every single atom was present originally with no more than its created potential. This is unlike macro-evolutionary theory (an unfinished continuum with expanding potentiality).

Creation was not ongoing, for we read, "His work has been finished since the creation of the world" (Heb. 4:3). How very different from the notion that new universes and new life forms are springing up, and that humans are evolving vertically! Even the stars, though incubating for centuries, are producing nothing new. In Genesis we read, "Thus the heavens and earth were finished and all the host of them [...] and God blessed the seventh day because on it he rested from all the work of creating he had done" (Ge. 2:1-2).

Once having made the universe, God didn't forsake it. Nor did he stop working, as we know from the laws of nature. Reformed theology makes a distinction between ***special creation*** and ***ordinary providence***, a distinction both biblical and scientific. Creation was therefore unlike God's continuing work of providence. Even with his ongoing provision, everything is winding down. Our lives, for example, are shorter than Adam's – and not just because of cigarettes, junk food, and neglect.

Early on, sin had not taken its toll, so fecundity (fruitfulness and longevity) continued awhile, whether because of friendly skies or God's desire to establish the human race. As Morris observed, "In the original economy, each individual life was conserved. [...] This *conservation principle* was drastically changed, however, with the imposition of God's Curse upon the world. Thenceforth, not only did death come in, with all living organisms destined to disintegrate and go back to their basic elements, but so do all other structures tend to become unstructured. Instead of a law of conservation of structure, there now prevails a universal law of breakdown of structure (morpholysis). Not only is there no more creation of order, but the reverse is taking place."[15]

"Information theory" says that information becomes garbled over time, as with audio cassette tapes played over and over again. It takes intelligence to push equations and genomes forward. And, outside agency! "Strange as it may seem", said Whitcomb, "this universal deterioration points to man's only true hope of immortality! For, if the universe has been evolving into higher and higher forms, then the biblical world-view and God's firm promise of eternal salvation to those who believe in him would be hopelessly discredited. On the other hand, the inexorable grip of the second law forces us to the conclusion that the earth was at one time more organized and integrated and beautiful than it is now. And this in turn points to an infinite and personal God who alone could have infused order and high-level energy into the universe at the beginning."[16]

Because of entropy, the cosmos is like an ill-fated gasoline tanker speeding downhill toward a catastrophic demise. Planet Earth is already showing signs of doom since its quality and order are declining. However, we need not fear a uniformitarian crunch, nor will the end come in the way that cosmologists predict. Those garbling this ask, "Where is this coming he promised? Ever since our fathers died, everything goes on as it has since the beginning of creation" (2 Pe. 3:3-8). But, "while people are saying 'peace and safety', destruction will come on them suddenly" (1 Th. 5:3), and this will not be a silent event! Rather, it will come with the a loud roar (and the sound of a trumpet) when the heavens shall roll up like a robe, once more defying the laws of the universe!

Attacking Sufficiency

During recent decades, there has been an intensive search for extra-terrestrials; 1947 was a banner year for them in New Mexico, as it was for flying saucers. During these same decades, the Bible has been battered. Believers have usually seen Scripture as genuine and trustworthy, but its sufficiency is under attack as never before. This attack is occurring on two fronts: placing personal experiences above the scriptures and appealing to external authorities. In combination, these two have a common goal. Though not countering the Bible directly, they are approaching it provisionally. Claiming that ultimate answers are found outside Scripture, they are suppressing its testimony.

Some say that the Bible is not a modern book, that it isn't a match for science. Were one to accept *that*, the Bible would suffer greatly, although it beats naturalism under any scenario, especially since scientists are now accepting both design and a beginning. Moses, however, mentioned only the sudden arrival of stars, implying immediate functionality and maturity. Although many see the universe as evolving, the psalmist saw it only "wearing out as a garment" (Ps. 102:26). Assuming more than Moses ever did, they are substituting "doubt" for "days". This is a strike at the heart of Scripture. Should it succeed, the Christian faith will regress rapidly, though this has gone unnoticed by the average person inundated with naturalism. Ridding themselves of the Supernatural, as if that were possible, people are dumbing down the Bible.

Geologists claim that rains fell on shales *initially*. Biologists say that chemicals became organic *spontaneously*. Paleontologists say that fossils were entombed *naturally*. Anthropologists say that humans were savages *innately*. Were this in fact true, one might be able to unravel the past, assuming only the present. But take a closer look! Dominating every branch of science there is a deep-seated dogma, couched in its own preferences, seeing in nature what is not in the Bible. The laws of nature do of course exist, and they are for our own good, but God does not hold himself to ordinary means alone. As stated in *The Westminster Confession* (Ch. 5), "God, in his providence, makes use of means, yet is free to work without, above, and against them, at his pleasure."

Knowing that the world never left God's hands, why equate him with nature's laws? Why ban him from the universe or weaken him, joining him with Satan's world of death? Why not accept him as *in control*? After all, he positioned the stars so accurately that birds and men can navigate by them. That said, it is a new day indeed now that scientists are embracing creation, as they're forced to do if they're honest. As a corollary, when *reason* interprets nature properly and *faith* reads the Bible correctly, the evidences can be weighed *objectively*.

The bottom line is this: If everything seems finely-tuned and tailor-made, the simplest explanation is that it *is* finely-tuned and tailor-made! Why force the facts into some fatherless fantasy alleging that evolution occurred simply because we "are", as in the humanistic version of the *anthropic principle*? Why not reclaim that principle? God is still matching atoms with molecules, stars with seasons, and hearts with praise. Towering over everything else is the forethought, creativity, and care of our Heavenly Father!

This is my Father's world, and to my listening ears
All nature sings and round me rings, the music of the spheres.
This is my Father's world; I rest me in the thought
Of rocks and trees, of skies and seas – his hand the wonders wrought.
(Maltbie D. Babcock, 1901)

[1] Michael Horton, *Putting Amazing Back into Grace,* Thomas Nelson Publishers, 1991, pp. 40,41

[2] Herbert Lockyer, *All the Miracles of the Bible,* Zondervan Publishing House, Grand Rapids, MI, 1961, p. 13

[3] Ibid, pp. 14,15

[4] L. Berkhof, *Systematic Theology*, Wm. B. Eerdmans Publishing Co., Grand Rapids, MI, 1981, p. 144

[5] Billy Graham, *Angels, God's Secret Agents*, Doubleday & Co., Garden City, NY, 1975, pp. 60,61

[6] L. Berkhof, *Systematic Theology*, Wm. B. Eerdmans Publishing Co., Grand Rapids, MI, 1981, pp. 148,149

[7] J. C. Whitcomb, *The Early Earth,* Baker Book House, Grand Rapids, MI, 1990, p. 53

[8] L. Berkhof, *Manual of Christian Doctrine,* Wm. Eerdmans Publishing Co., Grand Rapids, MI, 1984, pp. 111-116

[9] William Hendriksen, *New Testament Commentary on Colossians,* Baker Book House, Grand Rapids, MI, p. 75

[10] This section is distilled from a radio broadcast by David Feddes, *The Radio Pulpit*, The Back to God Hour, Vol. 45, #7, July, 2000, pp. 32-45.

[11] Henry M. Morris, *The Biblical Basis for Modern Science,* Baker Book House, Grand Rapids, MI, 1984, pp.77-86

[12] Hugh Ross(and others), *Mere Creation,* InterVarsity Press, Downers Grove, IL, 1998, pp. 365-369

[13] Stephen Hawking, *A Brief History of Time,* Bantom Books, New York, NY, 1990, p. 1333

[14] Norman DeJong, *God's Wedding Band*, Redeemer Books, Winamac, IN, 1990, pp. 30,31

[15] Henry M. Morris, *The Biblical Basis for Modern Science,* Baker Book House, Grand Rapids, MI, 1984, p. 91

[16] J. C. Whitcomb, *The Early Earth,* Baker Book House, Grand Rapids, MI, 1990, pp. 13-15

THE TENETS OF OUR THEORIES
(Chapter 7)

Philosophic Naturalism

Why is it so hard to come up with a definition for science, seeing its wonders every day? Because scientists bring *faith constructs* to their investigations, often saying, "Why bring God into the equation when it's so comfortable without him?"

Philosophic naturalism is the default mindset for the Western world. Dembski writes, "From biblical studies to law to education to science to the arts, inquiry is allowed to proceed only under the supposition that nature is self-contained. To be sure, this is not to require that we explicitly deny God's existence. God could, after all, have created the world to be self-contained. But for the sake of inquiry, we are required to pretend that God does not exist and proceed accordingly. [...] It remains logically permissible for the scientific naturalist to affirm God's existence but only by making God a superfluous rider on top a self-contained account of the world."[1]

Inundated with "enlightenment rationality", today's culture is taken with the notion that nature is autonomous, needing no outside input at all. "Nature spans everything from quarks to galaxy clusters. Most significant, we are part of nature. And with nature filling so many vital roles, it's fair to ask: What is nature? Definitions abound. Nature is the natural order. Nature is the realm of space, time, and energy. Nature is that part of reality described by natural laws. Nature is what scientists study – the domain of science. Each of these definitions is right as far as it goes. Implicit in these definitions, however, is a telling omission. In no instance do we find nature identified with creation."[2]

Nature is what our universe would have been, had there been no God. Such a universe would be hopeless, though many have adapted themselves to that very model. This is evident in the book, *Voices for Evolution* (National Center for Science Education), featuring statements from the Pope, Episcopalians, Methodists, the United Church of Christ, Presbyterians, the Lutheran World Federation, and several Jewish groups – all expressing respect for science *and* evolution as a part of science. The irony? Mainline Christianity and Jewry have accommodated themselves to naturalism while repudiating Genesis!

Naturalism sees evolution as "change over time", the kind we can all accept, as with bread rising from yeast. It goes further than that, however, touting evolution as the organizing principle for everything. According to evolutionism (usually called "evolution"), living things evolved through randomly cumulative changes involving reproductive isolation, adaptation, speciation, etc.

You name the sub-field and evolution is there, claiming that all creatures are related by a common ancestry, as in Darwin's "descent with modification". Many see this as God's methodology, though it contradicts both science and creation. The problem is, it requires ever increasing "faith"!

For secular biology teachers, evolution is "state of the art science". This is what the National Academy of Sciences claims in its booklet, *Science and Creationism*. Maintaining that creationism is incompatible with science, it says that students who are not told that evolution unifies the data are being cruelly short-changed. But the Academy's ideas are antiquated, "it having become obvious that naturalistic metaphysics can no longer drive science, as if to redefine its very essence."[3]

Naturalistic theories are "on the way out", says Dembski, "not because they are false (although they are that) or because they have been bested by post-modernity (they haven't), but because they are bankrupt."[4] "They have run out of steam because of the weakness of the arguments", never having been based on empirical rationality in the first place.

Creationism

There are two basic beliefs, and they cannot coexist. Either nature possesses its order **intrinsically**, or it derives it from an **outside source**, "a la creation".[5] Creationism traces order and design to the **Sovereign God**, "freeing science from shackles which were always arbitrary and have now become intolerable."[6] It is based on the **six-day model** and a prior commitment to **God's Word**. But when these enter into the picture, doesn't that compromise theorizing? Not when we admit that "the conceptual soundness of a scientific theory cannot be maintained apart from Christ,"[7] and that "Christ is never an *addendum* to a scientific theory but always a *completion* of it."[8] Once having accepted this, Christ is basic to every aspect of origins, even if people haven't a clue about him.

Creationists see science as fitting best with **the Logos**, the first cause, since the universe could never have arranged itself without him. As a corollary, they see creation beginning with perfection, contrary to the tenets dominating science for the past century. Within creationism, there are two subsets of belief: scientific creationism and biblical creationism.

Scientific creationism (creation science) is committed to two propositions: 1) a supernatural agent created the universe, and 2) the Genesis account is scientifically accurate. Given these requirements, the following tenets (jointly taken) define scientific creationism:

- There was a sudden creation of space, time, matter, and energy, from nothing, by a transcendent personal Creator.
- Biological life was supernaturally created; mutations and natural selection are insufficient to bring into existence all living "kinds" from a single cell or precursor organism.
- The major "kinds" were functionally complete originally; changes occurred within fixed limits (variation within kind); most genetic changes are downward as a result of harmful mutations or extinction.
- Adam and Eve were created uniquely (separate from the primates) with true knowledge, righteousness, and holiness.
- Geology, paleontology, and biology are best explained by catastrophism, primarily a worldwide flood.
- Planet Earth and its biological forms had a recent inception, ten to fifteen thousand years ago at the most.
- The laws of the universe have always been at God's command, including special intervention and miracles.
- The universe and its life forms have been impaired since the Fall, resulting in negative changes to the originally perfect Creation.
- Since a competent and volitional Creator purposed and made the universe, theological considerations are appropriate in all origins inquiries.
- The human mind is darkened and finite, but we can still explore the Creator's work scientifically, at least sufficiently to explain our place in God's plan.

Biblical creationism (with or without creation science) is committed to the following tenets:

- The Creator exists in three Persons (Father, Son, and Holy Spirit), each participating in the work of creation.
- The Bible (God's inspired/inerrant revelation) is authoritative – historically, morally, and scientifically.
- All things were created by God during six literal days of creation, the record of which is factual, historical, and clear – as recorded in Genesis 1:1-2:3 and Exodus 20:8-12.
- Adam and Eve exercised dominion over the earth as an implicit commission (sphere sovereignty), but sin distorted that dominion, culminating in the death of animate organisms and the separation of humans from their Creator.
- This alienation can be remedied through the blood of Christ, which is the key to the restoration of all Creation.

Scientific creationism, though not endorsed by all believers, has a high regard for the plain meaning of Scripture. However, the idea that the Bible is scientifically accurate has caused creation scientists some difficulty since the Bible is not strictly scientific. Nor can science speak exhaustively to the Bible's claims. Nevertheless, scientific creationism has made many positive contributions to the study of origins and is continuing to do so.

Creationism can be seen as a scientific endeavor, but it is more than that. It points to the Supreme Architect, Originator, and Governor of all things. Accepting his words, not merely those of some "expert", science can reclaim its Christian roots and recover its dialogue with theology. That is not the thrust of Howard Van Till's "creationomic science", however. Nor is it the basis for his "categorical complimentarity". Creationomic science (presumably a **concordant view**) assumes the co-authority of science and the Bible. Categorical complimentarity, according to Van Till, "divides all questions into two separate categories: internal affairs (the domain of the natural sciences), and external relationships (philosophy, theology, and ultimately Scriptural authority)."

Biblical creation is more careful than either of these two views. It grants priority to God's Word, acknowledging that Scripture and science are concordant only when correctly interpreted. That is the intent of this book: creationism, but not "creation science" as a movement. Studying origins from this perspective, we shall see that creation is incompatible with the naturalistic chronology in Chapter 3 (given its evolutionary slant). It is also at odds with theistic evolution, a viewpoint having no biblical warrant at all.

Simply stated, there is an "*a priori*" approach to theorizing: the grammatico-historical hermeneutic. Once having determined the Bible's claims (prior to outside influences, authorities, and evidences), they take precedence over all other claims. In other words, the evidences are to be tested by the Bible, not the Bible by the evidences. The bottom line? We are not to theorize beyond what is written (1 Co. 4:6).

Competing Cosmological Views

Genesis 1 tells us about the origin of space, lacking luminaries until the fourth day. As an alternative view, some say Moses didn't mean that the stars were created on the fourth day, arguing instead that Moses' reference to stars relates to their purpose rather than their arrival. Were that true, stars would have been present on Day 1, leaving ambiguity regarding Day 4.   A variation of this would be that the luminaries existed on the first day but didn't become visible until the fourth, due to a more stable water cycle by then, transforming the atmosphere from opaque to translucent.

Bible scholars have accepted numerous interpretations to accommodate the supposed antiquity of the cosmos, sometimes stretching the text beyond its natural meaning. The more obvious interpretation is that the astronomical bodies appeared on the fourth day, not initially. We see this from references to the "expanse". In Genesis 1:6, God says, "let there be an expanse." In Genesis 1:8, he calls the expanse, "sky". In Genesis 1:14, he says, "Let there be lights in the expanse." In Genesis 1:17, he mentions setting the stars in the expanse.

Holding competing views, Christians have followed at least three lines of argument in their theorizing:
>   *Arguing for a young universe:* holding to the primacy of Special Revelation, and literal interpretation.
>   *Arguing for an old universe:* holding to the co-authority of both revelations, and figurative interpretation.
>   *Arguing that the age of the universe is unimportant:* holding to general revelation as decisive and Special Revelation as inconclusive.

People claim allegiance to the Creator in each of these approaches, but there can be **only one correct view**, and that the most obvious, from Scripture itself. How then did creation become so fickle, if not through innovative exegesis? Why, for that matter, was everyone so excited when George Smoot and others announced in 1992 that they had found their hoped for ripples in space (background microwave radiation)? Every major newspaper headlined these "echoes of creation", moving Hawking to call them "the discovery of the century, if not of all time." But, as scientists were joyously applauding the "handwriting of God", new questions were already surfacing. Although the 3K background seemed to be an impressive prediction of the standard model, fitting with Planck's constant, there were reasons for doubt.

For starters, the sensitivity of the detector was in question, given the tiny temperature fluctuations. Then too, nobody could point to any single spot as the warmest, saying "this is the site of origin." And what about those massive, swirling galaxies, unevenly distributed in space, separated by gigantic voids, one great wall stretching across half a billion light years of space, countering the smoothness of the background? Even *rippled* inflation couldn't account for *such* lumpiness!

Adding yet another disquieting factor, today's galaxy clustering would have required tens of billions of years. But the cosmos isn't supposed to be that old! Counter-theories notwithstanding, imagine having a daughter hundreds of years older than yourself! Also, how much matter is there in the universe? Indirect evidence points to far more than scientists have been able to detect, so much more that up to 90% of it may be unaccounted for! But where is it, and in what form?

The abundance of lighter elements is not a clean prediction of the cosmic bang either, but rather an addendum to it, so obviously we must take a closer look. As Sten Oldenwald (a non-physicist) wrote in the Washington Post, "The Big Bang wasn't really big. Nor was it really a bang. It contains these basic elements: 1) pre-existing space into which the fragments from the explosion are injected, 2) pre-existing time we can use to mark when the explosion happened, 3) projectiles moving through space from a common center, 4) a definite moment when the explosion occurred, and 5) something that started it. Yet all these elements to our visualization of the Bang are completely false according to general relativity."

> *Pre-existing Space?* There wasn't any. Many of these theories of the earliest moments hypothesize a "mother space-time" that begat our universe, but you cannot at the same time place your mind's eye both inside this Mother Space-time to watch the Big Bang happen, and inside our universe to see the matter flying around. Yet this is what the fireworks display model demands that you do.
> *Pre-existing Time?* There wasn't any of this either! General relativity treats both space and time together as one object, called "space-time", which is indivisible.
> *Individual objects moving out from a common center?* Nope! As a mental anchor, many have used the expanding balloon as an analogy to the expanding universe. As seen from any one spot on the balloon's surface, all other spots rush away from it as the balloon is inflated. Yet there is no one point on the surface of the balloon that is singled out as the center.
> *Projectiles moving through space?* Sorry! I like to think of the shape of our universe as a "cosmic watermelon". [...] We see that its meat has always been present in the complete watermelon. [...] Like the meat of that watermelon, space has always existed in the complete shape of the universe in 4-dimensions.
> *Was there a definite moment to the Big Bang?* The moment dissolves away into some weird quantum fog. [...] General relativity is unable to describe this condition and only some future theory combining general relativity and quantum mechanics will be able to tell us more. We hope!
> *Something started the Big Bang:* At last we come to the most difficult issue in modern cosmology. We can trace the events leading all the way back to the chemists that created the gunpowder and wrapped the explosives. General relativity, however, can tell us nothing about the equivalent stages leading up to the Big Bang [...] This remains the essential mystery of the Big Bang, doggedly transcending every mathematical description created to describe it.[9]

Cosmologists say that the Bang wasn't so much an *explosion* as an *expansion of space and time* (neither of which existed initially). But correcting misconceptions doesn't solve all problems. How could the Bang have produced order and complexity, given the law of entropy? Says Oldenwald, "At this point common sense must give up its seat on the bus, yet it is precisely at this point that so many non-physicists refuse to be courteous, and who can blame them?"

Consider also these comments from Timothy Ferris, winner of the American Institute of Physics prize. Speaking as a *proponent* of the Bang, he nevertheless hedges about it in his book, *The Whole Shebang:*

> One problem is that while some observations indicate an age for the universe consistent with other measurements, some do not; if later observations hold up, something must be wrong. Another area involves the perplexing question of how, in a generally homogeneous universe, primordial fluctuations produced vast structures represented by superclusters of galaxies. Quite possibly related to this issue is the riddle of what constitutes the *dark matter,* nonluminous material that evidently holds the clusters together. Until these puzzles are resolved, we will not be sure that cosmologists are on the right track in working within the Big Bang context. And almost certainly there will be other vexations to come. The greatest of these surely is the question of how the universe came into being – which is itself a form of the philosophical riddle posed by Leibniz when he asked why there is something rather than nothing.[10]

Ferris doesn't pretend that the standard model is perfect or even true, but he sees only *it* as producing the universe – a macrocosm containing 100 billion galaxies, each with at least 100 billion stars, and a complex solar system including trillions of organisms, all requiring increasing organization and information. Why all this theorizing when the debate was settled long ago? As H. Morris wrote, "The primeval act of special creation is recorded in the first verse of divine revelation: God created the heavens (space) and the earth (matter) in the beginning (time). The cosmos is a *continuum* of space, matter, and time, with all three entities essential to a meaningful cosmos and all three coming into existence simultaneously."

Consistent with this, the psalmist wrote, "By the word of the Lord were the heavens made, their starry host by the breath of his mouth (Ps. 33:6). [...] Let them praise the name of the Lord, for he commanded and they were created" (Ps. 148:3-5). Now, isn't this cosmogony at its best?

Cosmogony and the Bible

But what is cosmogony? It is that aspect of cosmology (the study of the cosmos) dealing with the origin of the universe. Comparing evolutionary cosmogony with the biblical view, Morris wrote, "The fundamental evolutionary model does not really allow an absolute *beginning* of the cosmos. The cosmos, in this system, is the ultimate reality, self-existent from eternity. Evolutionary cosmogony starts with a cosmos in existence. Cosmogonists then attempt to explain how the cosmos developed into its present form from some primordial aspect, assumed or inferred. The fundamental creation model, on the other hand, assumes that the universe itself had a beginning. God alone is the ultimate reality. Space and time, as well as matter, did not exist until God brought them into existence out of nothing – by his omnipotence."[11]

Scientists have long feared that a finite beginning would mean an Infinite Creator. The fact that the universe had a beginning was hard for many to accept, but they were forced to concede such an event. As British astronomer Paul Davies said, "When scientists began to explore the implications of Einstein's time for the universe as a whole, they made one of the most important discoveries in the history of human thought: that time, and hence all of physical reality, must have had a definite origin in the past. If time is flexible and mutable, as Einstein demonstrated, then it is possible for time to come into existence and also to pass away again; i.e., there can be a beginning and an end to time. Today the origin of time is called 'the Big Bang'. Religious people refer to it as 'the creation'."[12] But time as we humans know it began with a *shining light* on a *rotating globe*, and both arrived within a *single day*.

As for the various cosmogonies, Davies divides them into four classes: "First is the orthodox scientific model of the universe that comes into existence at a finite time in the past and slowly degenerates towards a heat death [fitting with biblical creation, but not with the final trumpet]. Second is a universe that has a definite origin but progresses in spite of the second law of thermodynamics [an impossibility, given the laws of physics]. Third is the cyclic universe with no overall beginning or end, involving either strict repetition or statistical recurrences [neither biblical nor scientific]. Finally, there is the static (steady-state) universe, in which local processes may be degenerative or progressive but the universe as a whole remains more or less the same forever [rejected by almost every scientist]."[13] An ardent proponent of the Big Bang, Davies might be expected to support it wholeheartedly, but like Ferris he too has some doubts:

> Right from the start attempts by astronomers to "date the creation" ran into trouble. The age kept coming out wrong. There wasn't enough time for the stars and planets to come into existence. Worse still, there were astronomical objects that seemed to be older than the universe – an obvious absurdity. [...] In the early years of the subject, cosmologists could wave their arms and make the excuse that their data were still so woolly that a factor of two or three among friends was no reason for a dispute about fundamentals. However, in 1992 the Cosmic Background Explorer Satellite (COBE) provided what for most cosmologists was the clincher in pinning down the fine details of the big-bang theory. By measuring slight ripples in the background heat of the universe, COBE was able to inject a new level of precision into cosmological modeling. The snag is, the COBE data, combined with other recent observations, have only served to resurrect the age problem with a vengeance. [...] Some astronomers believe that, with a bit of fitting and fudging, the time scales can be fixed. [...] Others disagree and reject the entire big-bang scenario.[14]

In fairness, even the most fanciful of IMAX simulations couldn't rescue such an embattled theory, and the latest findings from Hubble are even more disquieting! Yet Ross (claiming the infallible Word) has written a spate of books fusing the Bang with Genesis! Seeing nothing beleaguered in the Bang model, he says, "Together, the Hubble, ROSAT, and COBE discoveries have helped solve the mystery of how galaxies and clusters of galaxies form. [...] With dramatic proof of the hot big bang creation event in hand, many astronomers have become willing to declare the implication of that proof: the existence of the Creator-God."[15]

Astrophysicist John Gribbin (University of Cambridge, England) believes as strongly in the Bang as Ross does, but his inferences from it are very different. Says he, "Before Charles Darwin and Alfred Russel Wallace came up with the idea of evolution, many people believed that the only way to explain the existence of so unlikely an organism as a human being was by supernatural intervention. But there is no longer any basis for invoking the supernatural. [...] It is now clear that the universe was not set up for our benefit, and that the existence of organic life-forms on Earth is simply a minor side-effect of an evolutionary process involving universes, galaxies, and stars."[16]

The problem is, Gribbin is as mistaken in denying the supernatural as Ross is in characterizing God by the Bang. Says Ross, "As helpful as big bang cosmology has been in attesting to the Creator's existence and transcendence, it has provided an even greater service in attesting to the Creator's personality."[17] But do we really need a presumed cosmogony to characterize God? Could he not have made things in ways so peculiar that we would fail repeatedly at characterizing him? We humans are so *different* from God! We can't even imagine one who is free from constraint!

Putting it bluntly, we can't say that Genesis supports the Bang or that the Bang supports Genesis. As Whitcomb said, "God alone can tell us how the world began, because no man was there to see it being created, and even if a human observer had been present, he could not have understood fully what he saw apart from God's own interpretation. [...] Even as God commanded Moses to 'put off his shoes' because the place whereon he stood was 'holy ground', so we must set aside our concepts of what could or could not have happened, and stand in God's presence, ready to hear and to believe what he has chosen to tell us about creation."[18]

Dating the Universe

Based on the speed and constancy of light and extrapolating backward, is the universe actually billions of years old? The most critical assumption is that starlight has always traveled at its present rate of speed, rather than slowing over time. The question is, has it always been fixed at 186,000 miles per second? Using the best tools of the day, Roemer measured it in 1675, declaring it constant. Twenty years later Cassini restated that view, but perhaps we should look at that again. The velocity of light seems, at the least, to merit some study.

The speed of light has implications all the way from cosmic space (and distance) to dating the universe. If light has been slowing, decaying, or traveling uniquely in the reaches of space, that might indicate a young earth on the order of thousands (not billions) of years. There is in fact some evidence for this. M.E.J. Gheury de Bray was probably the first to propose a decreasing speed of light, having deduced this from measurements spanning 75 years. Publishing his ideas in *Nature*, he wrote, "If the velocity of light is constant, how is it that, invariably, new determinations give values lower than the last one obtained?"

Consistent with this, 164 separate light measurements have been published during the past 300 years using 16 different techniques. In 1981, Australian astronomer Barry Setterfield reported that the speed of light had diminished so rapidly over three centuries that experimental error couldn't explain the change. Though decreasing only a percentage point (older results have greater error), this was statistically significant. Also questioning the limiting speed of light, R.Y. Chiao (U.C. Berkeley) demonstrated recently that light can be accelerated to near-infinite velocities, supporting findings from Princeton's NEC Research Institute (June, 2000) where light was accelerated up to 300 times its usual velocity. Russian cosmologist Troitskii (Radiophysical Research Institute, Gorky) concluded independently that the speed of light was ten billion times faster at "time zero" than it is today. He attributed redshifting to this decreasing speed of light, and Setterfield agreed with him, using a different approach.

Ask any cosmologist about the convincing supports for the Bang and right at the top will be background radiation, the speed of light, and redshifting (indicating cosmic expansion). The usual explanation is that the light from distant stars is redder than closer in. Astronomers attribute this to the wave-like "doppler effect", as in the lowering pitch of a jet's engines flying away from an observer. As Edwin Hubble explained it, the greater the redshift, the faster the individual stars and galaxies must be moving away from us, indicating an expanding universe. That, coupled with retro-calculated light, confirmed for him an ***aged cosmos***. This is questionable, though, given the peculiarities of light, the unknowns of space, and the effects of the Fall.

Distance is an assumption. The speed of light may have been stable for decades, but perhaps it wasn't always so. Triangulation may not even apply to curvilinear space. Redshifting is debatable too, since it may be partly from tangential light (the cosmos itself being in a spin). There is also the likelihood that far-off light is affected by energy loss – the "tired light phenomenon". Another possibility is that gravity can slow and bend light, seeing that black holes have such a strong pull that light cannot escape them. Some even say that distant light may be traveling in a totally unique way, not understood by anyone. Additionally, there is the problem of discordant redshifts. Certain cosmic structures, seemingly attached to each other and in the same locale, have dissimilar redshifts. But, as noted by Halton Arp, that would be impossible, contravening cosmic theory itself.

Arp (not a creationist) worked as an astronomer with Hubble at the Mt. Wilson and Mt. Palomar observatories before moving to Munich's Max-Planck Institute for Astrophysics. His observations on quasars and galaxies are world-renowned, but his ideas regarding discordant redshifts are not shared by most evolutionary cosmologists. Nonetheless, he has produced voluminous data questioning the theory that redshifts are proportional to distance. If he's right, some redshifts are unrelated to distance and/or cosmic expansion. That and other doubts caused him to write in his book, *Seeing Red*, "I believe the observational evidence has become overwhelming and the Bang has in reality toppled."

Arp may be an outlier, but others too are favoring a more evenhanded approach. Says Mitchell in his *Physics Essays*, "The better known and more effective scientists in this struggle are Anthony Peratt (Los Alamos National Laboratories) and Jayant Narliker (Centre for Astronomy and Astrophysics in India). Other prominent researchers fighting for the proper consideration of alternate cosmologies include Geoffrey and Margaret Burbridge, Fred Hoyle, Herman Bondi, Thomas Gold, and Eric Lerner."

Allowing for maturity, stars must have started out in various stages – mature, immature, and yet to be born – some with light ***"en-route"*** and others with their light ***touching the earth***. Earthlings would therefore have seen them whenever God intended them to be seen, some at their inception and others later on. Ultra-bright novas and supernovas would have exploded whenever God so ordained it, some becoming visible only now. This would fit with gradations of maturity and functionality, though not with standard uniformitarian theorizing.

As Aaldert Mennenga (Professor of Biology, Dordt College) explains it, "There are limits of extrapolation that must be observed. Those believing in Big Bang theory, for example, are on very slippery ground. The only way that a person could possibly calculate back to the Big Bang would be if after that initial moment everything would have developed strictly according to the laws of nature, and if we did actually and fully understand all those laws. Had there been anything else – *anything supernatural* – then of course the calculations would be wrong."[19]

Ross would argue that the Bang couldn't have occurred without supernatural activity, but God's ***supernatural*** must fit with the ***"six days"*** of his ***Word***. Little wonder then that the inter-net is filled with arguments involving claims and counterclaims regarding the cosmic bang, as in *"The Top 30 Problems with the Big Bang"* (Roy Keys Inc., 2002). The basic problem is that, whether appealing to "cold dark matter" or something else, cosmologists are resorting to unknowns to explain the *unknown*, which is both illogical and unthinkable. Moreover, said Mennenga, "If we read Genesis obediently, we know that Adam and Eve were created with the appearance of age, whether as adults or as young people, but not as embryos, fetuses, infants, or very young children. The perspicuity of Scripture demands this. If you deny the appearance of age, you have lost the very essence of divine creation."[20]

Amidst the Hype

No matter the hype, the Bang is still an *embattled theory*; the many band-aids holding it together are anything but convincing! As stated by D.B. De Young (professor and researcher in astronomy), among its missing links are these: missing origin, missing fuse, missing time, missing matter, missing antimatter, missing star formation, missing neutrinos, and missing life. But there are bigger gaps still: missing chronology, missing sequence, and missing "days".

Added to these concerns, the ***cosmological principle*** itself seems to be crumbling – i.e., the assumption that the cosmos is the same in every direction, lacking boundaries, edges, and a center. Summarizing his doubts concerning the current paradigm, Mitchell lists them as follows:

> ***Very old problems*** of singularity, smoothness, horizon, flatness, and the failed solutions of inflation theory.

> ***Newer problems*** relating to missing mass, the age of the universe, radiation from "de-coupling", a contrived chronology, abundances of light elements, and red shift anomalies.

> ***And problems newer yet*** involving inconsistencies of red shifts, curved space, inflation theory, decelerating expansion of the universe, and some additional logical inconsistencies.[21]

There is in fact growing evidence that the history of the universe was ***not*** that of the standard model. Moreover, wouldn't just ***one*** such discontinuity (mentioned by Mitchell) jeopardize the entire theory? Pressing the argument for a moment, how could ***any*** such theory ***resting on hypotheticals*** be the basis for confidence? Considering also "the fallacy of compounded assumptions" (Occam's razor), the Bang seems to be a huge intellectual edifice resting on few hard facts. Even its underpinnings are in trouble, so those claiming that the cosmological problem has been solved may be in for surprises!

People can be scholarly, yet ignorant, which is why "simple" folk look for answers while "wiser" ones seldom bother. True or not, shouldn't science afford more answers than questions? The problem seems to be the clash between presumption and science, the kind of science rooted in objectivity and proof.

There are alternative cosmogonies of course, such as Humphreys' "White Hole Theory", suggesting speedy cosmogenesis within the framework of relativity, expansion, and redshifting, but his ideas are no less fanciful than the others. So why not a fresh look at ***six day creation***? The data presumably so supportive of the Bang should be viewed instead as evidence for ***rapid creation***. Who but God could have spread out 100 billion galaxies in a single day, redshifted or not? All the probes, and all the equations – whether from Harvard, MIT, Stanford, and Berkeley, or from Germany, Russia and India – have failed to solve this puzzle!

The greatest concern is the Bang's incompatibility with the Bible, which is not to deny that God could have made the cosmos with a bang or bangs, or that expansion is illusory. Nor is it to debate the reality of dwarfs, nebulae, pulsars, and other cosmic wonders, some remaining to be understood and others still to be discovered. Science has shown that these spectacular bodies exist; they are born, they radiate, and they die, serving as testimonials to God's majesty, power, and glory. But did their light travel faster early on than today? If so, the universe could be ***rather young***.

From the outset, God was "forming" (***yatsar***), "making" (***asah***), and "creating" (***bara***) things by the word of his mouth. Whatever he made was orderly, complex, and functional, so why not everything arriving rapidly, getting right to God's purposes? Why force him to drag it out over eons? Had he wanted to say "billions of years", he could have said just that rather than "days".

Invoking the ***uncertainty principle***, scientists tell us that the universe arose from nothing, since its sub-particles can be generated from energy fluctuations in a vacuum. They point out also that the cosmos expanded exponentially during the earliest milliseconds. Given these scenarios, science has taken a step toward biblical creation. Could it be that the energy of creation, and starlight itself, produced the heat of the cosmos? The cosmos must have been highly unsettled until after the fourth day (witness the moon's impressive pock-marking)! It must have experienced an outburst of supernatural energy also, for to claim otherwise would be to tie the hands of God. The fact is, creation was a singular event, never to be repeated.

But why the "geocentricity" of the universe? Not because of the earth's location, since Planet Earth isn't necessarily at the center of the universe – though that may be a possibility (see pg. 176). The answer is, ours is the home for *saints* living as "strangers, in reverent fear" (1 Pe. 1:17). Considering Earth's preeminence, we should live holy lives, looking to the day of our redemption and speeding its coming, for we are "looking forward to a new heaven and a new earth, the home of righteousness" (2 Pe. 3:11-14).

As Morris put it, "of all the physical bodies in the universe, the earth is most important, then the sun and moon, then the stars. Therefore, the earth was created first (Ge. 1:1), then the two great lights to rule the day and night (Gen. 1:16), then finally 'the stars also' (Ge 1:16). This is the reverse of both the importance and chronological order imagined by evolutionists according to whom the universe evolved first, then its galaxies of stars, and finally the solar system, with the earth and moon somehow spinning off from the sun in the process. Although it is impossible to prove scientifically which of these two sequences is correct, the biblical order is more logical."[22]

Still, the plaintive cry of humanity is, "Where can we place our confidence?" The Latin for "confidence" is "con" (with) and "fide" (faith), but the faith of Davies and Gribbin is anchored in the evolutionary *joke* seeing the universe as an accident of no intrinsic value. Christians have fallen for absurdities too, thinking that if something is "scientific" it must be right. But is science really the judge of truth? As someone has said, "Science can be a companion to the truth but it isn't always its soul-mate. Thus, when people are wedded to some theory, they can suffer painful divorces when science is unfaithful."

Plausibility of the Myth

In my study I have an assortment of fossils: a trilobite, a dinosaur bone, nautiloids, foraminifera, sharks' teeth, an "ancient" fish, fossilized seedlings, etc. I prize these relics, having received them from my family, but one thing is certain: You can't buy a fossil without buying a philosophy! Attached to every one of them is a multimillion year "history", no matter its absurdity.

As C.S. Lewis said it so well, "Evolution is a *myth*, and myths die hard. [...] Perhaps nature was once different. Perhaps the universe as a whole is quite different from those parts of it which fall under our observation. But if that is so, if there was once a dead universe which somehow made itself alive, if there was absolute original savagery which raised itself by its own shoulder strap into civilization, then we ought to recognize that things of this sort happen no longer; that the world we are being asked to believe in is radically unlike the world we experience. In other words, all the immediate *plausibility* of the Myth has vanished. [...] It was all (on a certain level) nonsense, but a man would be a dull dog if he could not feel the thrill and charm of it. For my own part, though I believe it no longer, I shall always enjoy it as I enjoy other myths."[23]

People favoring cosmic evolution often favor biological evolution as well. The question is, which of the various views makes the most sense? Summarizing Gish's comments:

> *As all evolutionists believe*, chaos generated the cosmos, disorder was transformed into order; the complex arose from the simple. Everything is included – the whole family of reality: stars, galaxies, the solar system, the beginnings of life, all plants, animals, and man – including his consciousness, his ability to remember the past, cope with the present, and plan for the future. Even man's faith in God is nothing more than the product of an evolutionary process. The process is totally naturalistic and mechanistic, due solely to properties inherent in matter.

> *On the basis of Creation*, predictions concerning the inherent tendency of matter would be just the opposite of that predicted on the basis of evolutionary theory. If an omniscient, omnipotent Creator (the least we could say is that he was certainly adequate for the job) created the universe and all it contains, the universe would have started out in a state of perfection. Thus, matter would have no natural tendency to promote itself to higher and higher levels of order and complexity. If, however, something has happened since creation to change the original state (and obviously it has), the only effect possible would be to cause matter to change in such a way that it would now have an intrinsic tendency to become less ordered and less complex.
>
> *Now let us go out into the real world and take a look.* It is apparent, first of all, that matter does not have an inherent tendency or intrinsic ability to transform itself from disorder to order, from simple to complex. [...] There is, however, a natural law which describes just the opposite tendency – the Second Law of Thermodynamics.[24]

Evolutionists may mock this, claiming that order *can* come from chaos providing nature pours enough energy into it, but does nonsense generate intelligence? If so, why do our senses tell us just the opposite – that this never happens? A sobering addendum is this: If the Creator employed billions of years of universal decay to make man in his own image, he used the most wasteful, inefficient, and cruel processes *ever* to accomplish his goal!

"All Men are like Grass"

When replacing aortic aneurysms, surgeons cross-clamp the aorta. If the allowable time is exceeded, spinal paralysis will result. Providing you needed such an operation, would you allow me to proceed with it if I said, "Cross-clamping times are *theoretical*"? Of course not! Why then do people accept *origins myths*? Could it be the Western mind? "Can do" people, priding themselves in open-mindedness, like to figure things out. Action-oriented, but with little time for reflection, they turn to sound bytes and gurus, seldom checking original sources or the *Ultimate Source*. Though they have religious fervor of a kind, their theology is as shallow as their science, so they say, "Aha, evolution and the Bang!" But that isn't what the Bible says!

Framing the debate are two opposing viewpoints, supernaturalism vs. naturalism. Either God *is* or he *isn't*. Either he fashioned the universe as *he said he did*, or he *didn't*. People may finesse this, saying that if God exists he is either impotent or confined to ordinary processes, but God hates that mindset since it repudiates his *sovereignty*. Everything is then up for grabs and there is neither right nor wrong; neither authority nor accountability! People then make up the rules, claiming opinion as the arbiter of truth.

Consistent with this, the National Association of Biology Teachers (in their 1995 resolution) attributed biological origins to "the unsupervised, impersonal, unpredictable, natural process of temporal descent with modification". All biological organisms therefore come from mindless matter, mindless energy, and mindless process. But there is a stunning misperception here, for if evolution is our creator, that is the death of God! Everything reverts to relativism (lacking morality and values), leaving only "values clarification" and individualism. Having only a mindless creator, humans can impose their own will, doing what comes naturally. Sin is then redefined as "intolerance", and intolerant people are hated. The end result? The tables are turned, exchanging truth for a lie.

This leads to cultism, with its mantra: Follow the leader, modify your Bible, park your mind, and leave your family. Surrounded by such nonsense, people may see evolution as "purposeless change", but what do they mean by that? Claiming that knowledge comes from reason, they make up the evidence as they go along, basing their conclusions on perception. But they're left with loneliness and despair, since pessimism and hedonism have warped their minds. The upshot is an existential *'ism*, beginning and ending with man, without meaning at either end of life. Yet this is the opiate of modern society!

If God is sovereign, however, everything changes! The reason for existence is then clear, since morality has been established by a moral Being with whom people must reckon. Some don't see it that way, their having rationalized right and wrong as "traditions". And scientists themselves may not have expected things to end up this way, since the early rationalists had hoped mainly that the Age of Reason would set them free from superstition. Yet today's theorizers see science as explaining *everything*, leaving only *doom and gloom* in their universe.

How sorry we should be about their hoaxes, since the certainties of today will be laughable tomorrow! We must do more than grieve, though, because people will push their views incessantly, and these have captured the minds of many, including those of Christians. Believers are therefore easily disarmed, being so like the world that they cannot defend the truth!

Even in high-tech Silicon Valley, people are in the dark. Despite their best efforts, gravity pulls them into the dust every time. Sipping Starbucks Coffee in front of their dazzling computer screens, they can't even imagine **The Light**, being severely depraved. Viewing only the remains of a bygone world, they're unable to lift themselves up by science alone, since science (with all its twists and turns) can determine only what **is**, not how it **came to be**. But, even after all the nebulae have died out, there will be light, for God can bring people out of darkness into light.

In the last times there will be scoffers, following their own ungodly desires. Such people divide the world, having only their natural instincts, not the Spirit of God (Jude 18-20). Who then holds the key to knowledge? C.S. Lewis saw it in the hands of a variety of people, believers having the monopoly on truth. With that as the basic tenet, all disciplines are invited to the debate providing their logic, grammar, and rhetoric are framed by true knowledge, wisdom, and understanding. Truth, after all, is a matter of the Creator – not the creature.

The challenge for Christians? The **mind of Christ**, countering the hollow philosophies of this world. People may lay claim to the truth, but they must do so responsibly, for "if the trumpet does not sound a clear call, who will get ready for the battle" (1 Co. 14:8)?

> *All men are like grass,*
> *and all their glory is like the flowers of the field;*
> *the grass withers and the flowers fall,*
> *but the word of the Lord stands forever.*
> *(1 Pe. 1:24)*

[1] William A. Dembski, *Mere Creation,* InterVarsity Press, Downers Grove, IL, 1998, pp. 14,15
[2] William A. Dembski, *Intelligent Design*, InterVarsity Press, Downers Grove, IL, 1999, p. 97, 98
[3] Ibid, p. 85
[4] Ibid, p. 15
[5] Ibid, p. 99
[6] Ibid, p. 152
[7] Ibid, p. 209
[8] Ibid, p. 207
[9] Sten Oldenwald, *The Big Bang was NOT a Fireworks Display,* Washington Post, Astronomy Café Articles, May 14, 1997
[10] Timothy Ferris, *The Whole Shebang,* Touchstone, New York, NY, 1998, pp. 38,39
[11] Henry M. Morris, *The Biblical Basis for Modern Science,* Baker Book House, Grand Rapids, MI, 1984 pp. 135,136
[12] Paul Davies, *About Time,* Touchstone Books, New York, NY, 1995, pp. 17,18
[13] Ibid, p. 39
[14] Ibid, pp. 18,19
[15] Hugh Ross, *The Creator and the Cosmos,* Navpress, Colorado Springs, CO, 1993, p. 41
[16] John Gribbin, *In the Beginning,* Little, Brown, and Co., 1993, pp. 254,255
[17] Hugh Ross, *Mere Creation,* InterVarsity Press, Downers Grove, Ill, 1998, p. 371
[18] John C. Whitcomb, *The Early Earth,* Baker Book House, Grand Rapids, MI, 1990, pp. 19-21
[19] Aaldert Mennenga, *Dinosaurs at a Christian School, The Outlook*, Christian Reformed Fellowship, Inc., Grand Rapids, MI, June, 1990, p. 10
[20] Ibid, p. 10
[21] William C. Mitchell, *Physics Essays,* Volume 10, #2, June, 1997
[22] Henry M. Morris, *The Biblical Basis for Modern Science,* Baker Book House, Grand Rapids, MI,1984, p. 161
[23] C. S. Lewis, *Christian Reflections,* Wm. Eerdmans Publishing Co., Grand Rapids, MI, 1987, pp. 90-93
[24] Duane Gish, *Creation Scientists Answer Their Critics,* Institute for Creation Research, El Cajon, CA, 1993, pp. 157,157

THE DAYS OF CREATION
(Chapter 8)

Mists Driven by a Storm

These men blaspheme in matters they do not understand.
They are springs without water and mists driven by a storm.
(2 Pe.2:12, 17)

Strolling down the hospital corridor while awaiting a meeting, I paused at the portraiture of George Crile, father of thyroid surgery; one whom I have long admired, having adopted some of his surgical techniques. Soon I was with the Board of Governors to hear a quality report from an agency which had always in the past granted speedy accreditation since ours was a major teaching hospital treating kings and sheiks from around the world.

This year would be different, however. As if to prove their worth, these examiners were going for the minutiae, meaningless ones at that. Slipping into the second stage of anesthesia, I dreamt about Crile, who (though deceased) was far more effective even now than these surveyors. How should we respond to their prattle? Well, we would have to do some compromising, which is what we did, thereby assuring reaccreditation.

Compromise is helpful in the corporate world, but not in biblical exegesis. The Bible's details are not trivia. Paul said to Timothy, "Guard what has been entrusted to your care. Turn away from godless chatter and the opposing ideas of what is falsely called knowledge, which some have professed and in so doing have wandered from the faith" (1 Ti. 6:20). Why did Paul say this? Because, rather than receiving God's Word, many were willing to be deceived. Always seeking but seldom finding, they were "mists driven by a storm".

One way that this plays out is in the presumption that we need the "lens of science" to correctly read creation "days". Referring to this method, Berkhof wrote in his *Systematic Theology*, "The prevailing view has always been that the days of Genesis 1 are to be understood as literal days. It was only after the comparatively new sciences of geology and paleontology came forward, with their theories of the enormous age of the earth, that theologians began to show an inclination to identify the days of creation with long geological ages."[1]

Little wonder then that when this mindset was brought to Genesis, tensions resulted, as in the writings of Davis A. Young, professor of geology. Maintaining that Scripture can be explained by science, he wrote, "If it can be demonstrated beyond all doubt that Scripture demands a 24-hour view of the days, then the Christian scientist must accept that and, in effect, give up on geological science." Said he, "As a geologist I am quite delighted with this [day-age] interpretation, for I have become accustomed to thinking in terms of billions of years."[2]

Responding to Young's remarks, Whitcomb said, "How this approach honors the supremacy of Scripture or differs from straight-forward theistic evolution is not convincingly explained."[3] Nor, I would add, is this the approach of a responsible scientist, for it does not fit with the Bible and it doesn't fit with geology either, seeing geologists so divided over the data.

When we look to cosmology, paleontology, anthropology, etc. for our definition of "days", some pragmatic difficulties arise when extending them into ages. Vegetation appearing on day three is dependent upon creatures created on days five and six. How then would plants have survived for eons, without insects and birds? And what about the symbiotic relationships between plants and animals, some needing others for their very survival? More importantly, how could life itself have survived a lengthy series of geological ages, each morning with its eons of light and each evening with its eons of darkness? And how could God have looked upon these ages, with their eons of misery and death, proclaiming them "good"? Even a sixth grader could answer that!

The question is not whether some obscure scientist or theologian can come up with yet another reason to deny "days", but whether an honest exegetical study of the pertinent passages demands a non-literal interpretation. To determine this, we needn't be theologians, but we must consider the language and culture of the day as well as the meaning, purpose, and structure (genre) of the text. The primary question is this: Considering the overall context, and comparing Scripture with itself, was God referring to *undefined ages* or was he speaking about *literal days*? Remember, the answer must come from the most natural reading of the text, looking for its clearest message, as one would do in reading about the six day weather forecast.

What is at stake here? Chronology, sequence, and "days", nothing less than the reliability of the Bible! Consider also these contrasts from Ham and Taylor's *The Genesis Solution*:[4]

Evolutionism says: Flowering plants and pollinating insects evolved together through mutual benefit.
Genesis says: Plants were created on Day 3, insects on Day 6.   If these days were ages, how did flowering plants survive?

Evolutionism says: Stars existed before the earth.
Genesis says: Earth existed before the stars.

Evolutionism says: Man has been carnivorous, or at least omnivorous, from the beginning.
Genesis says: Man was originally vegetarian. Meat eating was not sanctioned by God until after the Flood.

Evolutionism says: Birds evolved from reptiles.
Genesis says: Reptiles ("creeping things") were created after birds.

Evolutionism says: Fish came into existence long before birds.
Genesis says: Both fish and birds were created on the same day.

Evolutionism says: Insects evolved long before the first birds.
Genesis says: Insects (including "creeping things") were created after birds.

Evolutionism says: Most of the earth's animals lived, died, and became extinct long before man even existed.
Genesis says: The entire original animal world was created only hours before Adam, at most forty-eight hours.

Evolutionism says: The first living things were sea organisms.
Genesis says: Full-blown land plants were created first.

Evolutionism says: Earth's plant life produced our oxygen-rich atmosphere.
Genesis says: Earth's life-supporting atmosphere was created before the plants.

Evolutionism says: The first fish evolved long before the first fruit trees.
Genesis says: Fruit trees were created before fish.

Evolutionism says: Matter has always existed in some form.
Genesis says: Matter did not exist until God created it.

Given these comparisons, why do the cognoscente of our day find it so hard to accept ordinary days? Stated differently, why can't they find proof for their eons? Because their views are not biblical and their proofs are not in the Bible!

Approaching the creation account from below, despite all the rhetoric about poetry, symbolism, etc., there is nothing unusual about its grammar or syntax, and we need not be experts to figure this out. Until verse 27 of Genesis 1, the characteristics of Hebrew poetry are lacking and the narrative is neither parable nor simile. Nor is it hyperbole, metaphor, or merely a story.

The terms "evening" and "morning" are no more unusual in the first chaper of Genesis than the same words occurring elsewhere in Scripture. The individual phrases, though describing incredible happenings, are spoken matter-of-factly. The nouns and pronouns are of the usual kind, consisting of common Hebrew words – words well understood during Old Testament times and not at all peculiar to either that culture or ours – despite the implications of *"tohu-bohu"* (chaotic void), *"bara"* (create), *"yatsar"* (forming), *"kun"* (founding), *"asah"* (making), *"aphar"* (dust), *"ruach"* (breath), and *"nephish chaya"* (living being).

Though the message is astounding, with its "forming" and "bringing forth", the language itself is ordinary, each "appearing" having occurred within a well-defined "day". And this is exactly how the early Jewish scholars and commentators understood these words.

(Extra)-Ordinary Creation Days

Applying Reformed hermeneutics properly, one could hardly see creation days as other than ordinary so far as their length is concerned. Why wouldn't days be *days* unless there is compelling Biblical evidence to the contrary, and wouldn't the same literalism apply to the chronologies and sequences of Genesis? As E.J. Young said, "If Moses had intended to teach a non-chronological view of the days, it is indeed strange that he went out of his way, as it were, to emphasize chronology and sequence for each of those days."[5] Although Young did waffle on the *length* of these days, the fourth century church father, Basil, was completely candid about them. Said he, "When I hear the word grass, I understand that grass is meant. I take it all in a literal sense. Therefore, let it be understood as it has been written!"

Genesis 1 is written in narrative prose, punctuated by a brief poem. Seeing it so plainly and unambiguously written, and knowing that there is literalism even in poetry, the first point in favor of ordinary days is the language itself. A second point is that the larger literary structure of any particular book must shape our thinking about its more discrete parts. Here too, the literal reading is the most harmonious if the overall context of Genesis is to maintain a meaningful relationship with the earlier chapters. A third point is that the literal reading is the only one supported by the remainder of Scripture. Moreover, the prophets, psalmists, and NT writers all confirmed the historicity of Genesis 1, just as Moses recorded it, and nowhere in the entire Bible is there any reference to days being ages or ages being days, although it is true that "with the Lord a day is *like* a thousand years and a thousand years are *like* a day" (2 Pe. 3:8).

Genesis 2 is synoptic, topical, and anticipatory, and some later chapters in Genesis use figurative expressions, but the book as a whole is chronological and sequential with nothing so unique that it doesn't come across plainly and factually to the average reader. Jesus himself never deconstructed these passages, and neither should we; nor does the language require (or even hint) that these days were eons. In fact, it is exceedingly difficult to imagine agrarian Hebrews winking at "days", proposing instead intricate triads and elusive language.

Adam knew what a day was! God defined it for him, calling the light "day" and the darkness "night" (Ge. 1:5). This is the exact terminology Moses used for the five days following the first, so there can be no question as to what God meant concerning the creation of all things in six ordinary days, after which there was one ordinary day of rest. These days were fixed from Day 1 of creation, so the burden of proof is on those who want them to refer to ages.

But isn't it true that the Hebrew "yom" (for day), can indicate a period of time, also? Yes, but not eons, and not as a rule. Grammatically and linguistically, "yom" lacks any signal for one to understand it as a figure of speech. When used figuratively, there is usually a linguistic signal (such as the English "as" or "like"). But when an ordinal number precedes it (the first day, second day, etc.) it is always an ordinary day and it cannot be read as millions of years.

What about the genealogies? Isn't it true that some names were omitted between the generations, allowing great antiquity for the human race? Let me say it as clearly as possible: It's hard to prove that any significant space was overlooked; perhaps a few hundred years, or a few thousand at the most, but no more than that. But couldn't the words "father" and "begat" skip over a few generations? Well, there's not much evidence for that. A careful look shows that the patriarchs fathered sons at specific ages for the time of the son's birth, and the genealogies are very clear about this. Except for minor exceptions in Luke 3, we have a remarkably continuous chronology from Adam to Noah, from Noah to Abraham, etc. (See Chapter 9, The Dawning of Humanity)

Even granting major gaps, one would have to come up with millions of years to fit the geologic time-scale. Insofar as real history is concerned, there is therefore no distinction between the first eleven and the remaining chapters of Genesis; they are all fully intelligible and genuinely historical. The pre-Abrahamic accounts are so real, in fact, that Jesus and his disciples spoke of them repeatedly. And every New Testament writer refers to them as absolute and authentic.

How about Adam's naming "the cattle, the birds of the air, and every beast of the field" during the sixth day, the same day in which Eve was created? Could he have both experienced loneliness and named all the creatures in a single day? The fact is, most of us feel lonely within moments after separation from a loved one. And as Leopold argued, "a limited number of animals might have been involved in the Garden"[6] (consistent with *basic types*, but not all the *sub-types*).

Remember, too, that Adam was of superior intellect, perhaps having a computer-like mind. His brain would have weighed no more than three pounds, but it was the ultimate model of complexity, processing information with cybernetic speed. He must have had unusual retentive capabilities as well, like certain autistic individuals today. Also, he was assisted in this naming, so he could have completed it in less than a day, the beasts and birds having been *brought* to him by God (Ge. 2:19).

Still, many have said that the activity of the third day, when dry land "appeared" and vegetation was "brought forth", could not have occurred within a 24-hour-period. But Grover Gunn (Foundation for Biblical Studies) said, "This argument overlooks the fact that the entire work of creation was supernatural."[7] God did take time for his creative activity, but he didn't limit himself to the slower processes of ordinary providence (as we see them today). Some things unfolded progressively, but only within boundaries so time restricted that only supernatural processes could have produced them.

As to whether or not these days were ordinary in length, the context is *very, very literal*. Remember, too, that biblical fidelity must reckon with seven sequential days, six of work and one of rest, for in the Book of the Law we read, "In six days the Lord made the heavens and the earth, the sea, and all that is in them, but he rested on the seventh day. Therefore the Lord blessed the Sabbath day and made it holy" (Ex. 20:11). God *spoke all these words* (Ex. 20:1) *in a loud voice* (Dt. 5:22), *writing them on tablets of stone* (Dt. 10:4). When the Israelites heard these words they came across as straightforward narration, to be taken literally and at face value – like the subsequent histories of Noah, Isaac, Jacob, Joseph, and his brothers.

Lacking real days, creation is meaningless, though Young (usually a defender of literal days) did comment, "God has not revealed sufficient for us to say very much about the length of those days."[8] Whitcomb responded, "It may be surprising to learn how strong are the biblical evidences supporting literal days if the indispensable and time-honored historical/grammatical system of biblical interpretation is accepted." Pointing out that "yom" requires ordinary days two thousand times in the OT, he went on to say:

- The terms "day" and "night" are described as periods of "light" and "darkness". This would be utterly meaningless if "day" and "night" are not parts of a normal day. In Genesis 1:14-19, the sun was created to "govern the day" and the moon to "govern the night". Again, "day" and "night" here must refer to parts of a normal day.

- The qualifying phrase, "the evening and the morning", attached to each of the creation days throughout Genesis 1, indicates a twenty-four-hour cycle of the earth rotating on its axis in reference to a fixed astronomical light source (not necessarily the sun in every case).
- A creation "week" of six indefinite periods of time would hardly serve as a valid, meaningful pattern for Israel's cycle of work and rest, as explained by God at Sinai.
- Since the word "days" in Genesis 1:14 is linked with "years", it is quite obvious that our well-known units of time are being referred to, their duration being determined not by cultural or subjective circumstances, but by the fixed movements of the earth in reference to the sun. Otherwise, the term "years" would be meaningless.
- Also, we must assume that the first three days of the creation week were the same length as the last three astronomically fixed days because exactly the same descriptive phrases are used for each of the six days.[9]

Summarizing these points, the Hebrew "yom", the words "day and night" and "light and darkness", the evening/morning formula, "days" linked with "years", and Israel's work/rest cycle are a combination leading to a chronological sequence of six contiguous and successive days – days of *ordinary length* and *extraordinary activity* based on God's *special providence*. Consider also the oceanic tides, a providential system tied to gravity and the moon. Joseph Pipa, Jr. (President, Greenville Theological Seminary) wrote, "When the dry land was separated from the water, the Spirit would have kept the water within its boundaries until the moon was created. Thus, the text implies acts of extraordinary providence during this process of creation."[10]

Claiming that these days were anthropomorphic, some have stretched them immeasurably, picturing creation in terms lacking any connection with time. There are of course anthropomorphisms in Scripture: In Psalm 18, for example, we find a literary device describing God's interaction with his people in terms of "smoke" ascending from his "nostrils". But illustrations such as these are not like God's visit to Abraham (in literal human form), or his literal work of creation where there are no anthropomorphisms at all. Thus, as Gunn insisted, "We must not confuse literary devices with literal events."[11]

Recall also that the Westminster Assembly of Divines (convened by the English Parliament in 1643) included in their Confession and Catechisms a statement that the world was created "in the space of six days", a phrase borrowed from Calvin, who wrote, "God himself took the space of six days for the purpose of accommodating his works to the capacity of men."[12] Some allege that the Divines never had this view in mind, implying that literal days are a fabrication of fundamentalists. But as Gunn pointed out, "There is no reason to believe that 'the space of six days' language found in the Westminster Standards means anything but the obvious and normal reading of the words. First, the interpretation of days as long ages, or normal days separated by long ages, is a position which arose long after the drafting of the Westminster Confession. Second, the very language of the Confession was used by Calvin to oppose Augustine's teaching of instantaneous creation."[13]

The bottom line? Volumes have been written disputing literal days, but Christians should give them no credence at all, for they are based on weird and worn assumptions. Rather than identifying with any of them, we must renew our commitment to Moses, who is telling us about genuine events, real people, a special garden, and an actual Fall. He is referring also to literal days, factual chronologies, and specific sequences – the sun, moon, and stars having been appointed for "signs to mark seasons and days and years" (Ge. 1:14). Receiving this from God himself, Moses wrote in such a way that every culture has been able to understand his words. These, therefore, are not words with which we can quarrel, for if Genesis is not reliable then God is not reliable either.

Alternative Day Theories

The doctrine of creation is under attack by those refusing to see the universe as working differently now than at first. Believers and unbelievers (alike) have rewritten "days" into "eons"; some arguing for creation *in* time and others for creation *with* time; some saying that ages came between the days, others that God created continuously.

How did people come up with these spins? Through their biases! Is it really so hard to see their bent? Bringing *a priori* evidences to the Bible, they have spoken instead of it rather than because of it. But why bother with their lengthy timetables when those proposing them stumble so badly over words like perfection, corruption, decay, death, flood, rainbow, and days?

Stripped of all humanistic presuppositions, Genesis 1 comes through with striking clarity, though some see it as illustrative, proposing alternative theories instead. By now these have all been thoroughly discredited, their being seriously flawed.

Two outmoded interpretations are the *gap theory*, placing lengthy ages between Genesis 1:1 and 1:3-31, and the *day-age theory*, suggesting days as periods of time. Two more current proposals are the *framework theory*, denying chronology and sequence, and *progressive creation*, envisioning supernatural causation but only where science has no explanation of its own – the so-called "god of the gaps" theory. These are all attempts at harmonizing science with Scripture, as in this summary from "*The Days of Creation*", a report to the 1999 Synod of the RCUS (Reformed Church in the US):

The Gap Theory (Reconstruction Theory) holds that there was a long interval of time between Genesis 1:1 and 1:3-31, during which God judged Satan, resulting in the waste and darkness mentioned in Genesis 1:2. But this requires changing the verb "was" in verse 2 to "became", and without that change there is no scriptural warrant for such a gap. Moreover, God made heaven, earth, and all the hosts of them within six given days, so the problems with the Gap Theory are fatal.

The Day-Age Theory (Geologic Age Theory or Concordist Theory) suggests that the days of creation were lengthy periods of time, corresponding to the "ages" of modern geology. The argument supporting this is that the Hebrew *yom* does not always signify a period of twenty-four hours. However, the most natural meaning is that the days of creation consisted of periods of light and darkness alternating in cycles of approximately twenty-four hours. Then too, even if "days" were geological ages, Genesis would still conflict with modern science since the Bible teaches a different chronology and sequence for creation.

The Punctuated Day Theory maintains that the days of creation were six ordinary days but that there were long intervening periods between these days. This view maintains literalness but relies too heavily on the findings of "science". Moreover, there is no biblical warrant for inserting eons between days; nor can this view accommodate the evolutionary development envisioned by paleontology.

The Framework Theory claims that the days of creation have nothing to do with time, but are forms or images designed by God to explain otherwise unintelligible acts of creation. Considerations supposedly compelling this non-literal interpretation are these:
- God rested from his creative activity on the seventh day, suggesting that the seventh day is an *eternal Sabbath* – not a normal day. If the first three days and the seventh were paranormal, perhaps the other days were not normal either.
- The sun was not created until *Day Four*. Since the sun is the instrument for measuring days, the first three could not have been days as we think of them.
- If the creation days were paranormal, God's modus operandi must have been *ordinary providence*. This would preclude any of the creation days from being ordinary in length since ordinary providence doesn't allow for time-consuming events like oceans evaporating or animals growing to maturity within such limited time-frames.[14]

The question is, do the concerns driving these alternative interpretations actually exist or are they based on misreadings of Scripture (faulty hermeneutics)? To answer that, we must look closely at biblical chronology and sequence.

Chronology and Sequence

The Gap Theory, while preserving sequence, dismisses chronology. To satisfy the geologic column, it presumes death and chaos followed by reconstruction and life. Though favored by Custance, Chalmers, Pink, Rimmer, DeHaan, and Scofield, this theory was rejected by Boice, who wrote in his *Genesis Commentary*, "It gives one of the grandest and most important passages in the Bible an unnatural and perhaps even peculiar interpretation – and it really does not settle the problem posed by geology. Geology shows us successive strata of the earth's crust containing fossils of earlier life forms. Advocates of the Gap Theory wish to account for these in the supposed break between Genesis 1:1 and 1:2, but at which point in this break did the judgment of God enter in? If it came after the laying down of the fossil evidence, then death was in the world before judgment. If the judgment came first, then the conditions arising from that judgment could not be as the second verse of Genesis describes them (a chaotic world submerged in darkness), for in such a world no plant or animal could survive."[15]

The Framework Theory claims that the days of creation are a literary framework unattached to chronology and sequence. Professor Arie Noordzij (University of Utrecht) first proposed this in his 1924 article, *"God's Word and the Witness of the Ages"*. Though championed by many, its arguments are easily countered. Those holding to the Framework see Genesis 2 as a second version of creation, their having reinterpreted chronology, sequence, and the interrelationships between Genesis 1 and 2. While it is true that the sequences and structure are different in the first two chapters, the exegetical key is this: Genesis 1 is driven by *chronological* concerns; Genesis 2 by *topical* concerns. Genesis 2 is clearly synoptic, topical, and anticipatory (not strictly chronological) and is therefore *not* the defining grid for Genesis 1 – not for its chronology, its sequence, or its days.

Dr. Meredith G. Kline, a major proponent of this theory, has written, "As far as the time frame is concerned, with respect to both the duration and sequence of events, the scientist is free of biblical constraints in hypothesizing about cosmic origins." According to Kline, the chronological sequences of Genesis 1 are determined by topical considerations from Genesis 2, but Young pointed out that the creation account ends with Genesis 2:3. Genesis 2:4 then begins with the phrase, "this is the account of", summarizing the preceding narrative with the intention of analyzing parts of it in greater detail. The wording in Genesis 2:5-7 is then like the title of a newspaper article, setting the stage for events to follow.

It is at this point that major errors are introduced by the Framework! Can it really be argued from Genesis 2:5 that God's creative activity involved only *ordinary providence*? The key is that Genesis 2:4 begins with *Elleh Toledoth* ("these are the generations of") phraseology employed repeatedly in Genesis. Whenever used, it introduces new knowledge built on prior information, and so also Genesis 2:5 builds on Genesis 1. The nature of the Toledoth is seen in the genealogies of Genesis 5 where each generation is the product (not the source) of prior patriarchal lineage. Likewise, Genesis 2 is the product of Genesis 1, although adding some new information. Interjecting subsequent information into what has already been presented is thus an indefensible hermeneutic, nailing down the fact that creation was from *extraordinary providence*, not God's everyday methodology.

Kline's hermeneutic has driven many to the conclusion that Genesis 1 cannot be factual, but his reading of Genesis 2 is erroneous regarding "evening and morning", "rain", "a man to work the ground", "extraordinary providence", "the eternal Sabbath", etc. In Genesis 2:2 there is a reference to Day 7 (the seventh day of whatever the first six were), so if the first six were of ordinary length then the seventh must have been ordinary also. Furthermore, although the words "evening and morning" are not mentioned in this verse, shouldn't we grant an alternate closing since the Sabbath is for rest, not labor?

Respected theologians (citing John 5:17 and Hebrews 4:3-5) have interpreted the "eternal Sabbath" as allowing creation days to be periods of time, arguing that the day of rest extends from creation into eternity. It is true of course that the writer compares God's rest (following creation) with the Sabbath of eternity, but *creation* refers to *beginnings* and *eschatology* to *end-times* (the eternal rest for God's people). Also, when the author explains that creation is to be understood by faith, it is a matter of revelation (not human inquiry) since the same writer says in Hebrews 11 that God created through his "spoken word", implying rapid creation. Hence, the lengthy view of beginnings rates only about a "2" on a credibility scale of "1 to 10". Accordingly, as E.J. Young concluded years ago, "There is no Scriptural warrant ever for the idea that this seventh day of creation is eternal."

In the Framework, much is made of the sun's absence until the fourth day. But Dr. Pipa observes, "It appears to me that God has actually spoken to the existence of light apart from the sun. In the series of rhetorical questions that God asks Job, he asks, 'Where is the way to the dwelling of light? And darkness, where is its place, that you may take it to its territory, and that you may discern the paths to its home? (Job 38:19,20)' [...] We know also that darkness existed as an ontological reality before the creation of the heavenly bodies. In this contrast, God is referring to the originally created darkness (not simply the absence of light), and the primordial light which God separated from the darkness."[16] The point is, the initial light was from **supernatural causation**, not **ordinary providence** (as in the Framework).

But rather than dwelling on every flaw of a failed hypothesis, perhaps we should focus on Kline's handling of the evidences. Kline is convinced that the six-day view pits Scripture against science, and ultimately against itself. However, the Framework pits itself against Genesis 1, calling it exalted prose, which is precariously close to calling it illusory. Regarding that method, Young said, "I cannot accept the so-called framework hypothesis which maintains that there are six pictures of creation and that they sustain no chronological relationship to one another. That is an easy way out of the difficulty, but I think it is insupportable."[17] It seems also to be a precursor to theistic evolution in light of the following questions:

- If pre-Adamic creatures *died*, how would one distinguish the Framework's death from theistic evolution?
- How would the Framework's morbidity and mortality fit with the God of the Bible?
- Why the need for some painfully convoluted hermeneutic if not to accommodate an assumed interpretation of the evidences, allowing for animal death?
- If pre-Adamic creatures *did not die* (no carnage before Eden), what was actually occurring during those lengthy ages required by the Framework?
- Whatever it was, how does it fit with the geologic column, where death and destruction are so plainly evident?
- Since one can neither prove nor disprove God's methods and timetable, why the appeal to the complexity and ambiguity of Scripture, rather than its more obvious reading?
- If the Framework is driven exclusively by exegetical concerns – i.e., the primacy of Scripture – why did this interpretation not arise until the 20th century?
- Since friend and foe alike agree that the literal reading is the most obvious, isn't the burden of proof on those reading it differently, redefining God's person, works, chronology, and sequence?

One might ask, "Why such a sustained focus on the Framework?" The answer is, because Kline's use of the historico-grammatical method is weak. In a footnote to one of his papers, *Space and Time in the Genesis Cosmogony*, he wrote, "In this article I have advocated an interpretation of biblical cosmogony according to which Scripture is open to the current view of a very old universe and, in that respect, does not discountenance the theory of the evolutionary origin of man." Given all this husk, there must be a kernel of truth somewhere, but it's hard to find! Creation, after all, involves **real history**, and in Reformed hermeneutics one should never forget that!

Summarizing The Framework, it is thematic and imprecise. According to this hermeneutic, forms and images supposedly help one understand an otherwise unintelligible Creation, but those holding to this see creation days as non-literal, non-chronological, and non-sequential, viewing them as metaphorical, semi-poetic, and figurative. Could this be why the Framework is so hard to explain and so impossible to swallow? But here is the more sobering question: Speeding down this slope, where are the **exegetical brakes** before we crash and burn?

For whatever reason, Kline's premises are tied to man's rationality and nature's laws. Consistently applied, this methodology will lead to a more serious problem: the rejection of not only the *first* Adam but also the *second*. Why then would this be tolerated, its having been so thoroughly discredited by lay and professional expositors alike?

Voice of the Church

The man without the Spirit does not accept the things that come from the Spirit of God,
for they are foolishness to him, and he cannot understand them, because they are spiritually discerned.
(1 Co. 2:14)

One of my patients, a rabbi, enjoyed sharing his theology with me. Asked about creation, he replied that rabbinical literature is a record of continuing controversy describing the contentions of individual scholars. Considering this less than helpful, I asked if he saw creation as the basis for the Jewish Sabbath. He did, but he dismissed creation days as a "story", seeing them as less important than Jewish life, Jewish customs, and Jewishness itself.

Ancient interpreters held an entirely different view. Hippolytus (A.D. 170-236) taught that the world was made in six natural days. Clement of Alexandria (A.D. 150-220), advocating recent creation, reckoned the time from creation to his own lifetime as less than 6000 years. Ambrose of Milan (A.D. 339-397), holding to 24 hour days, said that "God created day and night at the same time, continuing in their daily succession and renewal." Augustine (A.D. 354-420), believing in instantaneous creation, suggested that God didn't *need* six days to create. Along with that strange perspective, bordering on numerology, he claimed that it is difficult to say what kind of days these were, though maintaining that less than 6000 years had elapsed since the outset. Augustine did not, however, envision a long expanse of time as some have mistakenly said.

The Reformers were equally committed to literal days. Luther held to days as natural as our own, "days in which the sun moves from the east to the west." Calvin believed just as plainly in such days, saying that creation occurred "within the space of six days", accepting also the literal chronology and sequence of these days. He argued too that the days of creation are not merely a literary device, but "a literal space of time with a chronological interval." As if this were not enough, the Westminster Divines held to the same view – unanimously as it turns out.

The church's acceptance of alternative days is relatively new. During the middle of the nineteenth century there was a change of mind based on the influences of Lyell, Darwin, and Huxley. Capitulating to the ideologies of the day, Charles Hodge tried to square the Bible with the lengthy ages of Darwin, claiming that creation could be of undefined duration. Benjamin Warfield was of this opinion, also, given his leaning toward evolution.

Referring to these men, David W. Hall (pastor at Covenant PCA, Oak Ridge, TN) wrote: "I am happy to acknowledge the debt we owe to Hodge and Warfield. They were great home hitters, the Babe Ruth and Mark McGwire of their respective days. But even great hitters hit foul balls occasionally, and in the matter of the span of the creation week, they were far afield".[18] Commenting further, he said, "In all sincere respect, even though my fellow debaters claim the likes of Hodge, Warfield, and the Moderns, I feel safer standing with Luther, Calvin, Ambrose, the Westminster Divines, Turretin, and the long history of the church."[19]

Perhaps we should pause for a moment. The voice of the church does not determine Truth, but it may be helpful to note that, until the Scientific Revolution, the church affirmed six-day creation rather consistently. Two of its giants, Luther and Calvin, held that any pre-understandings to Scripture are not from the Spirit but from the mind that suppresses the truth. So, when people have their private interpretations (to which they are entitled), they are on their own, having forgotten the sweep of opinion over the centuries. Why should we be concerned about this? Because those who have been given a trust must prove themselves faithful (1 Co. 4:2), and faithfulness requires that we handle the Bible carefully.

As to whether or not creation days are a test of orthodoxy, the test of that is *faith in Christ*. We can differ about many things, but as long as we have *redeeming faith* we're on the right track, and we should tolerate each other. We should do more than that, however, for we must reflect our Maker as well, striving for unity while admitting that our confessions are subordinate standards. But creation days are indeed a test, for we are not to theorize beyond what is written (1 Co. 4:6). Creation is also a test of our fidelity to God's Word, and we must be careful regarding its Author. When we garble this we make it harder for people to trust in Christ, and if we do that we should be confessing and repenting.

Remember also that God gives us an opportunity to exercise our faith, and one way of doing that is through the faithful exegesis of Scripture. However, we should never label *literalists* "scientifically illiterate" or ***non-literalists*** "spiritually dwarfed".

As for the confessions of the church, some say there is a dearth of ecclesiastical statements concerning the length of creation days. Is this really true, or is there only a presumed silence? Digging deeper, we do find such statements after all. The Westminster Confession and its Catechisms have removed all doubt. Six day creation was maintained also in the post-Reformation literature of the sixteenth and seventeenth centuries, when prevailing opinion was that God made the world in six ordinary days.

The Heidelberg Catechism refers to creation days indirectly, since in Q/A 92 it connects the one day Sabbath with the six days of creation. If the days of creation were not the same as ours, this commandment would have to read, "God provided six images for creation and then rested forever". Putting it differently, should the word "day" mean a lengthy period in either or both instances, namely the six days vs. the seventh, this would render the entire commandment meaningless. So, the Catechism does teach six day creation and it tells us also about their length, seeing that these days had to be of equal duration for them to tell us anything at all about the Sabbath.

The Belgic Confession (Art. 5) does not specify the length of creation days, but it does insist that believers accept without any doubt all things in the Bible. Therefore, we must reject with all our hearts whatever does not agree with it (Art. 7). Nor may we subtract from it or add to it, as if human writings were of equal value. It follows then that the words of Scripture must be accepted, no matter what any scientist or theologian says to the contrary.

Even had the church never made such statements, that would not preclude them from being made today, for as Mordecai said to Esther, "Who knows but what you have come to royal position for such a time as this" (Est. 4:14)? There is after all a lot of bad theology in the world, and seeing creation days so badly maligned, shouldn't we be defending them? Moreover, given their charge to train leaders, wouldn't seminaries committed to Reformational theology have the highest responsibility in this regard? But here is my concern: Though God has gifted professors for this very purpose – to tell the truth – there is nevertheless a reluctance on their part to tell it like it is. And sometimes professors can lull us to sleep!

Springs of Living Water

Whoever drinks the water I give him will never thirst.
The water I give him will become in him a living spring.
(Jn. 4:13-15)

When we wrestle continually with alternative theories, we know they're in trouble, so isn't it time to trumpet the truth, seeing that it faded during the nineteenth century, never to recover? And what about evangelical churches with their low view of creation? How did they come to see "days" as so hypothetical when they are in fact so very plain, being at the heart of hermeneutics for centuries? Stated differently, how did some become so compromising when the Bible is so very clear?

Abraham believed God and it was credited to him as righteousness (Ro. 4:3). Speaking of Abraham, Paul said, "He is our father in the sight of God, in whom he believed" (Ro. 4:17). Today, however, many are placing a *question mark* where God has placed a *full stop*, appealing to "science" to bolster their theories. The truth is, there never was any biblical justification for these drawn-out days and there is no longer any scientific justification for them either, so why not drop all these preconceived notions, given God's incomprehensibility?

C.S. Lewis wrote in his *Reflections on the Psalms*, "A man can't always be *defending* the truth; there must be a time to *feed* on it."[20] But we must speak about it, as well, for though on the road less traveled (as Frost penned it), we Christians are still on the road best traveled. To travel it better, however, we must face the facts and state them squarely, since we seem to be at one of those junctures where the physical evidences are telling us that the Bible is true. Given the embarrassment of those whose ideologies have evaporated, there is now a fresh opportunity to re-instate biblical creation, but to make any progress we must embrace at least the following:

- *The literal reading of Genesis 1 is the most obvious and faithful interpretation of Scripture.*
- *Genesis 2, being synoptic, topical, and anticipatory, is not a second account conflicting with Genesis 1; nor is Genesis 2 the interpretive grid for Genesis 1.*
- *The pre-Abrahamic events, chronologies, sequences, and genealogies are not to be misread figuratively or otherwise – diminishing, distorting, or denying their factuality.*

Were we to accept these statements, could it be that some of our tensions would subside? But living in an alien world, I can hear the objections already. Here are a few of them and some suggested answers:

Statement: The literal position is just plain wrong.
Answer: Show me the compelling biblical texts to support such a statement.

Statement: Creation days are of secondary importance.
Answer: They are of concern today because of the slippage of doctrine and the fogginess of the Church's testimony.

Statement: The literal view ignores the evidences.
Answer: The evidences must be tested by the Bible, not the Bible by the evidences.

Statement: Galileo's telescope proved the Bible wrong concerning the sun's moving from the east to the west
Answer: The Bible often speaks in ordinary language, as we do today, but it is never wrong and it cannot be corrected. Regarding the heliocentric solar system, it can be validated, unlike cosmic history.

Statement: The literal position is fundamentalistic.
Answer: Luther, Calvin, and the Divines stood by the fundamentals of the faith, not evangelical fundamentalism per se.

Statement: The literal position is too explosive.
Answer: So was the long line of martyrs battling for truth.

Statement: The literal position is too constraining of science.
Answer: There is no such thing as fact-free science (from God's perspective), so origins theories are always to be formulated within the biblical framework. Similarly, we should be constraining ourselves, not God.

Statement: There is room for alternative positions.
Answer: The Reformed hermeneutic holds that the text can have but one meaning (the most natural) *prior to* the introduction of external influences, evidences, and authorities.

How pompous to think that humans could have any understanding at all, apart from God's Word! The objections will go on, but how long shall we halt between two opinions? Remember that Eve was taken physically, literally, and supernaturally from Adam's side. Conceding just this one point, the whole idea of reading creation in terms of ordinary providence is meaningless, even with a theistic twist. For a final question: Seeing alternative days as ill-fated as the Edsel, why not throw them into the incinerator, along with all the other fables? Considering the cost, why retrieve or recycle them? Why not just light the torch and let them burn? While some might not like the heat, perhaps they would enjoy the warmth and the light!

For God did not give us a spirit of timidity,
but a spirit of power, of love, and of self-discipline (2 Ti. 1:7).

[1] Louis Berkhof, *Systematic Theology,* Wm. B. Eerdmans Publishing Co., Grand Rapids, MI, 1941, pp. 153-154

[2] Davis A. Young, *Creation and the Flood,* Baker Book House, Grand Rapids, MI, 1977, pp. 18-22

[3] John C. Whitcomb, *The Early Earth,* Baker Book House, Grand Rapids, MI, p. 37

[4] Ken Ham & Paul Taylor, *The Genesis Solution,* Mater Books, Santee, CA, 1988, pp. 57-58

[5] E.J. Young, *Studies in Genesis One,* Presbyterian and Reformed Publishing Co., Philadelphia, PA, p. 100

[6] H. C. Leopard, *Exposition of Genesis,* Baker Book House, Grand Rapids, MI, 1942, pp. 130-131

[7] Grover Gunn, *Six Day Creation,* describing The Day Age Theory, Internet memo, 3/26/98

[8] E.J. Young, *In the Beginning,* The Banner of Truth Trust, Carlisle, PA, 1976, p. 43.

[9] John C. Whitcomb, *The Early Earth,* Baker Book House, Grand Rapids, MI. pp. 28-37, summarized.

[10] Joseph A., Pipa, Jr., *From Chaos to Cosmos: A Critique of the Framework Hypothesis,* Internet memo, 1/13/98

[11] Grover Gunn, *Six Day Creation,,* describing the Framework Hypothesis, Internet memo, 3/26/98

[12] John Calvin, *Commentaries on the First Book of Moses,* Baker Book House, Grand Rapids, MI, p. 78

[13] Grover Gunn, *Six Day Creation,* describing the 'position of Westminster Standards', Internet memo, 3/26/98

[14] Excerpted from, *The Days of Creation,* Report of the Special Committee to Articulate the Doctrine of Creation, Adopted by the 253rd. Synod of the RCUS, May, 1999, pp. 25-31

[15] James Montgomery Boise, *Genesis, An Exposition Commentary,* Zondervan Publishing House, Grand Rapids, MI, 1982, pp. 54

[16] Joseph A. Pipa , Jr., *Did God Create in Six Days?,* Southern Presbyterian Press, Oak Ridge, TN, p. 176

[17] E.J. Young, *In the Beginning,* The Banner of Truth Trust, Carlisle, PA, 1976, p. 43

[18] David W. Hall, *The Westminster View of Creation Days,* Internet Memo, 8/23/99, p. 1

[19] Ibid, p. 20

[20] C. S. Lewis, *Reflections on the Psalms,* Harcourt Brace & Co., New York, NY, 1958, p. 7

OUR FIRST PARENTS
(Chapter 9)

Planning for Adam

He who created the heavens, he is God; He who fashioned and made the earth; he founded it.
He did not create it to be empty, but formed it to be inhabited.
(Isa. 45:18)

In Hebrews 11:3, we read, "The universe was formed at God's command, so that what is seen was not made out of what was visible." This was God's *ex nihilo* creativity by which he made things supernaturally, from nothing in existence. To visualize this, try a little experiment. Lock yourself into a laboratory until you have created something *ex nihilo*. You'll need your sleeping bag, a cell phone, and plenty of food since you're likely to be there awhile! Yet the whole universe began in this way through the power of *divine fiat*.

Recounting how the Lord made the universe, Isaiah chose his words carefully. God founded (established) the earth, having made it *ex nihilo* (out of nothing), but he also fashioned and formed its inhabitants from materials previously made. So God was forming *(yatsar)*, founding *(kun)*, and making *(asah)* things as humans do, but he was also creating *(bara)* them as no human can.

When we humans make things, we start with something pre-existent, but we can't really create (*bara*) as God does. The word *bara* implies originality, purpose, and pre-planning, the process of introducing things by God's Word and Spirit. So exceptional is *bara* that it is used only three times when referring to origins: first, when God created the matter of the universe (Ge. 1:1); second, when he created living things (Ge. 1:21); and finally, when he created our first parents with their conscious being and living spirits.

When God spoke, things happened! That is not to say that everything appeared instantaneously, for God used formative processes as well: the heavens being "stretched out"; grass and herbs "coming forth"; the waters "beginning to swarm". With this in mind, note the words Isaiah chose. Matter was created *(bara)* from nothing, grass was made *(asah)* to grow out of the earth, Adam was formed (*yatsar*) from dust, having been created *(bara)* a "living being" and made *(asah)* into a recognizable form.

Whether arriving from precursor substances or not, everything appeared by the majestic, exclusive, and authoritative Word of God. Not only were his utterances commanding, they were consistent with his Being, reflecting the three Persons in the Trinity. God's voice was the source for all things, but he conferred with his Son (the Word, wisdom, and agent of creation) and with his Spirit (the power and might behind it all), as explained in *The Belgic Confession* (Art. 8).

If you haven't considered that voice, read what David said about it in his "Seven Thunders". We read in Psalm 29, "The voice of the Lord is over the waters" [as in waves and tides]. "The voice of the Lord is powerful" [as in tempest and calm]. "The voice of the Lord is majestic" [as in sunrise and sunset]. "The voice of the Lord breaks the cedars" [as in wind and fire]. "The voice of the Lord strikes with flashes of lightning" [as in rain and storm]. "The voice of the Lord shakes the desert" [as in quakes and faults]. "The voice of the Lord twists oaks and strips forests" [as in hurricanes and tornadoes]. Interestingly, God's thunders are mentioned also in Revelation 10:3 as *judgments on those refusing the truth*.

How God's Council must have rejoiced whenever he said, "Let there be", and there "it was"! First to appear was energy, powering up the sub-particles. Then came matter, filling the void. Then light, initiating chronology. Dark and desolate things were suddenly bright and beautiful! Whether or not photons turned into light-waves early-on, we don't know, but we do know that previously non-existent things sprang forth instantaneously. Each time there was the repetitive phrase, "He spoke and it was", signaling God's *fiat declaration*. Adam's arrival was totally unique, however. He didn't appear instantly, nor did he arrive through some lengthy process. Adam was so special that he was fashioned from clay and enlivened by the Spirit, his dust having had no latent potential at all.

Where are the equations for this creativity? The Bible is silent about them, and science hasn't discovered them either. What we do know is that Planet Earth preceded her cosmic cousins chronologically and sequentially, which boggles the mind.

Once God had illuminated the darkness, it was like flipping a switch. Absent pollutants, the full spectrum of light was displayed – like a gigantic floodlight penetrating the stratosphere. Time then sprang out of eternity, the waters parted, and the skies were established. The oceans then receded amidst splashing, spouting, and sizzling! Think about it! All that rumbling, grinding, and roaring! Bubbling springs, falls, and brooks! Precipices, plateaus, and canyons! Rivers, lakes, and deltas! Oozing cauldrons and spouting volcanoes! Jagged rocks, towering mountains, and even Tsunamis! How could anyone miss the Artist in this? Creation was so profoundly from God's hand that all original laws and processes are beyond human reach.

Who but the *Sovereign Lord* could have made such spectacular seascapes and vistas? He also made vaporous clouds, meandering rivers, and placid lakes, all bathed in the morning light, and all within a few days! Unbelievable you say? Not for him who walked on water and turned it into wine!

Nothing existed until God spoke it into existence. At his command ferns arrived before sunlight and fruit trees before fish. Fish appeared along with birds, and reptiles and insects came after them. Animals arrived hours before Adam, and all animate creatures were vegetarian. Holding otherwise is to tear the heart out of the Bible, which makes no more sense than dogs becoming dolphins or cows becoming whales.

But didn't animals come from other creatures? Not with "kind" locked into the record! Given this word, each creature was pre-programmed by genotype. Tulips come from tulips and dogs give birth to dogs. Correspondingly, no tulip will ever become a lily and no dog will become a cat. Why? Because the genome for dog spells D-O-G, chromosomes, genes, and DNA being as fully in God's plan as quarks, quasars, and supernovas.

Summing it up, Sproul wrote, "The Supreme Architect gazed at his complex blueprint and shouted commands for the boundaries of the world to be set. He spoke, and the seas were shut behind doors, and the clouds were filled with dew. [...] He spoke, and the earth began to fill with orchards in full bloom. The blossoms burst forth like springtime in Mississippi. The lavender hues of plum trees danced with the brilliance of azaleas and forsythia. God spoke once more, and the waters teemed with living things. The snail sneaked beneath the shadowy form of the stingray, while the great marlin broke the surface of the water to promenade on the waves with his tail. Again He spoke, and the roar of the lion and the bleating of sheep were heard. Four-footed animals, eight-legged spiders, and winged insects appeared. And God said, 'That's good'."[1]

Crowned with Glory and Honor

When I consider your heavens, the work of your fingers, the moon and the stars which you have set in place,
what is man that you are mindful of him? You made him a little lower than the heavenly beings
and crowned him with glory and honor.
(Ps. 8:3-7)

By the end of the fourth day, the stars had been flung into the farthest reaches, removing all doubt as to God's power and glory! He even "bound the beautiful Pleiades" and "loosened the cords of Orion", but he was still not content. Nor was he satisfied knowing the laws of the heavens (Job 38:31-33). He wasn't even fulfilled having made billions of galaxies, for while creation had ascended to an apex, the apex was yet to be occupied.

Spectacular though the newly-shining sun, moon, and stars were, they were surprisingly subordinate to Planet Earth. This was to be Adam's home! Yet, as Watts said it, "even Earth was too narrow to express God's worth, his glory, and his grace", for God had offered to the world a power so amazing that it would culminate in raising Christ from the dead and seating him at his right hand in the heavenly realms, far above all rule, authority, power and dominion (Eph. 1:19-22).

Why were Adam and Eve so late in arriving? Because God saw them as his crowning jewels! Unlike other creatures, humans were created for a relationship with God, one of compassion, companionship, and commitment. "God now stooped to the earth and fashioned a piece of clay. Lifting it gently to His lips, he breathed into it and it began to worship."[2] Why would God do this? Because Christ wanted to commune with that lump, though knowing full-well that he would sprinkle it one day with his own blood.

Commenting on this, Whitcomb exclaimed, "Of all living things on this planet, only man is self-conscious as a person; sufficiently free from the bondage of instinct to exercise real choices and to have significant purposes and goals." Man, and man alone, "has complex emotions including sadness and joy; appreciates art and music creatively; can make real tools; can be truly educated rather than merely trained; can use oral and written symbols to communicate abstract concepts to other persons and thus enjoy true fellowship; can accumulate knowledge and attain wisdom beyond previous generations and thus make genuine history; can discern moral right and wrong and suffer the agonies of conscience; and can recognize the existence and rightful demands of his Creator through worship, sacrifice, and religious service."[3]

Adam was a personal being with a spiritual nature, an eternal soul, a rational mind, and spectacular glory. Some say he wasn't even a real person, but the King James tells us, "through *one man* sin entered the world (Ro. 5:12). So there was truly an Adam, and he was special indeed. "God created him good and in his own image, in true knowledge, righteousness, and holiness, so that Adam might know God his creator, love him with all his heart, and live with him in eternal happiness to his praise and glory" (*The Heidelberg Catechism*, L.D. 3). Paul agreed with Adam's uniqueness, for he wrote, "Man did not come from woman, but woman from man" (1 Co. 11:8).

Most men have mothers, but humanity had its origin in one person, a ***man***, his name meaning "red man" or "red earth" (since Adam was formed from the ground). God then "breathed into his nostrils the breath of life" and Adam became "a living being" (Ge. 2:7). As Dr. John Murray (Westminster Theological Seminary) stated, "We have been specially-made, specially-endowed, and specially-appointed as image-bearers."[4] This was vested in Adam during the engagement of God's Council, before the world began.

When God made Adam it was not through his usual formula, "let there be". Instead, he said, "let us make man in our image, in our likeness, and let them rule over the fish of the sea and the birds of the air, over the livestock, over all the earth, and over all the creatures that move along the ground" (Ge. 1:26). Adam was stamped with God's character, denoting a sharp distinction between animals, "after their kind", and humans, "in God's likeness".

For Adam, there was elevation of a particular kind, since God had gifted him singularly. Thus, we should never conceive of people as somehow on a par with animals, since animals and people are not of the same stripe. Animals can reflect God's *glory*, but only humans reflect his *Being*, so Bavinck was right when he said, "The theory of the animal ancestry of humans violates the image of God and degrades man into the image of an orangutan." What is man then? "Many are stumped by this", said Schaeffer:

> For with the evolutionary concept of a mechanical, chance parade from atom to man, man has lost his unique identity. As he looks out upon the world, he cannot distinguish himself from other things. Quite in contrast, the Christian does not have this problem. He knows who he is. If anything is a gift of God, this is it – knowing who you are. It is on the basis of being made in the image of God that everything is open to man. Suddenly, personality does not slip through my fingers. I can understand the possibility of fellowship and personality. I understand that because I am made in the image of God and because God is personal, so now both a personal relationship with God and the concept of fellowship

as fellowship has validity. The primary factor is that my relationship is upward. Of course, I have relationships downward as well, but I am differentiated from all that is below me and I am no longer confused. [...] Also, I can see that all men are so differentiated from non-man that I must look upon them as having great value.[5]

Adam was so special that no suitable helper could be found for him among the animals. Nor could an animal be his soul-mate. "The Lord then caused the man to fall into a deep sleep; and while he was sleeping, he took one of the man's ribs and closed up the place with flesh. Then the Lord God made a woman from the rib" (Ge. 2:21,22). Imagine *that* appearing in a biology text! The world was readied for this, however, for a garden had been planted "in the east, in Eden", where all kinds of trees grew out of the ground, "trees that were pleasing to the eye and good for food" (Ge. 2:8-10). Here God equipped our first parents perfectly. Adam was the federative head, loving Eve with Christ-like love, and together they had dignity, dominion, and sanctuary.

In Paradise, Adam and Eve were of one flesh, Adam having become a tissue-donor. Human flesh, although now tainted, is still special to God – so much so that he will raise it anew, unlike what he will do for any animal. As for the guarantee of that inheritance, *The Heidelberg Catechism* assures us, "we have our own flesh in heaven", since Christ took on human flesh and is now our advocate with the Father (Q &.A. 49). How could anything be more convincing regarding our uniqueness? Why would we humans be so peculiarly differentiated from other creatures? Because, we are "sons and daughters of the living God", enjoying a relationship from above, unlike how other creatures relate to their Creator.

From Dust to Nobility

The Lord God formed the man from the dust of the ground
and breathed into his nostrils the breath of life,
and the man became a living being.
(Ge. 2:7)

Though given a soul, Adam was formed from dust. The Hebrew **aphar** (dust) appears over 100 times in the Old Testament, and never does it denote living matter. Adam's dust was as dead as that on our doorsteps until God breathed into it. And when God said later, "to dust you shall return", this was not living dust either, since **aphar** is nothing but the dust of Earth's crust, completely unlike living protoplasm. Likewise, when the text tells us that "man became a living being", it cannot refer to living forebears, or it would have to read, "a living being became a man", reading it backwards.

Putting it bluntly, primates don't become human! Adam did have a connection with animals, however, for just like them he was "formed out of the ground" (Ge. 2:19). The Hebrew "formed" suggests a potter fashioning clay, but there was something different about God's handling of animals' dust compared with Adam's. In creating animals, God said, "let the earth bring forth", but in making Adam he "breathed into his nostrils the breath of life" (Ge. 2:7). God did not say, "let the earth bring forth man", for there was an intimacy between man and his Maker that is nonexistent between God and other creatures. Also, there is no inference that the earth's dust had the power to transform itself into some creature which would later become an image-bearer.

In Adam's case, dead dust became spiritual, but first it had to become alive. So "the Lord God formed the man from the dust of the ground and breathed into his nostrils the breath of life, and the man became a living being" (Ge. 2:7). Adam was enlivened by God's breathing into an inanimate lump which was nothing special until God's Spirit was breathed into it. Understand also that the Hebrew, **nephesh chaya**, refers to "a living being", not a "living soul" (as wrongly worded in the King James). **Nephesh chaya** is generic to any living creature, so it is easily confused with Adam's soul. The human soul came from the Hebrew **ruach** (Spiritual breath) into Adam's dusty nostrils, so his clay became both **nephish chaya** and a soul, having received God's **ruach**.

We see then that the main difference between animals and Adam is the in-breathing of the Spirit. The fact is, had Adam descended from an ape, that creature would already have been a "living being" and God's **ruach** could not have made it again into a *"nephesh chaya"*. Thus, the soul cannot be interpreted as residing either in dust or in flesh, nor can "man" be defined as "hominid" or "brute".

Having received his soul, Adam was to exercise dominion over the earth and its inhabitants. This implies a supervisory delegation on the part of him who entrusted his sovereignty to mankind. Man then became God's vice-regent, subordinately authoritative over nature, along with his Master. Adam's domain included "every living creature" (Ge. 1:28) – even the *dinosaurs* – for the psalmist wrote, "You made him ruler over the works of your hands; you put *everything* under his feet; all flocks and herds, the beasts of the field, the birds of the air, and the fish of the sea" (Ps. 8:6).

God blessed our first parents, saying, "Be fruitful and increase in number; fill the earth and subdue it" (Ge. 1:28), and still today all things (including the environment and human propagation) are under human dominion. In other words, we have the responsibility for them.

Human nobility is not in the flesh, however, for we have lost the perfection of our genes. We have a postural dignity suitable for Christ's dwelling within us, but our authority is not from our strength, size, intelligence, or cranial capacity. These have all declined, so our pre-eminence is from God's "image and likeness". And when "likeness" is added to "image", there is an extension of God's nobility directly to us, elevating us above all other creatures – giving us inexpressible value in the eyes of our Creator. But human supremacy is not in humanity per se, since human dominance does not reside in DNA alone.

The Human Genome

All flesh is not the same: Men have one kind of flesh,
animals have another, birds another, and fish another.
(1 Co. 15:39)

It was an Austrian monk who took the first step toward biology's "book of life". While growing peas in his monastery garden in 1856, Gregor Mendel set out to determine how hereditary traits are transmitted. All living organisms have cells with central nuclei and surrounding cytoplasm, but the question was, "Where are the hereditary elements, in the nucleus or in the cytoplasm?" And what is the hereditary material that is passed from one generation to another?

Mendel's experiments involved the physical features of plants, not their cellular components, but he set the stage for *cellular biology*. Years later, staining cells and watching them divide, biologists discovered nuclear threads (chromosomes) appearing just before cells split. Soon thereafter, they discovered that cells contain many different chromosomes varying in size and shape, but it wasn't yet clear that these contained Mendel's hereditary factors.

In 1902, W. Sutton theorized that each chromosome carried its own set of genes. He then demonstrated that chromosomes occur in pairs, one from the mother and the other from the father. Human cells were found to carry 23 pairs, 22 of which are similar, the 23rd being different in males and females, determining their gender. In males, the 23rd pair consists of two dissimilar chromosomes (x and y). Contrastingly, in females there are two similar x chromosomes making up that 23rd pair.

Working with fruit flies, Thomas Morgan confirmed that genes lie on chromosomes and determine hereditary traits. Genes consist of proteins and DNA (Deoxyribonucleic Acid). DNA consists of four building blocks (called nucleotides, or bases): Adenine (A), Guanine (G), Cytosine (C), and Thymine (T). In 1952, Hershey and Chase (using radioactive tags, bacteria, and viruses) discovered that DNA is the hereditary genetic material. And in 1953 Watson and Crick (Cambridge, England) came up with the final evidence, unraveling DNA's structure and establishing a sure footing for *molecular biology*.

DNA consists of two strands of nucleotides intertwined as a "double helix" (twisted ladder). Each strand compliments the other. Knowing the sequence of one helix, biologists soon determined the sequence of the other, and within a decade they had discovered that a single gene (a piece of DNA) contains the information for making a specific protein. Many genes working together produce the proteins that form an organism and keep it functioning. These findings marked the end of one era and the beginning of another, and from there it was a short step to saying, "We need to determine the sequences for all the genes."

Mapping the genome is relatively new research. The Human Genome Project, an international effort begun in 1990, is initiating a revolution that will lead to improved diagnostics, newer drugs, and better treatment of certain diseases. Some say we will have our unique codes imprinted on smart cards, enabling physicians to tailor-prescribe treatment for each person's genetic pattern. But the final map will still have gaps which cannot be filled using present technology.

The human genome, though seemingly intelligible, is far more complicated than had been expected. The whole assemblage shouts intelligence and design, though there is still no chemical explanation for what it means to be a *person*. The biggest surprise, using the most sophisticated of search engines, is the limited number of genes in humans. That number had been estimated at 100,000 but it has shrunk to approximately 30,000, only twice that in roundworms.

Since half our genes are like those in the lowest animal forms, the question arises, "Are we less complex than had been thought?" There is more to be learned of course, but the answer may be that each cell reads its encoded information in many different ways. Importantly, while researchers had previously labeled 97 percent of human DNA as "junk", they now think that even junk DNA has functions, though they're not always sure what these may be. Functional or not, many see these snippets as evolutionary remnants, and therein lies the rub! Perhaps those empty strands – those silent gaps – are actually reminders of how far we have fallen from our original garden-perfect state. After all, Adam performed inconceivable feats! And he lived to be 930 years old!

Human chromosomes are 40% DNA and 60% protein (individual proteins are the subject for fancier studies). Six billion base pairs of DNA are tightly packaged into 46 chromosomes where the genes carry sufficient information for making all the proteins and enzymes in the human cell. DNA, and therefore all of life, is made up of the previously-mentioned A, T, C, and G nucleotides. The proteins themselves are made of amino acids, but the instructions from DNA (for the assemblage of amino acids in the cell) are not direct. RNA (Ribonucleic Acid) is the intermediary, and it differs from DNA in its structure and function. RNA is single-stranded, enabling it to exit the nucleus and enter the cytoplasm where proteins are made.

The information making a person unique is written into DNA. If it were a book, and one could read ten letters per second, it would take eleven years to recite the whole 10,000 page book! As it turns out, your DNA is 99.9% identical to mine, subtle differences in genes accounting for the variability in individuals. In all organisms there are small variations (polymorphisms) differentiating one organism from another, each blueprint discoverable by gene sequencing. We know also that defective genes can cause hereditary diseases, a single misplaced letter sometimes producing lethal consequences.

This information will dwarf the current catalog of genetic knowledge. For better or for worse, it will have consequences (ethical, legal, and social) involving the creation and control of mutations, alteration and elimination of biological characteristics, the selection and determination of fetal gender, etc., all of which can affect future generations. Mapping the human genome is thus a cause for both celebration and caution.

Francis Collins, Director of the Human Genome Project, claims that this is the most important effort ever, surpassing the moon landing. Scientists hope that it will provide an intellectual perspective into *who we are* and *where we originated*. If it could be determined which DNA sequences code for certain organs and structures, then it might be possible to determine *whether or not evolutionary descent occurred*. However, if an organism is presumed to have descended from another, it must be shown that there is a genetic succession of viable transitional organisms serving as a continuum from prior ancestors. Conversely, if no such succession is demonstrated, it should be possible to say that descent didn't occur. In either event, people are looking to the genome to solve questions of origins and migrations, and therein lies the potential for mischief.

There is a saying in anthropology, "Every skeleton has a voice." Working with DNA markers, scientists theorize that humans came from Africa or Israel, diversifying from there and moving rapidly around the globe. To trace when and how certain ancestors first populated Europe, geneticists are studying mitochondrial DNA. Unlike nuclear DNA, mitochondrial DNA is in the cytoplasm. It is inherited only from one's mother, passing unmixed and unchanged from one generation to the next. Mutations of mitochondrial DNA occur more frequently than those in nuclear DNA, so these are viewed as a *time clock* to the past. Were that indeed true, and were one to compare two persons' mitochondrial DNA, the differences between them might determine the length of time that certain individuals shared an ancestor and what kind of ancestor that might have been.

National Geographic put it this way: "Scientists all over the world are using mitochondrial DNA to re-create migrations of ancient peoples across Africa, the Americas, and everywhere between. It's important to keep in mind, however, that the exquisite diversity in our mitochondrial code that allows us to trace these events is a classic exception that proves the rule. In most of the rest of our genes (99.9% of them), every human being is exactly the same. Most of the variations in the remaining one-tenth of a percent don't bunch up into geographic regions or racial groups but instead are spread around the globe. Put another way, the snips and snippets of code that make one person unique are scattered about in other genomes all over the world, binding us all together in a splendid tangle of interrelationships."[6] Using these markers, scientists postulate that Europeans descended from a lengthy chain of mothers and grandmothers dating back to 11,000 to 14,000 years ago, 10 percent tracing to 50,000 years.

As scientists are assembling entire genomes, they are relying on *presumed mutational rates* embedded in *cybernetic chips*. But what else is in these chips? Keyed into their memory banks is the idea that evolutionary descent is as natural as motherhood itself! So what do we end up with? Computerized "conclusions" based on mitochondrial myths and anthropological biases! And if the data streams don't fit, they can always be reconfigured into some new proposal!

But even having the letters in proper order, the pages can still be scrambled. Reading them, geneticists are discovering substantial similarities among creatures. A third of the genes in *nematodes* (roundworms) are shared with humans. Many of those in chimpanzees are so similar to human genes that something else must be producing the morphological differences – namely the *proteins themselves*. Even bacteria are our cousins in code, so the most profound secret of genes may be the unmistakable unity of everything alive, which sounds like Moses had it right all along, linking Adam with dust like that of the animals (Ge. 2:7).

Basic Types and Family Trees

God made the wild animals according to their kinds, the livestock according to their kinds,
and all the creatures that move along the ground, according to their kinds.
(Ge. 1:25)

Sequenced DNA has been called "the periodic table for humans", "the blueprint for life", "the code of codes", and even "the holy grail of humanity". With all this allure, the Human Genome Project can easily become a religion. Stated differently, while the pursuit of knowledge is our mandate, the "book of life" can become a nightmare rather than a dream, particularly when neo-Darwinian assumptions are brought to it.

Keep in mind that nothing in the genome negates the fact that "kinds" reproduce after their kind, which is always the norm. Though DNA is a miracle, remember also that the data can be misleading when combined with the idea that human and animal flesh are *one*. The truth is, any commonality is from a *common Designer*, not a *common ancestry*!

Some think there are only two kinds of living organisms, plants and animals, but even the category, "species", can be defined in various ways. The common definition is that they are potentially interbreeding groups which, when reproductively isolated, are no longer able to interbreed. As finer and finer divisions are made, only certain specific creatures seem to have enough in common to allow their interbreeding in the wild. These are said to be of the same *species*, like Darwin's finches.

Taxonomists are interested in such groupings as they relate to the classification of flora and fauna around the world, but what had been a workable system for years is shaking to the core. Maverick biologists are now proposing that people abandon the traditional ranking, junking a system developed over 250 years ago by the Swedish botanist, Carolus Linnaeus. Why? Because morphologic similarities can be measured more precisely now than ever before, by gene sequencing. Scientists are far from understanding these sequences fully, however, so they cannot (as of now) use them for taxonomy. Classifications are being redefined nonetheless, including kingdom, phylum, class, order, family, genus, and species.

A major difficulty is still the "species problem". Given today's science, how does one define the term? A final definition doesn't exist, but clarifications have been offered. Frank Marsh, a taxonomic biologist whose ranking by "basic types" goes back to 1941, has coined the term *"baramin"*, from the Hebrew *"bara"* (to create, shape, or fashion) and *"myn"* (species or kind). Hybridizing organisms are of one created kind, or "baramin", and this idea is gaining acceptance. Siegfried Scherer (Director of the Institute of Microbiology, Technical University, Munich) says that basic types are like the current "family" with its potential to diversify.

What are the advantages of such a definition? There are many, says Scherer. "First, it provides a category whose members share the same morphogenetic pattern; second, it builds on the wealth of interspecies hybridization data already available, but rarely used in classification; third, the data can be augmented by artificial insemination or artificial pollination; fourth, this approach allows one to define the basic taxon without reference to other species, defining the higher taxa in terms of hierarchical rank; fifth, basic types provide a taxonomic rank above the species level, directly comparable within all kinds of sexually reproducing organisms; sixth, this method leaves plenty of room for using morphological similarities in defining genera; and seventh, this system does not involve major changes in nomenclature."[7]

Where did basic types originate? According to Scherer, "they are thought to share a common ancestor that is more primitive than their descendants. Accordingly, the available biological data should fit evolutionary models and should demonstrate transitions between fossil groups that may be considered as basic types. Alternatively, basic types might have originated by design." Clearly then, taxonomic arguments can be made by either side – by creationists as well as evolutionists.

Though not primitive at all, basic types may have existed at certain times in history, such as before the Flood, after which there could have been rapid speciation, sub-types branching off from the originally created "kinds". This would account for a lesser number of animals in the Garden and fewer sub-types in Noah's Ark. Such bursts of speciation are not mentioned in Genesis, but the diversity of races descending from Noah does seem to imply genetic pluri-potentiality producing a variety of physical features, color variations, etc. If such differentiation did indeed occur, creationists see it as happening at certain specific times in history, ending as quickly as it began – by the hand of God and for his own good purposes.

Basic types can be fascinating, and amusing. Rev. David Feddes (*The Radio Pulpit*, Oct., 2000) writes, "Have you ever heard of a zorse, a zonkey, a beefalo, a cama, or a liger? A zorse is from mating a zebra and a horse, and a zonkey is a cross between a zebra and a donkey. A beefalo is a cross between buffalo and domestic cattle, also called a cattalo. Veterinarians mated a camel and a lama, naming it 'Rama, the cama'! And how about ligers (the product of lions and tigers)?" Mules (usually sterile) result from mating horses with donkeys. But how do hybrids relate to Genesis 1?

Apparently, basic types existed from the beginning. Certain creatures do interbreed successfully, so they may trace back to their original "kinds", endowed with information capable of producing a variety of descendants. Science writer Margaret Helder comments, "If these speculations are correct, then the created animal kinds in the Ark might have been as few as 2000, assuming that the baramin were roughly comparable to the *family* level recognized in our present taxonomic classification schemes. Alternatively, if creation kinds are comparable to the *genus*, rather than family level, there would have been about 16,000 different kinds of animals on the Ark."[8] The fact is, had all of today's species been in Noah's Ark, its capacity would have been severely taxed.

Baramin can be diagrammed, but diagrams aren't proof. Considering the lines of descent for various data sets, improved scenarios may come from computer simulations, but the mathematical task will be daunting. Yet this methodology could actually distinguish which organisms are of separate baramin. While not all assumptions will prove valid, newer insights will emerge with time. "The important thing", says Helder, "is that creation-based questions are being asked and creation-based research is being pursued." As a result, taxonomic information will expand exponentially.

For now, evolutionists are squabbling over their centuries-old family tree, a tree incorporating evolutionary dogma. Those favoring its restructuring say that there aren't enough branches (ranks) in the traditional system to encompass *remote evolutionary growth spurts*. Also, they are concerned about the mass of information arriving at such a dizzying speed as to make taxonomy confusing – so much so that some would rather not touch yet another "tree". In the opinion of William Burger (Curator of Botany, Field Museum, Chicago) this reclassification is "moronic". But it's probably unavoidable.

What would replace the current family-tree? A new one as free-floating as evolution itself! Under the new system, humans would still be classified as Mammalia, but biologists would no longer care if ours is a class, superclass, or some kind of giga-superclass. The category "species" would be abolished and humans would go by the single name *"sapiens"*. The evolutionary lineage would then be as follows: Single-celled Eucaryotes produced Metazoans (multicelled animals). Metazoans gave rise to chordates, having cartilage supporting the nerves along their backs, and they became animals with backbones: *hominoids, hominids, early humans, and then us*. But what rubbish, compared with biblical creation!

As scientists are redefining taxonomy, "phylogeny" is returning as a consideration. Phylogeny? It's a fancy word for *evolutionary descent*, reaching back to Ernst Haeckel, the German Darwinist who popularized the phrase, "ontogeny recapitulates phylogeny", meaning than the human embryo (with its pharyngeal pouches and gill slits) retraces evolutionary development from fish to amphibian to reptile to mammalian to hominid to human. This has been thoroughly discredited, of course, but it remains in the heart of those seeing subhuman primates as climbing the evolutionary branches.

The phylogenetic approach seemed workable in 1981, when first applied to a single gene, but that is no longer true. Carl Woese (University of Illinois) studied a specific gene for synthesizing proteins. Comparing variations of that gene from different species, the family tree was seen as branching into two primal kingdoms: 1) single-celled organisms found in scalding springs and oil wells, and 2) multicellular organisms branching into plants and animals. But now that entire genomes have been decoded, the old phylogenetic tree has toppled, since if all organisms had evolutionary forebears, the primeval cell would have been implausibly complex, no matter the taxonomic ranking.

Even so, the newer nomenclature seems inevitable. Why? Because evolutionists are interested in more than just a better classification. What they really want is an enhancement of their theories, which is perhaps the major reason for their revisiting the family tree in the first place.

As the "tree of life" is becoming more evolutionary, researchers are discovering new categories to insert into its branches. Consistent with this, putting it in today's language, humans are in the kingdom *Eukarya-Metazzoa*, phylum *Chordata*, subphylum *Vertebrata*, superclass *Tetrapoda*, class *Mammalia*, order *Primata*, family *Hominidae*, genus *Homo*, and species *sapiens*. But where are the hominids? To answer that, see *Figure 2*.

THE EVOLUTIONARY MYTH

THE MORE SCIENTISTS dig, the more hominid species they find. Most are distant cousins that went extinct without progeny; others are our direct ancestors

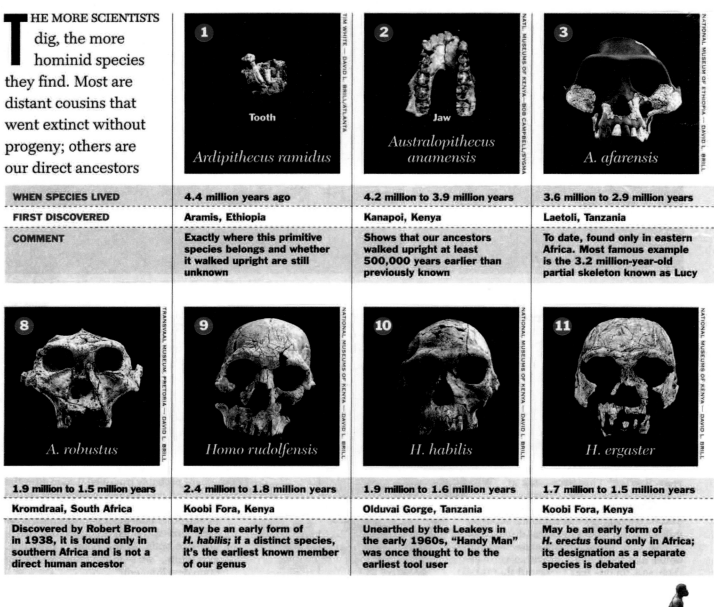

	Ardipithecus ramidus	**Australopithecus anamensis**	**A. afarensis**
WHEN SPECIES LIVED	4.4 million years ago	4.2 million to 3.9 million years	3.6 million to 2.9 million years
FIRST DISCOVERED	Aramis, Ethiopia	Kanapoi, Kenya	Laetoli, Tanzania
COMMENT	Exactly where this primitive species belongs and whether it walked upright are still unknown	Shows that our ancestors walked upright at least 500,000 years earlier than previously known	To date, found only in eastern Africa. Most famous example is the 3.2 million-year-old partial skeleton known as Lucy

	A. robustus	**Homo rudolfensis**	**H. habilis**	**H. ergaster**
	1.9 million to 1.5 million years	2.4 million to 1.8 million years	1.9 million to 1.6 million years	1.7 million to 1.5 million years
	Kromdraai, South Africa	Koobi Fora, Kenya	Olduvai Gorge, Tanzania	Koobi Fora, Kenya
	Discovered by Robert Broom in 1938, it is found only in southern Africa and is not a direct human ancestor	May be an early form of *H. habilis*; if a distinct species, it's the earliest known member of our genus	Unearthed by the Leakeys in the early 1960s, "Handy Man" was once thought to be the earliest tool user	May be an early form of *H. erectus* found only in Africa; its designation as a separate species is debated

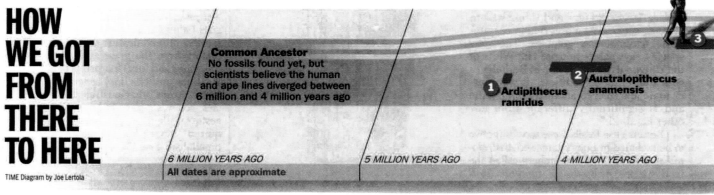

HOW WE GOT FROM THERE TO HERE

TIME Diagram by Joe Lertola

Common Ancestor
No fossils found yet, but scientists believe the human and ape lines diverged between 6 million and 4 million years ago

1 **Ardipithecus ramidus**

2 **Australopithecus anamensis**

6 MILLION YEARS AGO
All dates are approximate

5 MILLION YEARS AGO

4 MILLION YEARS AGO

Figure 2: *All in the Family* (© Time, Inc., 8/23/'99, reprinted by permission) – captions & footnote (*) added.

HOMINOIDS, HOMINIDS, & HUMANS

A. africanus

TRANSVAAL MUSEUM, PRETORIA — DAVID L. BRILL

3 million to 2.3 million years
Taung, South Africa
First ancient human ancestor discovered in Africa, it was once thought to be *the* missing link between apes and humans

A. aethiopicus

NATIONAL MUSEUMS OF KENYA — DAVID L. BRILL

2.8 million to 2.3 million years
Omo Basin, Ethiopia
May be an ancestor of *A. boisei* and *A. robustus*. The fossil above, found by Richard Leakey's team, is called the **Black Skull**

A. garhi

NATIONAL MUSEUM OF ETHIOPIA — DAVID L. BRILL

2.5 million years
Bouri, Ethiopia
The newest hominid species to be identified, it may have been the first to use stone tools and eat meat

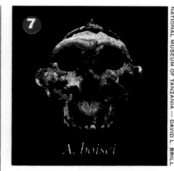

A. boisei

NATIONAL MUSEUM OF TANZANIA — DAVID L. BRILL

2.3 million to 1.4 million years
Olduvai Gorge, Tanzania
First ancient hominid found by the Leakeys. This skull's huge molars earned it the nickname "Nutcracker Man"

H. erectus

AMNH — DAVID L. BRILL

1.7 million to 250,000 years
Trinil, Indonesia
Discovered in 1891, it may have been the first hominid to use fire and the first to migrate out of Africa

H. antecessor

JAVIER TRUEBA — CONTACT PRESS IMAGES

800,000 years
Gran Dolina, Spain
May be the last common ancestor of both Neanderthals and modern humans; species designation debated

H. neanderthalensis

MUSÉE DE L'HOMME, PARIS — DAVID L. BRILL

200,000 to <30,000 years
Neander Valley, Germany
Overlapped with *H. sapiens.* Earlier forms extending back to 600,000 years are sometimes called *H. heidelbergensis*

Homo sapiens

ISRAEL ANTIQUITIES AUTHORITY — DAVID L. BRILL

Earliest known fossils date to about 100,000 years ago. Other fossils from Africa that are between about 1 million and 100,000 years old probably include ancestors of modern humans

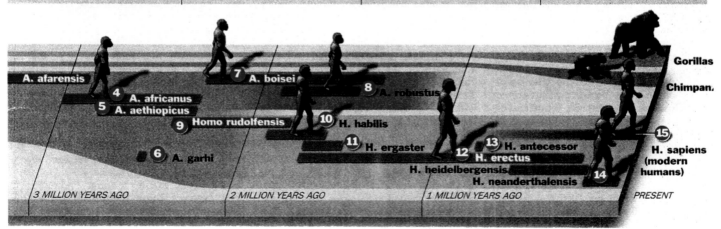

* Note carefully, the scraps of skull and globs of clay!

Voice of the Hominids

Some say all hominids could fit into a single coffin, but there are now thousands of such supposed hominid fossils. Complete skulls and skeletons are rare, however, consisting mostly of fragmentary remains.

Hominids were purportedly pre-human (leading to man), whereas hominoids include apes, humans, and hominids. *Homo* is generic for man, and *pongid* for apes (chimpanzees, orangutans, gorillas, siangs, and gibbons). Thinking about them, who could forget Peking man (an ape), Java man (a gibbon), Nebraska man (a pig's tooth), and Piltdown man (an outright fraud), all proposed as intermediates between apes and humans? Truth is, there are apes and there are men, but there have never been ape-men, though many have tried to reconstruct them from scraps of skull and globs of clay.

The ape-men of years ago have all but disappeared, but researchers are coming up with others. Paleontologists had postulated a single hominid line, starting with an upright-walking species, *Australopithecus afarensis*, famously represented by "Lucy" (a 40% complete skeleton of an extinct ape found in 1974, in Ethiopia). But that scenario is now being challenged by the famed Leakey family who claim to have found a long-lost cousin, *Kenyanthropus platyops* ("flat-faced man of Kenya"), dating back to between 3.5 and 3.2 million years ago. According to *Time Magazine* (April, 2001), "Old flat-face could displace *A. afarensis* as a link in the human lineage; or it may be part of a branch leading to *Homo rudolfensis*, a species with a strikingly similar face, having lived in East Africa between 2.4 and 1.8 million years ago." Says *Time*, wearily, "You find something beautiful and new, but the conclusion is you actually know less".

The proposed lineage of sub-humans is neither continuous nor uniform, but researchers are still clinging to it, maintaining a progression from *Ardipithecus ramidus* (4.4 million years ago) to *Homo erectus* (1.7 million to 250,000 years ago) based on increasing brain and body size, decreasing tooth size and skeletal robustness, increasing use of tools, etc. If we choose to believe this, hominids must have arisen from stooped primates, becoming erect on their own, but they would have been hopeless competitors in a struggle from which only *Homo sapiens* emerged triumphant.

According to evolutionists, it's a battle for survival involving false starts, failed experiments, bloodshed, and death. "Humans are no exception to this, no matter what we might like to think", said Ian Tattersal, anthropologist at the American Museum of Natural History.[9] The *Neanderthals*, vanishing 30,000 years ago, represented only a recent version of that contest. They were evidently an interesting but temporary side-branch to humans, incapable of artistic expression or abstract thought, having only short life-spans. But the *Neanderthals* of Skhul and Tabun (Mt. Carmel) are described by French paleontologist, John Piveteau, as "being torn from the same layer as *Homo sapiens*, suffering a veritable regression yet having the mark of human origin."[10] In other words, they were **human all along**, albeit diseased, deformed, and devolving from Adam.

Concerning skull size, anthropologists are wary of equating it with intellectual capability. Why? Because the cranial vault of an average American measures about 1,400 cubic centimeters vs. that of *Neanderthals* measuring 1,300 to 1,425 cubic centimeters, sometimes exceeding our own. Brain dimensions can tell us nothing about evolution, and other skeletal features tell us equally little, since even today we find prominent brows, slanted foreheads, stooped backs, large teeth, and strange looking extremities – whether because of degenerative changes or genetic drift – whether in Alaska, New Zealand, Rhodesia, the Congo, or in Mount Hermon.

Evolutionists say the relationship between *Homo sapiens* (100,000+ years ago) and the *Neanderthals* (200,000 to 30,000 years ago) is unclear, but *Homo erectus* descended (1.9 million to 1.6 million years ago) from *Homo habilis*, or from some fossil currently assigned to *habilis*. Thus, the journey of *Homo sapiens* wasn't a steady march from primitivism to perfection, but rather a turbulent tale of repeated failures and animalistic behavior leading to culturally complex, technologically savvy creatures like us.

According to *Time Magazine*, "While all the answers won't be in for some time, experts have identified several key transitions in our evolutionary chronicle. The first, which happened around the time we diverged from the apes between 6 million and 4 million years ago, was the development of bipedalism – two-legged walking rather than the kind of locomotion Tarzan learned from his adoptive ape family. The second, occurring 2.5 million years ago, was the invention of toolmaking – the purposeful crafting of stone implements rather than just picking up handy rocks – transitioning to meat eating. Then, somewhere between 2 million and 1 million years ago, came the dramatic growth of the brain and our ancestors' first emergence from Africa. Finally, a few hundred thousand years ago, our own species learned to use that powerful organ [the brain] for abstract thought, which quickly led to art, music, language, and all the other skills that have enthroned humans as the unchallenged rulers of their planet."[11]

How did *Time* come to its remarkable conclusions regarding *transitioning, meat eating, and enthronement*? From bits and pieces of age-old road-kill, labeling human remains, "sub-human"! Also, by relying on presumed mutational rates while ignoring the fact that mutations are harmful (not helpful)! Yet, despite these highly speculative methods, one is expected to accept the "findings" with a **straight face**!

The question is, did carnivores climb the evolutionary tree? Cannibals too? If so, did they transmit their brutishness to me? Could I be more brutish than you simply because of some ancestral fluke? Does that explain my nobility, or lack of it? The contrasting view is that Adam's habitat, nutrition, and genes were superior to ours, but these deteriorated drastically, producing wide-ranging morphologic decline in his descendants. Seeing humans in that context, we must forget about any evolutionary tracks!

The Bible tells us that Adam mirrored God perfectly and Eve came from his rib, countering a sub-human female's giving birth to "Baby Boy Adam". It tells us also that humans are image-bearers, though imperfectly so. In other words, there is a godly image in each of us, and if hominids can rob us of *that*, then the principle of Scripture's self-verification is forfeited.

From Genesis, we know that our first parents were rational, spiritual, and immortal – right from the outset. Knowing the basis for their nobility and needing to ask no questions about origins, they spoke intelligibly with God, thus negating any progression from proto-man to godly man. But where do the hominids fit in? Isaiah said the earth was "formed to be inhabited", not as a burial ground for hominids (Is. 45:18). So Paradise could not have come from the jungle! Nor did hominids predate Eden! Stooped clunkers could never even have imagined language, literature, art, and music. Nor could they have understood epistemology.

Cornelius Van Til said he knew what he knew by questioning those supposedly in the know. Said he:

> I see the strong men of biology searching diligently through hill and dale to prove that the creation doctrine is not true with respect to the human body, only to return and admit that the missing link is missing still. I see the strong men of psychology searching deep and far into the sub-conscience in order to prove that the creation and providence doctrines are not true with respect to the human soul, only to return and admit that the gulf between human and animal intelligence is as great as ever. I see the strong men of logic and scientific methodology search deep into the transcendental for a validity that will not be swept away by the ever-changing tide of the wholly new, only to return and say that they can find no bridge from logic to reality, or from reality to logic. And yet I find all these, though standing on their heads, reporting much that is true. I need only to turn their reports right side up, making God instead of man the center of it all, and I have a marvelous display of the facts as God has intended me to see them.[12]

Epistemology aside, how can one explain Adam to those refusing humans without hominids? Perhaps we should remind them that mitochondrial DNA (from mother to daughter) shows no human as coming from *other than* a human mother. With the exception of Adam and Eve, we all had mothers stamped *"Homo sapiens"*, not *"subhuman primate"*. Though not looking to the genome alone for all the answers (as if deifying science), it should come as no surprise that human DNA is connected with one person, and *she* of Adam's line. There is, after all, a final authority! But it isn't science.

Dawning of Humanity

Reading creation literally (excluding gaps) places the dawning of humanity at about six thousand years ago. Adam lived 130 years before his son, Seth, was born. When Seth had lived 105 years, he became the father of Enosh. Enosh lived 90 years until he became the father of Kenan. When Kenan had lived 70 years, he became the father of Mahalel. When Mahalel had lived 65 years, he became the father of Jared. When Jared had lived 162 years, he became the father of Enoch. When Enoch had lived 65 years, he became the father of Methuselah. When Methuselah had lived 187 years, he became the father of Lamech. When Lamech had lived 182 years, he had a son named Noah. When Noah was 500 years old, he became the father of Shem (Ge. 5:3-32).

Barring major gaps, Noah's Flood would have occurred 1656 years after the creation of Adam, or about 2400 years before Christ. Abram was born 292 years after the flood. Counting the years from Shem to Abram, as in Genesis 11, one arrives at a time-line of just under 2000 years for the pre-patriarchal lineage (from Adam to Abram), as confirmed in Luke 3 and 1 Chronicles 1). We are told also that "Noah was six hundred years old when the floodwaters came on the earth" (Ge. 7:6) and that "there were fourteen generations from Abraham to David, fourteen from David to the exile, and fourteen from the exile to Christ" (Mt. 1:17). Thus, the timeline from Adam to Christ may have been as brief as 4000 years plus a few generations.

With the exception of Cainan's unexplained placement between Arphaxad and Shelah, recorded in Luke 3, the genealogical records are remarkably complete, outlining a trail of specific personages at definite times for genuine redemptive history. Toying with the numbers solves nothing since unbelievers care so little about history. Moreover, their world of brutality was never the salubrious Garden where Adam lived for 930 years (Ge. 5:5). Though not knowing Adam's birthday, or Abram's, insertion of gaps will not result in a chronology significantly exceeding 10,000 years (15,000 at the most). Greater antiquity than that is from **working** the numbers, not **counting** them.

The numbers notwithstanding, where did Adam start out? Did he originate in Africa (as many think), or in the "Eden of the East", the world of the Patriarchs? If he did come "out of Africa", as the evolutionary books insist, where is the evidence? And shouldn't we question it, given the absence of trails and the paucity of tracks? Also, shouldn't anthropologists rethink cranial contours, postural variations, and other skeletal features since many of these are so easily attributable to human entropy?

Think again about hominids compared with Adam. *A. garhi* (2.5 million years ago) was supposedly a toolmaker, linking Lucy (3.6 to 2.9 million years ago) with the first humans. Among *garhi's* fossils were the bones of animals butchered with stone implements. The marks on an antelope's jawbone suggest that hominids used a sharp stone to remove its tongue. Nearby, another animal's tibia shows chop marks indicating that the bone was scraped free of meat and bashed open for its nutritious marrow. The question is, did sub-humans make these tools and engage in this behavior, allowing ape-men to shift to a fat-rich high energy diet?

Return with me to the Apostle who wrote, "Since by man came death" (1 Co. 15:21, KJV). Carnivorous behavior could never have been in God's original plan, for to accept that as normative is no longer accepting the Bible in faith. Unlike death's coming from hominids, God himself said, "To all the beasts of the earth and all the birds of the air and all the creatures that move on the ground, everything that has the breath of life in it, I give every green plant for food" (Ge. 1:30).

What caused carnivorous behavior then? The Curse and the Fall! These aren't real to secularists, however, so they fancy *Homo rudolfensis* living in filth and squalor 2.5 million years before *Homo sapiens* (whom they see arriving 100,000 years ago). Humans would then have lived for thousands of years alongside *Neanderthals*, perhaps interbreeding with them amidst all kinds of exploitation. The question then arises, was there a **real Adam** and did he live **100,000 years ago**? Or, did he appear **much more recently**, as recorded in the genealogies?

Suppose these generations were stretched to fit the evolutionary view. The gaps would add up to 100 millennia! Can you imagine any record (verbal or written) being transmitted accurately over the intervening, interspersed generations – especially with perishable materials, primitive storage, nomadic wanderings, marauding, and pillaging? God could have preserved these records regardless, but who would have thought it important to note a specific age for certain patriarchs, omitting whole generations between them? What sense would that make? Why would these genealogies have been recorded in the first place? And how could any such record relate to the Savior when whole generations were never included as in his lineage or of his Spirit?

Arguing for "ancient man", some have said that our calendar is not that of the ancients and that our reckoning was not theirs, either. But God said, "Let there be lights in the expanse of the sky […] and let them serve as signs to mark seasons and days and years" (Ge. 1:14). Weren't these the markers for the ancients as well? Why then wouldn't years be *years*? Why, for that matter, wouldn't generations be *generations* and fathers *fathers*? Aren't the scriptures plain enough?

As Morris wrote, "There seems to be no reasonable conclusion but that the compilers of these lists (under the guidance of the Holy Spirit) intended them to be understood as essentially complete records of the messianic line leading from Adam through Noah to Abraham, and finally to the founder of that nation through whom one day the promised 'seed of the woman' would appear. […] We conclude, therefore, that the biblical chronology must be taken at face value and that no comparison with the standard evolutionary chronology is possible at all, either for the earth as a whole or for man in particular."[13]

To think otherwise, re-classifying **history** as **prehistory**, is to expunge the historicity from Genesis, wrenching redemption from the record. As Norman DeJong said wisely, "Anyone who gets pushed off the proverbial fence and admits to being an evolutionist will refuse to accept the historicity of Genesis 1-11. Such rejection will come, not because of careful exegesis of the biblical text, but because that person has been culturally conditioned to reject the clear teaching of Scripture. He has been taught by parents, by historians, by biologists, by anthropologists, by geologists, and even by theologians to question the veracity of Genesis 1-11. With that kind of conditioning, the reaction is predictable: those prehistoric myths may be interesting, but they certainly are not true."[14]

Garden of Eden

***The Lord God took the man and put him in the Garden of Eden
to work it and take care of it (Ge. 2:15).***

Granting naturalism, one could hardly stop at human evolution, raising issues for the entire creation account. Those refusing Adam and Eve as real people see them as arriving from evolutionary processes, but injecting such a view into Genesis (detaching humans from redemptive history) just doesn't work. Once we accept that method, epistemology suffers, as does ontology and teleology. It is then only a matter of time before logical consistency erodes the remainder of the Bible.

Evolutionary man differs vastly from the cultured couple in Paradise. In Eden they were given tasks including agriculture, animal husbandry, horticulture, oceanography, metallurgy, language, art, feeding, caring, and nurturing. Had God not equipped them for these duties, they would have failed miserably. However, as *The Westminster Confession* (Ch. 4) asserts, "He created them, male and female, with reasonable and immortal souls […] having the law of God written in their hearts and the power to fulfill it."

That would be a foreign concept to those claiming "Mother Nature" as their creator (enabling to all her evolving creatures). This might be a homey perspective to some, but it is no more hopeful than naturalism itself.

As for the cavemen, they were descendants of Adam, though not as vigorous as he. Having only rudimentary skills and no moral insight, they lived in harsh surroundings, suffering from many deficiencies. What crops they planted were threatened by pillaging, pests, and ineptitude. Encumbered by danger, disease, and death, they were trapped in their surroundings: cold, dark, damp, and encircled by savages. A pathetic environment, indeed, with its heathen practices and smelly corpses! No wonder they resorted to cannibalism, having wandered so far from the blessings of God.

How unlike the Eden of Adam where a comely river branched into four, overflowing with beauty and bounty. Here God ordained marriage and the family for companionship, affection, commitment, and procreation. Here Adam and Eve walked blamelessly with their God, enjoying his favor. Here they rested in the shelter of the Almighty, praising him daily. Worshiping him in the splendor of his holiness, they were strengthened by his presence. This was the place for poetry, praise, and promise, pleasurable to Adam's senses and in tune with the Maestro!

On a tragic note, we are now aliens and strangers in the world, "for all have sinned and fallen short of the glory of God" (Ro. 3:23). What nobility we still have is from him who is willing to share with us his person, his presence, and his promises, "for his anger lasts only a moment, but his favor lasts a lifetime" (Ps. 30:5). Even the patriarchs, the progenitors of Christ, had a gradual shortening of their life-spans related to the Fall, the Flood, and genetic failure. However, the antediluvians (living before the Flood) had an advantage; they lived longer than we, perhaps due to the earth's protective envelope.

God had the right to destroy what he had made, since our first parents had forsaken him. And the Curse impacted everything! All creation was blunted, including man and his dominion. But still there is **hope!** We can be ransomed and healed, and we can still exercise a degree of dominion, though our neglect is evident wherever we look.

In this weird, complex, and fragmented world, we have a wonderfully redemptive God. He is the God of the Garden, and of the mountains. Satan lurks in the valleys (the Valley of Desolation, the Valley of Despond, and the Valley of Death), but Christ was identified with the mountains: the Mount of the Beatitudes, the Mount of the Transfiguration, the Mount of Olives, Mount Calvary, and Mount Zion (the "City of God"). Christ is also the Lily of the Valley, and one day "every valley shall be raised up, every mountain and hill made low; the rough ground shall become level, the rugged places plain" (Isa. 40:4).

As a father has compassion on his children,
so the Lord has compassion on those who fear him;
for he knows how we are formed,
he remembers that we are dust.

(Ps. 103:13)

[1] R.C. Sproul, *The Holiness of God,* Tyndale House Publishers, Inc., Wheaton, Ill., 1998, pp. 8-10

[2] Ibid, p. 10.

[3] J.C. Whitcomb, *The Early Earth,* Baker Book House, Grand Rapids, MI, 1990, p. 120

[4] John Murray, *Lecture Notes, Systematic Theology,* Westminster Theological Seminary, 1962

[5] Francis Schaeffer, *Genesis, in Space and Time,* InterVarsity Press, Downers Grove, IL., 1972, p. 48-53

[6] National Geographic, *Secrets of the Gene, Vol. 196, No. 4,* October, 1999, p. 75

[7] Siegfried Scherer, *Mere Creation, Basic Types of Life, Evidence for Design from Taxonomy?,* InterVarsity Press, Downers Grove, IL, 1998, pp. 195-211.

[8] Margaret Helder, *Pushing the Envelope of Creation-Based Biology, Christian Renewal,* September 6, 1999, pp 14,15

[9] Michael Lemonick & Andrea Dorfman, *Time Magazine, How Man Evolved,* Aug. 23, 1999, p. 51

[10] Walter Lammerts, *Why Not Creation?,* Baker Book House, Grand Rapids, MI, 1970, p. 350

[11] Ibid, pp. 52-53

[12] Cornelius Van Til, *Why I Believe in God,* published as a pamphlet for the Committee on Christian Education, Orthodox Presbyterian Church – summarized electronically by Jonathan Barlow, 1996.

[13] Henry Morris, *The Biblical Basis for Modern Science,* Baker Book House, 1984, pp. 124-125

[14] Norman DeJong, *God's Wedding Band,* Redeemer Books, Winamac, IN, 1990, p. 47

PARADISE FRUSTRATED
(Chapter 10)

Adam's Dig

Suppose Adam had in Paradise a modern-day back-hoe. Digging with it in the Garden one day, he discovered a skeleton – not just any skeleton but one seemingly human with a modest cranium, a hunched back, and over-sized brows. This would startle any building contractor, but imagine Adam's horror as he clawed through mounds of dirt, finding petrified thistles, calcified serpents, dinosaur eggs, fossils with ingested animal parts; even burnt bones, rudimentary tools, and battered skulls! What might he have said during the cool of *that* day? "All these dead and dying things? Hosts of extinct species? Father, did your 'very good' include all *this*?"

Now picture another scene: Adam, expelled from Paradise, questioning, "Father, you rebuked the serpent, saying, 'you will crawl on your belly'. You said to me, 'I give to you and all creatures every seed-bearing plant to eat'. You punished sin with the curse of death, but what we see doesn't fit your words! Who caused this, *we or you*? And *why*?" A pastor has written:

> Few of us look at death as a friend. It's a by-product of the Fall, and something we could do without. [...] But life on this earth without at least *some* things dying with frequency would, it seems, be impossible. [...] What would happen, for instance, to a forest's ecosystem if the deciduous trees didn't give up the ghost annually? [...] Doesn't it seem appropriate that the millions of tiny animals in plankton get filtered through the whale's baleen and lose their lives to support the whale's mass? If we look only at these kinds of deaths and many similar deaths, death doesn't seem so objectionable. It apparently is necessary for other things to live.
>
> As Christians, most of us have rather naïvely believed that death came into the world at the Fall. [...] Where can inquiring minds turn to find out if death existed before the Fall? Our primary source for this inquiry is not the Bible but Creation itself. Not everything God wants us to know is revealed in his Word; much is also revealed in God's world, which is "before our eyes like a beautiful book". [...] This beautiful book shows abundant evidence that creatures were dying for a long time before people were even created, let alone before they fell from grace.
>
> When paleontologists bring the fossil record before us, we see that life is indeed very, very old and that many things died before creation and the fall of humankind. [...] Anyone who's been to a museum and has seen the skeletons of predatory dinosaurs knows that these galloping gourmets carried their cutlery in massive sets of jaws. They were predators – they fed on other animals. They first entered the fossil record around 245 million years ago but had all died out by 60 million years ago. That means that a massive amount of carnage – death – occurred before the fall. [...] We must remember that the Bible writers, though fully inspired by the Spirit as they wrote, knew little or nothing of the creatures from the eons before them.[1]

These are not harmless statements. They claim that: 1) "our primary source for this inquiry is not the Bible but creation itself", as perceived by paleontologists in the fossil record, 2) Bible writers "knew little or nothing about creatures of the past", 3) creation occurred over "eons" of time, and 4) "a massive amount of carnage occurred before the Fall". Note also the lack of differentiation between vegetative death, which God allowed, and fleshly death, which he abhorred.

May we trivialize death in this way? Can we really say that pre-Adamic death squares with Scripture because death is required in our own ecosystem? Not at all! In the Book of Romans we read, "For the creation was subjected to frustration, not by its own choice, but by the will of the one who subjected it, in hope that the creation itself will be liberated from its bondage to decay." We read also that "the *whole creation* has been groaning as in the pains of childbirth right up to the present time", not because death is natural but because nature was *frustrated* (Ro. 8:20-22). Thus, we must reject the notion that millions of animals died and countless species became extinct before Adam's arrival, a view conflicting with his naming "all the animals" and his having dominion over "every living thing".

Consider also the fact that Adam lived in a world of exclusively herbivorous animals, no matter how carnivorous they are today. The greater concern, however, is that pre-Adamic death is the antithesis of him in whom is *life* (Jn. 1:4). As we read in Acts 3:15, John 8:44, and Hebrews 2:14, the "Author of Life" is not like Satan, "the murderer from the beginning," the "devil holding the power of *death*". Christ wanted nothing to do with Satan's biosphere of death! In fact, he died to destroy it!

"If man emerged by way of animals, finding death awaiting him when he appeared on the stage of history, then man does not *bring* death – he *inherits* it!" So said Dr. L. DeKoster. "Can the Jesus of Christianity, who assumed man's flesh to die for man's sin, be the 'Jesus' of any evolutionary cult which breaks the causal connection between sin and death? Nothing is more at odds with Christianity and the Bible! Christianity says (by way of St. Paul's inspired Word): 'As sin came into the world by one man, and death through sin' (Ro. 5:12). Note well: '*and* death', not by inheritance from the animal, but '*through sin*'. For Christianity, death is unnatural – 'the *wages* of sin' (Ro. 6:23). For 'theistic evolution', death is quite natural; the wage of an animal ancestry. The distinction is clear: death as understood in Christianity vs. death as misunderstood in evolutionary theory. For Christianity, sin leads to death. Death is the penalty which God pronounced upon sin. But to hear that, you have to take Genesis as *real history*."[2]

When Calvary is cut loose from the Fall, the result is a ready acceptance of death. The fact is, what *once was* became *de-created*, and it deteriorated from there. As Calvin said, "Many things now seen in the world are rather corruptions of creation than any part of its proper furniture. Ever since man declined from his high original, it became necessary that the world should gradually degenerate from its nature. [...] At the present time, when we look upon the world corrupted, as if degenerated from its original creation, let that expression of Paul recur to our mind, that the creature is liable to vanity, not willingly, but through our fault – and thus let us mourn, being admonished of our just condemnation (Ro. 8:20)."[3]

We see then that the noxious things of this world (e.g. bacteria and viruses making us sick) were created by God, but by him as an avenger. Were this an evolutionary world, these are what Adam would have found in Eden, but the Bible tells us otherwise: that what we see now is only what is *left*, and it's all *our* fault!

Web of Life

Think of a rabbit in the jaws of a coyote. A brutal world indeed! Yet the "web of life" seems to require that certain creatures serve themselves up for the good of others. Why? Because there is an intricate web in which energy is exchanged between those that eat and those that are eaten. This chain begins with the sun's energy, captured by photosynthetic plants called *producers*. Energy then passes to *consumers*, organisms relying on other organisms for their sustenance. Certain consumers eat producers; others eat other consumers; still others eat both. One could also say that there are primary consumers (herbivores) and secondary consumers (carnivores).

Even dead things pass their energy to the living, as when scavengers (*decomposers*) break down organic remains. In his textbook, *Biology, The World of Life,* Wallace describes these wretched end-processes. "Decomposers [primarily fungi and bacteria] generally feed by secreting digestive enzymes into their food and absorbing the breakdown products. They are somewhat unusual: unlike animals, they readily digest the cellulose-laden corpses of plants and the nitrogenous wastes of animals. In so doing, they produce carbon dioxide and water, as do consumers, but in addition they release sulfates, nitrites, nitrates, and other mineral ions. Without decomposers, our world would be a far different place, a corpse-strewn, mineral-deficient wasteland."[4]

Today's web, with its cyclical death and decay, is as indispensable as energy itself, though it seems chillingly cruel with its bloody encounters and repulsive interactions. Louis Pasteur studied these processes, working with beef broth, maggots, and putrefaction. Eventually, he demonstrated the bacterial cause of anthrax, a scourge ravaging both cattle and people. This led to an explosion of knowledge in bacteriology, mycology, virology, etc. We now know that within hours of an animal's demise there will be dramatic changes. Decomposers (normally checked by bodily defenses) will attack the corpse and obliterate it. Although we don't know exactly how the Law of

Entropy worked initially, these processes involving spoliation and putrefaction (though required today) would have been out of place in Paradise.

In our own bodies, intestinal bacteria synthesize vitamin K, an essential factor in blood clotting. They live, multiply, serve their purpose, and die, but would they have died in a pristine world? The answer is, "death came from *sin*", not by "*design*". Besides, creation was a completed process, and things worked differently in the beginning. Organisms harmful now might have been helpful then, though we cannot say with certainty that some of them even existed. As for teeth and claws, one way of looking at them is that they were ideal for ripping vegetation, therefore not in themselves indicators of carnivorous behavior. Plants, too, might have been altered by sin, though they were eaten before the Fall (presumably dying in the process). But plants were never given the "breath of life" as animals were, and that is the critical distinction.

For teasers, would elephants have crushed ants in Paradise? Would Adam have ruptured his spleen when falling from a tree? Could Eve have fractured her ankle? Would there have been pain and suffering in this idyllic setting? We know that pain is useful, like any of our five senses. We know also that God said to Eve, "I will greatly increase your pains in childbearing" (Ge. 3:16). By implication, then, there might have been some discomfort even in a perfect world. Eve must have had healing capabilities too. But what about Adam's bleeding?

Honesty confesses ignorance. Reaching too far into a bygone world, we have only conundrums for which there are few answers. But why should we need them when the essence of faith is Christ, not nature? Couldn't the Almighty have reshaped ants, ankles, and spleens as quickly as a rubber ball resumes its shape when crushed?

Admittedly, it takes a leap to believe in Paradise, but it need not be blind. Though lacking certain particulars, we know that the universe is groaning in the wake of sin. That, not the web of life, is the cause of our woes, and it is a cycle of despair – beginning with sin and ending with death. Christ, however, gives us hope! Imagine Lazarus' corpse showing no putrefaction after three days!

Entrance of Entropy

Eden's processes involved cohesion, integration, and vitality, unlike today's disorderliness, dissolution, and death. The systems of this world are sad and lonely results of a universal cause. Entropy is everywhere, having entered "through a man" (1 Co. 15:21). From the time of Adam, it affected both humans and animals (Ro. 5:14). Says Morris, "There has been a drastic amendment to the second law! No death of sentient life, either animal or human, was intended in God's original creation. [...] But now everything is proceeding back again to the dust, according to the second law of thermodynamics."[5]

The **de-creation principle** is broad indeed, "involving the loss of useful energy, the loss of order, and the loss of information."[6] It applies to all processes (inorganic and organic), which is why the Bible points to entropy as universal, producing physical, biological, and sociological deterioration. "This corresponds with the loss of order which we detect through the physical sciences (physics, chemistry, geology, engineering, astronomy, etc.), life sciences (zoology, physiology, medicine, etc.), and the behavioral sciences (psychology, sociology, anthropology, economics, etc.)." As far as we ourselves are concerned, "entropy impinges most directly and painfully in the phenomena of aging and death", phenomena which are the sad destiny of all.[7] Overwhelmed by these awful processes, Adam became lower than dust, having become rebellious dust. "Many died by the trespass of that one man" (Ro. 5:15), as did trillions of creatures since then.

Regarding the devolution of biological organisms, we read:
- As for man, his days are like grass, he flourishes like a flower of the field; the wind blows over it and it is gone, and its place remembers it no more (Ps. 103: 15-16).
- Man's fate is like that of the animals; the same fate awaits them both: as one dies, so dies the other. All have the same breath [...] all come from dust, and to dust all return (Ecc. 3:19-20).

Regarding the devolution of the cosmos, we read:

- In the beginning, you laid the foundations of the earth, and the heavens. […] They will perish […] they will all wear out like a garment (Ps. 102:25-26).
- Lift up your eyes to the heavens, look at the earth beneath it; the heavens will vanish like smoke, the earth will wear out like a garment, and its inhabitants will die like flies (Is. 51:6).

When sin entered, the changes in the world were profound. The Bible tells us, "The whole world is under the control of the evil one" (1 Jn. 5:19). Death affected all creatures down to the cellular level. What had been an ecology of life became an ecology of death, and **all nature** was changed. The rocks were affected too, so the **whole creation** is now groaning in its bondage to decay (Ro. 8:21,22). Given such slippage, today's chronometers may no longer reflect true history.

Taking of Life

Once, casualties were everywhere! "Everything that moved on the earth perished: birds, livestock, wild animals, all the creatures that swarm over the earth, and all mankind – everything on dry land having the breath of life in its nostrils" (Ge. 7:21-22). Why not fish, too? Because God's curse was not like ours. His judgment involves the value he places on life, as expressed in two words: **breath** and **blood**. Interestingly, animals and people share the same air and hemoglobin – and the same fate. Incidentally, when treating trauma victims, the two immediate requirements are oxygen and blood. Is it any wonder then that God sees life as hinging on these same two requirements?

In the Pentateuch, blood is associated with atonement. The Levitical laws were instituted because God hates defiled things, not to mention dead and dying things. These were kept outside Israel's camp since God's purity demanded it. In the same way, had there been anything repulsive in the original Creation, God could not have declared it "good". Nor would he have created a repugnant world to begin with, since he is the antithesis of defilement. Knowing this, it makes no sense to view pre-Adamic death as coming from God's holy and loving hand. Also, the hundreds of millions of organisms that surrendered their blood and breath could never have been our ancestors, for God destroyed them in **anger**, not in **love**.

But that isn't the end of the story! Death was defeated by him who gave his blood and breath for that which was lost. So much did he despise death that he swallowed it up forever (Is. 25:8). And he who holds "the keys of death and Hades" (Rev. 1:18) is coming again as the "destroyer of death", bringing "life and immortality" to believers (2 Ti. 1:10). Death is, after all, the **last** enemy, not the **first**, and Christ came to earth to "put it under his feet" (1 Co. 15:26), not under Adam's.

Accordingly, when we see our planet in the throes of death, we can be certain that Adam would have encountered none of it except that of plants. The reality is, creatures in Eden lived in total harmony, for God could not have allowed them to consume each other without repudiating his character. Nor would his curse have had any meaning had Adam not sullied something pure. Had it been otherwise, God would have relinquished himself and the Cross would have been in vain.

Broken Things can be Restored

Reading the Bible carefully, it says all things have been committed to Christ, "through whom all things were made and without whom nothing was made" (Jn. 1:3). These are parallel and repetitive statements. When we find such phraseology, it is usually for a reason such as 1) stating the subject as truth, 2) emphasizing the relatedness of all aspects of it, and 3) imprinting it on our hearts and minds. Having said that, read these verses thoughtfully, focusing on the words, "things", "all things", "created things", "these things", "the former things", and "everything":

Ge. 1:31: God saw all that he had made and it was "very good".

Ge. 7:21: Every living thing that moved on the earth perished.

Isa. 65:17: Behold, I will create new heavens and a new earth. The former things will not be remembered, nor will they come to mind.

Mt. 11:27: All things have been committed to me by the Father.

Ac. 3:20-21: Jesus Christ must remain in heaven until the time comes for God to restore everything, as he promised long ago through his holy prophets.

Ro. 1:25: They exchanged the truth of God for a lie, and worshiped and served created things rather than the Creator.

1 Co. 15:26-27: The last enemy to be destroyed is death. For he has put everything under his feet.

Col. 1:15-16: By him all things were created; things in heaven and on earth, visible and invisible. [...] All things were created by him and for him.

Heb. 1:1-4: In these last days he has spoken to us by his Son, whom he appointed heir of all things [...] sustaining all things by his powerful Word.

Rev. 21:4: He will wipe every tear from their eyes. There will be no death or mourning or crying, for the old order of things has passed away.

Rev. 21:5: He who was seated on the throne said, "I am making all things new!"

The language in these texts is sequential, repetitious, and interrelated, describing a cosmos ***created, de-created, and re-created***. Note how carefully the authors crafted their words:

- The term "all things" is synonymous with "created things", "everything", and "these things". It can refer to things in heaven and things on earth: inanimate things, animate things, and heavenly things – things existing from early on as well as into eternity.
- All things were originally "very good" because they were created by God, for him, and through him. Once created, God upheld them by his ordinary providence.
- Throughout history, people have worshiped created things rather than the Creator. Therefore, everything that moved on the earth perished (both animals and humans), except for those in the Ark.
- The Bible mentions two categories of things: 1) the "old order", called "the former things", and 2) "reconciled" or "restored" things, also called "new things".
- Christ died to renew everything, but unregenerate people and angels will not participate in this renewal.
- ***Only the old order – fallen things – can be restored***. The world of entropy as we know it.

Had the world remained perfect following the Fall, it could not have been (technically) restored. Nor would it have needed to be. Conversely, if the old order was operative in Paradise, why would it need to be "liberated from its bondage to decay and brought into glorious freedom" (Ro. 8:21)? Were God to restore such a broken world to its original, he would be bringing it right back to that old realm of corruption, making no sense at all. Hence, it is the post-Adamic world of confusion, not the pre-Adamic world of coherence, that needs to be restored.

Christ came not only to destroy Satan's work, but to restore his own (1 Jn. 3:8). The King James insists, "The creation *itself also* will be delivered from the bondage to corruption", implying that nature's fall was *additive to* human corruption (Ro. 8:21). Regarding that, Hoeksema wrote, "The former things shall have passed away (being those of the present economy). These things shall pass away forevermore. They can never enter into the new creation to spoil and mar its bliss, and there shall be no fear of them ever entering again."[8] They are passed away because death has been judged and that aspect of God's program, which was of Satan, is *finished*. Since our world has no element of perfection left in it, the former things must *disappear*.

The fact is, "the Son of Man came to save what was *lost*", so redemption is cheapened by those who naturalize death (Lk. 19:10). As Ham and Taylor put it, "If animals died before Adam, the foundation of the gospel is cut at its roots. [...] If everything is evolving upward, and thus getting better and better, what was God's curse all about? [...] And why doesn't the Bible clearly reveal the true source?" After all, Christ's sacrifice is driven by a perfect Paradise, a real couple, forbidden fruit, and original sin. "Without that original sin and those literal circumstances, who (or what) would need to be redeemed?"[9]

Ask yourself a simple question. "Would anyone restore a *new* car?" The answer is obvious, isn't it? We don't restore new things. We restore old, broken things – but things with potential. God, however, sees no potential in the old order (myself included) because it insults his character. Yet, thanks to his mercy, he is willing to restore them, and me!

God's restoration, however, is not like bringing an old Chrysler back to life. In God's perfect plan, the Chrysler *disappears*, never again matching the original. The new creation will be what "no eye has seen" (1 Co. 2:9), nor has it entered into our imagination. God is going to restore everything as he promised long ago by the holy prophets (Acts 3:21), and he will wipe away every tear (Rev. 21:4). Happily, there will be no more suffering, no more pain, and no more death!

God couldn't begin this project, however, until he had sacrificed his Son. Imagine that! Were I to restore an old Chrysler, I could start now, providing I had the resources, but God's restoration can begin only after the curse is lifted. Why? Because the old order violates his nature! He couldn't touch it, so to speak, without Calvary! Once we understand this, we find the Bible dashing all arguments favoring pre-Adamic death, and in a remarkably convincing way.

The Wolf and the Lamb

Christians can look forward to an amazing future, for sin shall be no more in the new heaven and earth (Isa. 66:22). The language describing this is often symbolic and spiritual, but the word pictures do come through as verbal whisperings of a real and glorious future, based on a real and glorious past. Think about that as you picture this:

- The wolf and the lamb will feed together, and the lion will eat straw like the ox. […] They will neither harm nor destroy on all my holy mountain (Isa. 65:25).
- In that day I will make a covenant for them with the beasts of the field and the birds of the air and the creatures that move along the ground. Bow and sword and battle I will abolish from the land, so that all may lie down in safety (Hos. 2:18).
- I will make a covenant of peace with them and rid the land of wild beasts so that they may live in the desert and sleep in the forests in safety (Eze. 34:25).
- The wolf will live with the lamb, the leopard will lie down with the goat, the calf and the lion and the yearling together; and a little child will lead them. The cow will feed with the bear, their young will lie down together, and the lion will eat straw like the ox. The infant will play near the hole of the cobra, and the young child will put his hand into the viper's nest. They will neither harm nor destroy in all my holy mountain, for the earth will be full of the knowledge of the Lord as the waters cover the sea (Isa. 11: 6-9).

These are apocalyptic visions pointing to end-times. As Kuyper wrote in his *Calvinism and Science*, "The Apocalypse returns to the starting-point: 'In the beginning, God created the heavens and the earth.' Creation is his wonderful handiwork and, though marred by sin, it opened the way for a still more glorious revelation in its restoration". Christ's restoration, says Kuyper, "is and ever will be the salvation of that which was first created, by virtue of its capacity as God's handiwork and as a revelation of God's attributes."[10] The key is that *the original perfection was lost*, only to be *restored*.

Comparing the last three chapters of Revelation with the first three of Genesis, there is a reversal of the Curse. Sin is atoned, death is assuaged, and heaven is gained. Once death and Hades are thrown into the lake of fire, perfection and dignity are restored, and creation regains its original worth (Rev. 20:14). The outcome is twofold: Sinners are reclaimed and all things are renewed. When our corruptible souls become incorruptible, then *all* of Paradise will be restored.

Abraham Kuyper, a gifted theologian and statesman, saw this with unusual clarity. In his book, *The Revelation of St. John*, he said Christ's restoration involves a backward look at our *origin in perfection*. Though history became tainted, it will have a perfect ending, a *terminus in perfection*. Between these two poles, everything operates within the realities of today. There is, however, a commonality at both poles, a "connection of perfection", for though Paradise was lost it will surely be regained.

Said Kuyper, "What is told of the future of this earth and of this solar system is all-embracing and affords no room in God's holy doing for a consummation alongside of and entirely apart from our world. It is, and always shall be, the world God Almighty has created, which he (in spite of all the sins of angels and men) has in its broad dimensions upheld and maintained, and which at the time of the end he will so bring out to a perfect form that it will correspond to his purpose of creation – *his original plan* – now no more susceptible of corruption."[11]

Knowing this, why do people struggle with the future? Because their view of the *end* is tied to their view of the *beginning*, lacking perfection at either pole. Christians have a better answer, recalling that the wolf and the lamb will come together. That would be a bloody encounter today, but the prophets knew it wouldn't be so in the future – contingent on the most bloodstained thread in history, "the blood of the covenant."

Covenantal Relationships[12]

There is a redemptive aspect to history, beginning with **creation/perfection**. Adam was in a perfect environment where there was no death. It was from perfection that he started out, imperfection being abnormal. Rightly related to his Creator and perfectly equipped as vice-regent, he carried out his Father's will over the created order. Following the **Fall and judgment**, however, all revelation became redemptive in character and focus. When **redemption/grace** entered the scene, it was centered in the sacrifices of the temple and the blood of the Cross. History itself is moving toward **consummation/restoration**, when everything will revert to **creation/perfection**. This is the four-fold doctrine of redemption, based on the completed work of Christ.

Though Adam was perfect, he could never have figured out God's will on his own. While in the Garden, God revealed it to him so that Adam and Eve could maintain their righteousness by obeying certain commands, the "*creation ordinances*". Directed to Adam, he was to obey them joyfully as a responsible steward over the domain God had given him.

The Ten Commandments are built on these ordinances, and there is a relationship underlying them involving 1) God's moral will at creation, 2) God's moral will when he redeemed Israel out of Egypt, 3) God's moral will as he brought it into the Life of Israel in Canaan, and 4) God's moral will as delivered in Christ's Sermon on the Mount (built upon by the Apostles in the Epistles). God's will has never changed, although it has been amplified. It will be the standard for our judgment, met through the blood of Christ.

In the Creation Ordinances there are several binding pronouncements, as follows:
- Procreation: be fruitful and multiply
- Geographic Distribution: fill the earth
- Dominion/labor: Adam was given tasks
- Marriage: "For this cause shall a man leave his father and mother."
- Tree of Knowledge of Good and Evil: "Do not eat of the tree."
- Sabbath: six days of work; one of rest

Following the Flood, God's moral revelation had an incremental expansion when he said, "If man sheds man's blood, by man shall his blood be shed" (Ge. 9:6), at which time capital punishment was established. God also permitted humans to use animal flesh to expand their food supply.

Generations later, God broke into the life of an idolater who lived in Mesopotamia – worshiping the gods of that place. The Lord entered his life graciously and Abram responded to the call to leave Ur of the Chaldeans, though he didn't know where he would be going. So total was Abram's surrender that his faith was "counted unto him as righteousness" (Heb. 11). Here was a man through whom the covenantal promises would come, since God had said to the Serpent, "He [Christ] will crush your head, and you will strike his heel."

Abram responded to God's call, and he was blessed. He knew that salvation would come through him to every nation of the world (Gal. 3). But he was childless! So he and his wife devised a scheme involving Hagar, and Ishmael was born. For us to understand that God's covenant was fulfilled by divine initiative, not human scheming, Sarah gave birth to a son whose name means "disbelief". It was in Isaac ("Laughter") that the covenant would be fulfilled, through Jacob, by deception. This involved divine initiative, so election stands because of inheritance, not human accomplishment.

Jacob had twelve sons who ended up in Egypt. There God broke into the life of Israel, removing them from Pharaoh's domination. Addressing them later at Mt. Sinai, God gave them the Ten Commandments. These were given upon self-identification by him who offered his undeserved grace, releasing Israel from bondage. God redeemed Israel saying, "I am the Lord your God, who brought you out of Egypt, out of the land of slavery" (Ex. 20:2). But here is an important point. Never once did God say, "keep these commands and I will redeem you". Rather, his commandments were given to an **already redeemed people** in the form of a "Suzerain/vassal Covenant", coming from the King of Kings to the children of Israel.

Like all contracts, the Law of God had provisions and requirements.:
*   It began with self-identity: "I am the Lord, your God, who brought you out of Egypt" (Ex. 20:2).
*   It indicated favor to Israel: redemptive grace, bestowed by the Suzerain (King).
*   It promised blessings if the people would honor their Great King: i.e., if they would obey joyfully, they would have a life of "beatitude", or bliss.
*   It declared consequences and curses for violations of the covenant (a feature of many secular covenants as well).

In these covenants there is a connection between "no other gods" and "no images". It comes down to a few simple questions: Who wrote the commandments; how did he write them; and did any other part of God's Word come to humanity in this way, **written in stone by the finger of God**? Isn't the very way these commands were produced and spoken so unique that it should signify for everyone and for all time that these were not merely the words of Moses, but of God? Israel knew this! God had demanded that they purify themselves for days before standing at the foot of Sinai. Whenever God spoke the mountain trembled in smoke, and the Israelites were so terrified that they begged Moses (alone) to deal henceforth with this awe-inspiring Deity.

After providing the Law, God demanded strict allegiance to it, an allegiance still required of us today. Among its demands were two positive commands: 1) keep the Sabbath – "remember to keep it holy", and 2) honor the home – "your father and your mother." God also announced two negatives applying to humanity: 1) no killing, and 2) no adultery. Additionally, there were three social obligations: 1) no stealing, 2) no false witness, and 3) no coveting. Underlying these commands was a strong affirmation of holiness based on the sanctity of God's name, his image, his day, parental relationships, sex, life, property, truth, and possessions.

For failing to keep the Law, God offered a remedy, his Covenant of Grace. To Calvinists, the Covenant of Grace and the Covenant of Redemption are nearly identical. The Covenant of Redemption is between the Father (representing the Trinity) and the Son (representing the elect). On the basis of that unique relationship, God established his Covenant of Grace, extending salvation to the elect through his **blood and Spirit**.

Covenantal theology involves a delicate tension between the faithfulness of God and the sinfulness of man. The first evidence of this is the "protevangel covenant", the maternal promise in Genesis 3:15. Then came the covenant with Adam, declaring Adam's dominion. The ensuing covenant with Noah involved all flesh, including nature and animals. Later came the Abrahamic Covenant, sealed with circumcision, followed by the Sinaitic Covenant, anticipating the New Covenant and providing a way for sinners to meet the demands of the Law. Rooted in grace

– not works – the New Covenant was superior to all earlier covenants. It could be received by faith, through baptism and communion, and bread and wine replaced the old sacraments.

Having received the Covenant of Grace, "all who rely on observing the Law are under a curse, for it is written, 'Cursed is everyone who does not continue to do everything written in the Book of the Law'." We see then that "no one is justified before God by the Law, because the righteous will live by faith" (Gal. 3:10-14). Yes, we must still honor the Law, but we can do so joyfully (out of gratitude), since Christ fulfilled its demands.

In none of these covenants did God enter into a casual relationship with humans. The Bible points consistently to a "bond" tying people to God, much as when couples seal their vows with tokens and pledges. In our kinship with our Savior there is a "bond-in-blood", a life and death attachment between God and humanity, a thread woven throughout Scripture. We see it in the sacrifice of animals, in the circumcision of Abraham's household, in the Passover lamb, in oblations at the Temple, and in the blood of the Cross. We remember it also in the wine of the New Covenant, and we shall see it more gloriously when we drink it anew in our Father's kingdom (Mt. 26:29).

Each of these covenants involves an agreement between God and his people. In each instance he spoke to humans about sin, its consequences, and its payment. This concentration on cause, effect, and remedy is so pervasive that we cannot escape the fact that God hates sin, death, and pollution. But "just as sin entered the world through one man, and death through sin", we can "receive God's abundant provision of grace, the gift of righteousness, through one man, Jesus Christ" (Ro. 5: 12-18). This is the "blood of the covenant which is poured out for many" (Mt. 26:28). A happy ending indeed for us Christians!

Knowing the remedy for corruption, we have something to shout about! Not only can *we* rejoice, but so can ***all Creation***. But one day God will display his power and glory even more amazingly than when he first made the universe! As Horton said fittingly, "Christ came not only to save sinners (1 Ti. 1:15); he came also to save the world" (Jn. 4: 42). We see then that "God is concerned about saving individuals, but he is concerned also about saving the world which he created."[13] This means that, while the Cross is central, we must be clear about its scope, for not only did Christ secure new creatures, he secured a new heaven and earth!

When we understand what the frustration of Paradise was about, we can better appreciate the God of Creation, the God of the Cross, and the God of history. Obeying him who towers over everything, we must exercise our mandate over Earth's air, water, land, and creatures, treating them all with respect. While not worshiping this planet or its inhabitants, we Christians should be the best of environmentalists. Alternatively, mistaken views of Creation translate into idolatry and/or failed stewardship – as when nature is worshiped (or disrespected), when creatures are exalted (or devalued), and when things are deified (or neglected).

As a final comment, Calvin wrote, "The proper study of man begins with the image of God." Therefore, in the community of the redeemed we value that image and protect human life. But when truth breaks, culture breaks! It breaks because people have little regard for either God or humans. This plays out in people's attitudes toward abortion, infanticide, euthanasia, cloning, frozen embryos, stem cell research, genetic manipulation, organ procurement, the disabled, end-of-life care, animal rights, and the arbitrary taking of human life by those holding others in contempt for whatever reason. So, remember this:

If we keep our voices silent, all creation will rise and shout!
If we keep our voices silent, then will the very rocks cry out!

(from Luke 19:40)

[1] Mark Tidd, *Did Death Happen Before the Fall?*, The Banner, Grand Rapids, MI, 6-3-'91, pp. 6-8

[2] Lester DeKoster, *Warning: Darwinese is Spoken Here*, Christian Renewal, Lewiston, NY, June 20, 1988

[3] John Calvin, *Commentaries on The Book of Genesis*, Baker Book House, Grand Rapids, MI, 1993, Vol. 1, pp. 104-105

[4] Robert A. Wallace, *Biology, The World of Life*, Scott, Foresman, & Co., London, England, 1990, pp. 600-603

[5] Henry M. Morris, *The Biblical Basis for Modern Science*, Baker Book House, Grand Rapids, MI, 1984, p. 196

[6] Ibid, pp. 199-200

[7] Ibid, pp. 201-202

[8] Herman Hoeksema, *Behold He Cometh*, Reformed Free Publishing Assoc., Grand Rapids, MI, 1969, p. 678

[9] Ken Ham and Paul Taylor, *The Genesis Solution*, Master Books, Santee, CA, 1988, pp. 65,66

[10] Abraham Kuyper, *Lectures on Calvinism*, Wm. Eerdmans Publishing Co., Grand Rapids, MI, k1953, pp. 118-120

[11] Abraham Kuyper, *The Revelation of St. John, (translated from the Dutch)*,Wm. Eerdmans Publishing Co., Grand Rapids, MI., 1963, pp. 337-345

[12] Material in this section is by permission of Dr. James Grier, *Lectures on the Ten Commandments; The Law in the Life of the Christian"*, Cornerstone University, Grand Rapids, MI., September, 1999.

[13] Michael Horton, *Putting Amazing Back into Grace*, Thomas Nelson Publishers, Nashville, TN, 1991, p. 86

FROM DESIGN TO THE DESIGNER
(Chapter 11)

Chemical Evolution to Pre-biotic Soup?

Then God said, "let the land produce vegetation: seed-bearing plants and trees" …
And there was evening, and there was morning – the third day (Ge. 1:11-14).

Did life evolve billions of years ago from simple chemicals, mindless matter, and purposeless processes? Evolutionists are so taken with this idea that they will violate their own rules to save it, but the Bible says nothing about evolution or random assembly. The truth is, living things were whole and functional from the beginning, and genuine science will never contradict this.

Keep in mind that creationists and evolutionists work with the same information. The universe is the same for both of them, but their perception of it differs, as does their interpretation. J.D. Morris wrote in the prologue to the book, *Radioisotopes and the Age of the Earth* (ICR, 2000), "Since neither creationists nor evolutionists can go back in time and observe past events, neither can rightly claim their view of origins to be scientifically proven. Thus, both are on an equal scientific footing, so honesty demands modesty regarding their claims. The issue can be addressed scientifically only by comparing which of the competing views handles the data better, and which is better able to make predictions of new experimental and observational results."

Evolutionary biologists claim that living organisms came from sea fissures, tidal pools, and pre-biotic soup. Russian biochemist, Alexander Oparin, theorized in 1924 that the earliest molecules assembled themselves in primal oceans. In 1928, British biologist J. Haldane looked also to the seas, proposing that amino acids and sugars were the substrates for life, forming from the action of ultraviolet rays on simpler chemicals. He believed also that terrestrial creatures evolved from primordial scum. Speculating on the requirements for such emergence, J.D. Bernal (1947) stated certain conditions which might have produced sufficient concentrations of the essential building blocks, transforming them into macromolecules for life. As Robert Wallace pictured it in his biology text, *The World of Life:*

> Our home was lifeless […] a dead unchronicled ball of matter covered by a very thin layer of hot swirling gases. The surface was hot, molten, and volcanic. In time, the surface began to cool and solidify. […] Heavy billowing clouds, miles thick, surrounded the darkened sphere. The murky blackness was continually split by bright, spewing gapes in the earth and thunderous lightning from above. Water vapor condensed and fell to the sterile earth, immediately exploding from the heat – to be lifted skyward with a crackling hiss. It is difficult to imagine that this seething place would, in time, give rise to something called life. Hydrogen and nitrogen together form ammonia. Because of this, it is assumed that the atmosphere of the earth was composed not mainly of nitrogen, but of ammonia. By the same token, there would also have been a great deal of water, formed by the union of oxygen and hydrogen. Of particular importance, carbon would have tended to join with hydrogen to form methane. Methane is an organic molecule of the sort associated with living systems.[1]

According to Wallace, life appeared somewhere between 4.1 billion years ago (when the earth's crust cooled) and 3.5 billion years ago (when the planet became populated by bacteria). These bacteria left fossilized remains (stromatolites), indicating that they had become somewhat advanced. But where did they come from? Says Wallace, "The answer leads us directly to the origin of life", noting also that "conjecturing about how life began seems both fruitless and safe" since "one can never be proven right and it is impossible to be proven wrong." "Nevertheless", says he, "it is a good intellectual exercise which helps us to understand scientific reasoning." Then he makes a bizarre proposal: "Let's ignore all the problems associated with the question, gird our loins, and tread into an arena littered with dead guesses."[2]

Dead guesses? Was the early world oxygen-poor, or was it bathed in oxygen? Was it really the primal oceans where molecules first interacted? If so, how did they form and where was the energy for their interaction? Wallace opines, "It turns out (fortunately for our story) that there are a number of sources of such energy. For example, the sun produces a variety of types of radiation. Another source of energy is heat. Remember, the earth's surface was still far from placid; the searing landscape was constantly jarred with violent eruptions, and molten or hardened rock covered much of the earth's surface. Lightning continually streaked earthward from the dense, heavy clouds, jolting molecules of the earth below."[3]

Examining this closely, the basic evolutionary proposal is that the early atmosphere contained hydrogen, carbon monoxide, carbon dioxide, nitrogen, ammonia, and methane, but little or no free oxygen. Such an atmosphere would have been toxic to cells, though its *reducing* quality might have favored the formation of organic molecules, the prerequisites for life. But first we must understand what oxidation and reduction mean. Chemical reactions require transfers of electrons, involving oxidizing and reducing agents. Oxidation is detrimental to chemical evolution, so an oxygenic environment would have blocked biogenesis whereas a reducing environment could have favored it.

Those claiming that the primitive atmosphere was *reducing* (enabling chemical evolution) say that: 1) oxygen was not present initially, and 2) under these conditions, molecules such as water, carbon dioxide, and ammonia would have yielded their electrons, allowing them to react with each other to make new molecules. Listing their arguments in 1984, Drs. Thaxton (molecular biologist), Bradley (materials science engineer), and Olsen (geo-chemist) pondered as to whether or not life could have evolved under such conditions. Citing the inadequacy of all such theories in *The Mystery of Life's Origin*, they presented the following scenario which they clearly **could not** support:

> In the upper zones of the primitive atmosphere, there would have been little if any free oxygen with which ultraviolet light could interact to produce an ozone layer such as presently protects all living things from lethal doses of ultraviolet. Instead, ultraviolet would irradiate the reducing atmosphere to form amino acids, formaldehyde, hydrogen cyanide, and many other compounds. At lower altitudes these same organic compounds would result from the energy in electrical storms and thunder shock waves. Synthesis would be occasioned at the earth's surface by wind, blowing gases of the reduced atmosphere over hot lava flows near the sea.[4]

Were this in fact true, rain would have washed simple compounds (formed in the atmosphere) into the seas where they might have reacted with the ocean's molecules producing organic chemicals. Further reactions could then have taken place in tidal pools having the consistency of a hot dilute soup, brewing up the precursors for life. This broth would have thickened in basins, lakes, lagoons, etc., allowing adsorption of organic compounds (amino acids, sugars, purines, pyrimidines, etc.) onto catalytic clays. These could then have promoted the polymerization of simple molecules into macromolecules (lipids, peptides, carbohydrates, and polynucleotides). From these there might have come DNA, RNA, protocells, cells, and living creatures. **Biochemical predestination** would then spell out the origin of all living things.

Hoping to confirm this, Stanley Miller built an airtight apparatus through which four gases (methane, ammonia, hydrogen, and water vapor – all supposedly present in the early atmosphere) were circulated past electrical jolts simulating lightning. Allowing these to circulate in his charged chamber for a week, Miller was surprised to have produced organic compounds – including amino acids, the building blocks for proteins. Follow-up experiments simulating early conditions (adding a petcock and cooling device) yielded detectable amounts of some of the biochemical precursors for living cells. With these results in hand, there seemed to be at least theoretical support for the early stages of chemical evolution. Fifty years later, however, Miller's soup has evaporated. Why? Because a far stronger argument can be made *countering* chemical evolution.

Miller's device collected chemicals in a trap that never actually existed in the primordial world. Nor could tidal pools concentrate the soup, since dilutional factors would have prevented its thickening. Even had such thickening occurred, ultraviolet light would have been damaging, consuming essential precursor chemicals. Electrical discharges would have been harmful too (at least as harmful as helpful), so outside energy (no matter its source) would have prevented progress. Also, these experiments assumed a reducing atmosphere, but there is mounting evidence for an oxygenic primitive earth (even tiny concentrations of oxygen would have inhibited biogenesis).

Oxygen or ultraviolet? Pick your poison. But there are other concerns as well. Miller's currents bore no relationship to the energy of lightning, geothermal vents, volcanic heat, and shock waves. Nor did his experiments take into consideration the production of oxygen by photosynthesis, the equally harmful photo-dissociation of water, and the multitude of amino acids required to produce a living organism. Or, for that matter, the irrationality of biochemical evolution in the absence of informational pathways.

Where are we then in our current state of knowledge? Dean Kenyon (Professor of Biology, San Francisco State University) remarks that scientists have come up with only destructive, disorderly, pointless processes:

> The experimental results to date have apparently convinced many scientists that a naturalistic explanation for the origin of life will be found, but there are significant reasons for doubt. [...] In most cases, the experimental conditions in such studies have been so artificially simplified as to have virtually no bearing on any actual processes that might have taken place on the primitive earth. [...] Other aspects of origin-of-life research have contributed to my growing uneasiness about the theory of chemical evolution. One of these is the enormous gap between the most complex "proto-cell" and the simplest living cells. [...] In my view, the possibility of closing this gap by laboratory simulation of chemical events likely to have occurred on the primitive earth is extremely remote.[5]

Kenyon goes on to describe the intractable problem of the spontaneous origin of left-handed optical isomers. Living cells contain amino acids with side groups of atoms on the left only, but the amino acids produced in the laboratory are always 50 percent left-handed and 50 percent right-handed, like those in nonliving matter. What's more, some twenty different amino acids are needed to produce the proteins in a single cell, each as decidedly left-handed as the five hundred amino acids in the smallest living creature. Who knows the odds against them having acquired left-handedness in the evolutionary scheme, but they're estimated at 10 to the 123rd power!

Evolutionists claim that sunlight contributed sufficient energy to drive the equations forward, but chemical evolution would have conflicted with the second law of thermodynamics. H. Morris explains, "It is utterly naïve to think that the contradiction between evolution and the second law can be resolved simply by saying that the earth is an open system and evolution is maintained by the sun's energy. [...] What is the marvelous mechanism that converts the sun's energy into the age-long growth process from some 'simple' replicating chemical in a primeval ocean to the present world of organic life, including man? These questions must be answered before the evolutionist has the right to expect men to believe his philosophy. In the absence of such a directing structure and implementing mechanism, the evolutionary process is utterly contrary to scientific law and can be sustained only by faith in pure magic."[6]

As a matter of fact, there is even more bad news for chemical evolution. Geologists have demonstrated from metal oxides (iron oxide, uranium oxide, etc.) in the **deepest rocks** that oxygen existed in the **earliest atmosphere**. Planet Earth **always** had free oxygen and it couldn't have been very low, even early on, since considerable amounts of metal oxide exist.

Another difficulty for the evolutionary view is that analysis of sediments has shrunk the time interval for chemical evolution down to at most a few hundred million years.[7] Not only is that far too short a time for biological origins, according to evolutionism itself, but the earliest rocks show **no trace of pre-biotic soup**. Thus, it has become increasingly clear that the emergence of life from the oceans is no longer sustainable. "We may therefore with fairness call this scenario the myth of the prebiotic soup", said Thaxton, Charles, and Bradley.[8] But why not just "ignore all these arguments and trudge on into an arena littered with dead guesses", as Wallace suggests? Because that would be trusting science over Scripture, and flimsy science at that!

The Bible doesn't leave us guessing, which is what its "perspicuity" is all about. Genesis 1 tells us that the earliest life was vegetative, preceding the sun by a day. Plants predated animals, providing creatures with food and oxygen (by photosynthesis). But plants need animals as much as animals need plants, so God (given his orderly plan) created them both within a few days. The Bible tells us also that life originated on land, not in the seas.

Thermal energy existed early on, but we don't read about rain or lightning – only about streams and mists watering the surface of the ground (Ge. 2:6). Nor do we read about oxygen, although we *are* told about "the breath of life". As for ozone, perhaps it wasn't needed early on (for shielding), granting an initial greenhouse canopy. But such an envelope might have contained at least some ozone, as ours does today, which would have been ruinous to chemical evolution.

Pre-biotic Soup to Living Cells?

One of the major hurdles for evolutionary progress is the shift from soup to cells. This requires more than amino acids, sugars, and energy. Biological advancement implies sufficient information to drive transcription, translation, and cell replication, but none of these could have entered into the picture without a driving force directing inorganic substrates (building blocks) to become organic. That engine is DNA, but the odds against its emergence by chance are so bleak that they're estimated at one in ten, followed by 155 zeros, which is more than anyone could display on a calculator.

The now-familiar DNA molecule is the stuff of genes consisting of inheritable packets of information aligned in chromosomes. With its twisted staircase of nucleotides, it was acclaimed (by Watson and Crick) as the "secret of life". Chromosomes are very precise in their behavior and they are important in cell replication, a process involving mitosis, reassemblage, and reduplication.

Replicating even the simplest cell involves spindle-formation, hydrogen bonds, base sequences, enzymatic reactions, messengers, membranes, transcription, and translation, all requiring biochemical/molecular interplay. Too complex to consider here, these all depend on DNA and RNA. But where are the pathways for these elaborate molecules, and how well are they understood?

Though not conceding special creation, Wallace remarks, "Complex flowcharts, stroked chins, and remarkable electron microscope photographs of cell interiors may lead some people to believe that the 'great questions' have been answered, and all we need now is to tie up a few loose ends. Nothing could be further from the truth. In fact, we have barely touched the hem of the garment. [...] It seems that the intense research efforts in this area are currently overmatched by some very fundamental questions that, so far, have simply refused to yield."[9]

Scientists do know enough to give them an appreciation for the ***irreducible complexity*** of all biological systems. As Denton wrote in his *Evolution, A Theory in Crisis*, "Biochemical knowledge about living systems, accumulated over the past twenty years, has provided a vast new body of information by which to assess evolutionary claims and, as a result, a number of interesting problems have arisen."[10] We know, for instance, that the information in living organisms comes by way of a genetic ancestry. But where did it originate? Clearly *not* from precursor organisms, nor by jumping the bridge from inorganic chemicals to living cells.

According to Denton, "If we think of the cell as being analogous to a factory, then the proteins can be thought of as analogous to the machines on the factory floor which carry out individually or in groups all the essential activities on which the life of the cell depends. [...] Just as different sentences are made up of different sequences of letters, so different proteins are made up of different sequences of amino acids. In most proteins the amino acid chain is between one hundred and five hundred amino acids long. [...] Most proteins consist altogether of several thousand atoms folded into an immensely complex spatial arrangement. Proteins which perform different functions have completely different overall 3-D structures and functional properties. [...] Although proteins are amazingly versatile and carry out all manner of diverse biochemical functions, they are incapable of assembling themselves without the assistance of nucleic acids."[11]

So we're back to needing DNA (the blueprint), transcription (replicating the gene's sequence), RNA (the photocopying process), and translation (decoding), all of which are key to the making of proteins. "The synthesis of proteins by the cell is thus achieved as a result of a remarkable and intimate relationship between one class of molecules – the proteins – and another quite different class of molecules – the nucleic acids. Nucleic acids contain the information for the construction of proteins, but it is the proteins which extract and utilize that information at all stages as it flows through this intricate series of transformations."[12] Summing it up, *to have cells we need proteins but to have proteins we need cells*. We now know not only of a break between living and non-living things, but also that it is the most dramatic and fundamental of all the discontinuities of nature.[13]

There is complexity beyond that, however, for molecular biology has proven that even the simplest of cells are micro-factories with thousands of exquisitely designed pieces of molecular machinery, more complicated than the most sophisticated of space machines. Explaining this, Behe writes in *Darwin's Black Box*, "Even systems that at first glance appear amenable to a gradualistic approach turn out to be major headaches on closer inspection – or when the experimental results roll in – with no reason to expect that they will be solved within a Darwinian framework."[14]

Quoting Klaus Dose, a prominent "origin-of-life" researcher, "More than 30 years of experimentation on the origin of life in the fields of chemical and molecular evolution have led to a better perception of the immensity of the problem of the origin of life on Earth rather than to its solution. At present, all discussions on principal theories and experiments in the field either end in stalemate or in a confession of ignorance."[15]

Referring to biology's contributions, Behe says, "Scientists working on the origin of life deserve a lot of credit; they have attacked the problem by experiment and calculation, as science should. And although the experiments have not turned out as many hoped, through their efforts we now have a clear idea of the staggering difficulties facing an origin of life by natural chemical processes. In private, many scientists admit that science has no explanation for the beginning of life. [...] As a result, evolutionary biology is stuck in the same frame of mind that dominated origin-of-life studies in the early fifties."[16]

Summing up the arguments, "The world of molecular machinery, coding systems, informational molecules, catalytic devices, and feedback control is totally unique to living systems and without parallel in non-living matter". As Denton points out, "Nothing illustrates more clearly just how intractable a problem the origin of life has become than the fact that world authorities can seriously toy with the idea of panspermia [seeding from elsewhere in the cosmos]. The failure to give a plausible evolutionary explanation for the origin of life casts a number of shadows over the whole field of evolutionary speculation."[17]

To generate even the most basic cells we're face to face with *missing information links*, an *insurmountable barrier to the evolutionary dream*. But there are barriers related to mutations, as well. The very earliest cells supposedly arrived after a long period of pre-cellular evolution. This "is presumed to have begun with a primitive self-replicating molecule which slowly accumulated beneficial mutations enabling it to reproduce more efficiently. Over eons of time, it gradually evolved into a complex self-replicating object acquiring a cell membrane, metabolic functions, and eventually all the complex biochemical machinery of the cell. As the outcome of a perfectly natural process, driven by chance and selection, life is now widely viewed as an inevitable process."[18] Yet, according to biology itself, meaningful mutations seldom happen.

Soup never advances to cells! It's just the opposite, in fact! DNA-laden cells, functional from the outset, assemble chemicals by themselves, assuring their own survival. This is a rich ancestral heritage, driven by the *existing genome*, and all replication systems are essentially the same. Rather than having sloppy systems for copying themselves, cells have proof-read mechanisms supplying the information, defining the pathways, and managing the complexities.

Moreover, as Denton describes it, "The size, structure, and component design of the protein synthetic machinery is practically the same in all cells. In terms of biochemical design, therefore, no living system can be thought of as being primitive or ancestral."[19] This is hardly a picture of pre-biotic chemicals assembling themselves into cells! It is, however, a profound statement regarding the hidden things of God, and his wisdom!

Living Cells to Whole Organisms?

And God said, "Let the water teem with living creatures,
and let birds fly above the earth across the expanse of the sky" (Ge. 1:20).

Cells make up tissues, tissues make up organs, organs make up organisms, and organisms make up the biological world.

The development of biological organs exceeds vastly the complexity of cell formation, even in the simplest organisms. Protozoans are single-celled organisms (e.g., ameba) existing in warm ponds and swimming holes. Tourists encounter them with unpleasant after-effects, especially in developing countries. They can be seen only under the microscope, yet they have mini-structures – organelles, and cilia for locomotion. Covered with these hair-like appendages, ameba swim purposefully, bending around corners. But how simple are their organelles, and why do they function so well?

To begin with, all organ systems have structure and functionality. Protozoans may have cilia, but these must be structurally sound for locomotion to occur. Behe pictures it as follows: "When a cilium is sliced crossways and the cut end is examined by electron microscopy, you see nine rod-like structures around the periphery. [...] Each of these nine microtubules is seen to actually consist of two fused rings. Further examination shows that one of the rings is made from thirteen individual strands. The other ring, joined to the first, is made from ten strands. Summarizing briefly, each of the nine outer microtubules of a cilium is made of a ring of ten strands fused to a ring of thirteen strands."[20]

Continuing the discussion, while ciliary structure is complex, so is its function. Translating the esoteric into plain English, Behe offers this simplified version of it: "Imagine several smokestacks made of tuna cans that are tightly held together. The tuna can smokestacks are connected by slack wires. Attached to one smokestack is a little motor with an arm that reaches out and holds on to the tuna can in a neighboring smokestack. The motor arm pushes the second smokestack down, sliding it past the first one. As the smokestacks slide past each other, the slack wires begin to stretch and become taut. As the motor arm pushes more, the strain from the wire makes the smokestack bend. Thus the sliding motion has been converted into a bending motion."[21]

Having studied protozoa myself, and done some river paddling too, I know that forward propulsion would require every component of the cilium to be precisely engineered, not just the anatomical machinery but the biochemical as well. Otherwise, there would be lots of splashing but very little swimming. *Function* is at least as complex as *structure*, and both are more complex than had ever been imagined prior to molecular biology. So the challenge of engineering persists. And why do cilia form in the first place? Behe explains that in terms of a biochemical challenge:

> The cilium contains tubulin, dynein, nexin, and several other connector proteins. If you take these and inject them into a cell that lacks a cilium, however, they do not assemble to give a functioning cilium. Much more is required to obtain a cilium in a cell. A thorough biochemical analysis shows that a cilium contains over *two hundred different kinds of proteins*; and the actual complexity of the cilium is enormously greater than what we have considered. All the reasons for such complexity are not yet clear and await further experimental investigation. Other tasks for which proteins might be required, however, include attachment of the cilium to a base structure inside the cell; modification of the elasticity of the cilium; control of the timing of the beating; and strengthening of the ciliary membrane.[22]

Now for a more complicated structure: not an organelle, but a full-blown bacterial flagellum. To function efficiently, this tail-like appendage needs an even more complicated structure, an "acid-driven, rotary motor". But for this to exist, both the mechanical and biochemical requirements increase significantly! The engineering thresholds are so demanding in fact that flagella are the focus of ongoing research, each needing a paddle, a rotor, and a motor!

Moving on to bacteriophages (ultramicroscopic agents parasitizing bacteria), biologists know from nucleotide sequencing that there are pages of letters for their individual DNA sub-units, consisting of over 5000 sequences in a single bacteriophage. This is minuscule, however, compared with our own DNA. So why all this complexity? Because of the gene pool of ancestral parents, placed there by an all-wise Creator. Biogenesis is just that *simple*, and just that *complex*.

Lower to Higher Forms?

God made the wild animals according to their kinds, the livestock according to their kinds,
and all the creatures that move along the ground according to their kinds.
And God saw that it was good (Ge. 1:25).

Did cold-blooded animals become warm-blooded? Did worms (e.g, nematodes) become insects (arthropods)? Did eels (invertebrates) become cats (vertebrates)? Was there an inevitable progression from frogs (amphibians) to snakes (reptiles) to birds to mammals to man? The answer was "obvious", and it gained a wide following, but evolutionism has faded so badly that even the most implacable Darwinist must keep reminding himself that what we see *wasn't designed* and has no purpose except its own.

The question is, what is evolution? Evolution is a *flexible word*. In its simplest form it means *"change over time"*. Most often, it describes the lengthy process by which life came from nonliving material, requiring no outside agency except matter and energy. That was Darwin's definition and it is still in vogue today, claiming the descent of all life forms from a common ancestor by "random chance and undirected processes". Whether spelling out the mechanisms or not, keep in mind that whole populations, not just individuals, supposedly evolved. But in what increments, small steps or giant leaps?

Classic Darwinism holds to incremental variation – the gradual accumulation of small mutational changes over time, resulting in inter-species transformation. Darwin believed in descent with modification (always over time), though he had no clue regarding chromosomes and DNA.

Like Darwin, anyone can study finches and fossils, looking for ascendancy. But, though believing in such changes, Niles Eldredge (American Museum of Natural History) and the late Stephen J. Gould (Professor of Geology, Harvard and New York Universities) were struck with the absence of transitional fossils. Yearning for answers, they concluded that life forms may have persisted for long periods of time, changing unpredictably and abruptly into totally different "kinds". To Eldredge and Gould, evolution meant long periods of "stabilization" during which organisms changed little if at all, punctuated by abrupt episodes of rapid change – "punctuated equilibrium". How did they come up with this? By moving from Darwinism to neo-Darwinism. As Behe recounts it:

> In the first half of the twentieth century, the many branches of biology did not often communicate with each other. As a result genetics, systematics, paleontology, comparative anatomy, embryology, and other areas developed their own views of what evolution meant. Inevitably, evolutionary theory began to mean different things to different disciplines; a coherent view of Darwinian evolution was being lost. In the middle of the century, however, leaders of the fields organized a series of interdisciplinary meetings to combine their views into a coherent theory of evolution based on Darwinian principles. The result has been "evolutionary synthesis", and the theory called neo-Darwinism.[23]

Eldredge and Gould pictured large segments of DNA transitioning from one organism to another, producing thousands of macro-evolutionary changes within a few generations. This followed Goldschmidt's failed hypothesis proposing large-scale genetic leaps producing creatures so radically different that a bird might have hatched from a reptilian egg. Commenting on this, R. Maatman (Chemistry Professor Emeritus, Dordt College) wrote, "Goldschmidt advocated a wholesale chromosomal rearrangement that he called 'the systemic mutation' as the novel genetic process to account for speciation – by observations of *Drosophilia* [fruit fly] chromosomes. While natural selection usually eliminates such individuals arising from systemic mutations, occasionally it might allow them to propagate as *'hopeful monsters'* under special circumstances."[24]

By now, these monsters have all but disappeared, being so bizarre that Darwin himself would have balked at them. But, though defunct, they have found their way into neo-Darwinism, re-defined as macro-leaps occurring when and where needed, transmitting desirable traits to future generations. With this as the working hypothesis, new organisms are always possible given changed circumstances and perceived need (e.g., reproductive isolation and/or alteration of the environment), always allowing *time* to manage the *leaps.* The problem is, macro-evolution doesn't occur in any meaningful sense, and micro-evolution is insufficient for change.

Micro-evolution is a misnomer. It can rearrange existing genomes but it cannot create new genetic material. "Micro-evolution has to do with fluctuations of characteristics within a given set of information – a set fixed within created boundaries which cannot be crossed. Macro-evolution would imply that a whole new set of information has been produced and that this new set actually crosses boundaries into new kinds. But it is simply not true that all creative processes are the result of a two-part phenomenon, micro- to macro-, allowing new species to develop from existing ones. So the issue is one of fluctuations within prescribed limits vs. the arrival of entirely new information."[25] Lacking the latter, there can be no real change.

Creationists admit that micro-evolution occurs within limited parameters; witness the offspring of Adam and Eve diversifying from a common ancestral pair into all the races of the world. The question is not whether this happened (or if it still does), but whether or not it tells us anything about the requisite processes for generating new organisms.

As Phillip Johnson expresses it, "The difficulties with both the micro-mutational and macro-mutational theories are so great that we might expect to see some effort being made to come up with a middle ground that minimizes the disadvantages of both extremes." But no such ground exists, either in science or in the Bible.

What about fruit flies? Experiments with fruit flies have accomplished nothing structurally or functionally. They have generated only senseless information, ridiculous morphology, and randomly disorganized misfits. Fruit flies (geneticists' pets) may show morphologic changes under certain conditions (e.g., irradiation), but the resultant mutations are pointless, generating no forward direction, purpose, or benefit. So today, not only do we have 21st century mathematicians concluding that neo-Darwinism is impossible, but its mutations are seen as purposeless – producing sick flies, crippled flies, sterile flies, and dead flies, but always and only *fruit flies*. No matter the modification, *fruit flies* don't become *house flies*. They may mutate, but they never *trans*-mutate! Why? Because mutations are letter-changes within an existing code; they don't produce new taxonomic "kinds."

Forward mutations are not to be confused with the elimination of peppered moths subjected to predators, or bacteria exposed to antibiotics, since these changes will revert when the causative factors are reversed. Mutations are in fact very rare, occurring only once in every ten million duplications of a DNA molecule. They are also random and useless, if not frankly harmful. Stressing this, Jonathan Wells (molecular/cellular biologist, U.C. Berkeley) points to London's moths and Darwin's finches as "icons of evolution", the likes of which prove nothing regarding revolutionary change, though they do attest to immutability of species.

As for neo-Darwinism, it is elegantly simple. According to Wells, it can be stated in four propositions: "Every organism develops according to a program encoded in its genes (which is to say DNA). DNA is the hereditary material that transmits traits from organisms to their descendants; new traits occasionally arise because of DNA mutations; and natural selection produces both microevolution (*below* the species or genus level) and macroevolution (*above* the species or genus level) by favoring advantageous traits and thereby increasing the frequency of genes in the population."[26] But where is the evidence?

Lacking the fruits of their theories, neo-Darwinists are embellishing them by bringing homology (morphologic similarities) and embryology (fetal development) back into the discussion. They point to interchangeable genetic material in early embryogenesis producing either useful morphogenesis (e.g., new organs from stem cells) or congenital anomalies (morphogenesis gone awry). In the minds of some, these interchanges confirm that major genetic alterations can be achieved during the initial stages of life – seeing also that DNA snippets (modules) can be readily exchanged (spliced) during gene-altering experiments.

To evolutionists, this fits with the discovery that arthropods and chordates share a common family of genes considered important in determining body patterns. These so-called "homeotic genes" are present in all animals, and evolutionists are excited about them. As it turns out, though, homeotic genes are raising more questions still, so some are calling them rubbish. Says Wells pointedly, "The universality of homeotic genes is supposed to be due to their presence in a common ancestor, but the preponderance of evidence suggests that the common ancestor lacked the features that those homeotic genes now supposedly control – and from a Darwinian perspective this is a serious problem."[27]

Furthermore, if these genes are so nonspecific as to make fruit-flies sprout legs where there should be eyes (or antennae where there should be wings), or if the same genes can determine structures as radically different as a fruit fly's leg and a squid's eye, then homeotic hopefuls are telling us very little about useful assemblage. Nor can they tell us how whales became mammals or how dragonflies became "helicopters" (hovering in space, doing high-speed turns)! Truth is, homeotic genes tell us nothing about how organisms are formed. "As they turn out to be more and more universal, the control they exercise in development turns out to be less and less specific."[28]

On a lighter note, just how attractive would a female fruit fly be to the male with a leg protruding from her eye? More to the point, if meaningful macro-evolution is how things worked, why don't we see it happening?

Higher Animals to Persons?

Why would protozoans want to swim in the first place? If it was so important for bacteria to become people, why do we find them looking like the stromatolites of old, even in Silicon Valley? Lacking a Master-plan, what is the likelihood of apes becoming people? Where are the pathways for change, informational or otherwise? Did we humans mutate upward because of innate pre-disposition? And what about our spirituality? Is it from self-determination, or from God?

Some say organisms only *appear* to have been designed, but Crick had another idea. Knowing that DNA could never have arisen by chance, he theorized that creatures from elsewhere contributed the bits and pieces for life, sowing their seeds on Earth. But "panspermia" is as comical as saying that evolution happened simply because we *are*, as in the naturalistic version of the ***anthropic principle***.

How about the "emergent property of matter", as Sagan coined it? Well, could a band of marching army ants spell the word G-E-N-O-M-E, lacking a plan? Could tone-deaf amateurs perform an orchestral opus without instruments, scores, and a director? Not in a million years! We've never seen anything like it and we never will! Even the simplest of organisms need nuts and bolts for their emergence, and the absence of these has blocked all evolutionary routes. The problem is, chance assembly (coincidence) doesn't work! It produces only disorderly marchers, discordant music, and deranged monsters, and mathematicians have complained about this for years!

Whole volumes have been written about a single organ and function, and every organic system shows its own exquisite engineering. Consider also the complexity of the human body, which contains 100 trillion cells. If unwound, the DNA in a single cell would be more than six feet long. Each gene is like a sentence containing information no less specific than written codes and human language, telling the cell to manufacture a particular protein needed for the construction of a complete organism. Confronted with such specificity, need I remind you that we are spectacular gene-machines?

Our bodies have spindle-like muscle cells capable of kinetic work, cylindrical cardiac cells enabling contractions of the heart, bone cells producing corpuscles (carrying oxygen and fighting infection), gastric cells secreting acid and mucin, neural cells sending and receiving messages, retinal cells perceiving light and color, and even germinal cells enabling our reproduction.

Each cell was designed to respond in ways beyond the scope of these pages. But it is in our *personhood* that we enter into the temple of God, since there is no anatomical explanation for it. Having dissected the central nervous system, I can say with confidence that neural tracts don't explain sentience, which is why neuroscientists have no vocabulary for consciousness, conscience, and the soul. Nor can these be explained by Darwinism, since it sees the brain only as a computer. We might ask then, are we merely machines without souls? Is our humanness from our being *Homo sapiens* in lineage? If we believe that, we're denying him who said, "Father, into your hands I commit my spirit" (Lk. 23:46).

The Bible tells us that we were "fearfully and wonderfully made", but without supernatural agency there is no rationale for this – or for human emotions, awareness, rationality, and spirituality! Humans can't generate something new and innovative (genetically) from something non-existent. Evolutionists admit this too, if they're fair and honest, since there is no natural pathway for man's uniqueness. This is a very real problem for neo-Darwinists! Any wonder then as to why some would prefer to rid themselves entirely of conscience?

Believers, on the other hand, rest comfortably with spirituality, though they too can be misled, framing their arguments poorly or avoiding personhood entirely. Most of us can read, however, and nowhere is there a map for mankind's ascendancy. The gulf between brutes and humans is so wide that it cannot be bridged naturalistically. Only God can bestow godliness, and this poses a serious dilemma for those trying to harmonize evolution with the Bible.

It was that very problem with which Darwin struggled until his death. By the late 1830s, he came to view Special Revelation as "utterly incredible". Recounting this, Nancy Pearcey (Executive Editor for Colson's award-winning radio program, *BreakPoint*) wrote, "Darwin's intellectual journey seems to illustrate the old adage that if one rejects a Creator, inevitably one puts something else in its place. In Darwin's case, he assigned godlike powers to the laws and processes of nature"[29]

Unlike Darwin, those revering God have deep intellectual strength. "Not by might nor by power, but by my Spirit", says the Lord Almighty (Zec. 4:6). Even were evolutionists right, why would God have thought it necessary to evolve humans over eons, destroying countless misfits in the process? Why wouldn't he implement his plans directly, without *first* generating *a world of despair*? The answer is clear isn't it? ***God never made misfits in the first place!*** Nature shows no such trail, and neither does Scripture.

But what if people could mimic God? Since much of the world is synthetic already, couldn't we create life, substituting ourselves for the Divine and gaining our independence in the process? Am I wrong to think that such reasoning makes one profoundly egotistical? And exhausted? But wait, wasn't life brought forth already by humans? Yes, by the magicians in Egypt (Ex. 7:11-13). However, this was from Satan, so shouldn't we avoid seeing ourselves as gods (2 Ti. 3:5)? God gave us the cultural mandate, not the freedom to play God, so we are rebelling against him when we look for signs and wonders (2 Th. 2:9). These will be pursued until the end of time, but *real* signs and wonders are from "the Spirit, the water, and the blood" (1 Jn. 5:8).

Supernatural Causation

With the technology revolution in full swing, robotic surgery is here to stay. In modern surgical suites, the surgeon is seated at a console. The usual lines and tubes are all suspended from booms, leaving so much ambient space that a number of observers can be accommodated in the room. Surgical procedures are displayed on monitors and performed using touch-screens, voice-activated computers, smart instrumentation, etc. Every maneuver is caught on video, and (though humans are still needed) surgical assistants are disappearing. Even those second coffee-cup tremors are no longer of concern since they can be digitally eliminated. Pulsating organs can be stopped too, by virtual imaging. But where is the patient? In a sterile pod on an ergonomic table attached to remote systems. As we surgeons would say, "The patient is in good hands", just not touching hands! If this seems Orwellian, you might be comforted knowing that teleconferencing can connect your surgeon with real-time consultants anywhere in the world, right from the console and on camera.

High-tech doesn't just happen, however. It requires intelligence, information, design, and effort. Seeing these same requirements at work in the universe, why not accept them in creation? The reality is, the pursuit of knowledge is committed to a *framework* working in *one of two ways*:

    Either: Science is *open* to supernatural causes, in which case it can be objective, inviting verification and criticism.

    Or: Science is *closed* to supernatural causes, in which case it is subjective, fostering confusion and cover-up.

Of the two alternatives, creationism is committed to the first, evolutionism to the second. Science must therefore be freed from its bondage, for as Dembski says, "If we prescribe in advance that science must be limited to undirected natural causes, then science will necessarily be incapable of investigating God's interaction with the world. But if we permit science to investigate intelligent causes (as many sciences already do) [...] then God's interaction with the world, insofar as it manifests the characteristic features of intelligent causation, becomes a legitimate domain for scientific investigation."[30]

The question is, if God energized the particles and the fields, is this religion or could it be science at its best? Knowing the answer, a new breed of researchers is offering design arguments as a *preliminary wedge between two views*, "uniting the divided and dividing the united", as Johnson puts it. This may drive the argument back toward *supernatural causation*, where it belongs, though that has not happened as of now.

Science vs. "Science"

Design theorists are reverse engineers, retro-engineering things shown to be designed.[31] Investigating how these were produced, they are finding plenty of things attributable to design, especially in the biological world. One could argue that secular scientists know this too, for they are design theorists at heart, albeit in naturalistic clothing. Rather than admitting to design, however, they are increasingly vocal, belittling those holding to the supernatural – insisting that science and religion be separated. Yet the very persons who insist on this are eager to use their own science as a basis for pronouncements about religion.[32]

According to P. Johnson, "the literature of Darwinism is full of anti-theistic conclusions, such as that the universe was not designed and has no purpose, and that we humans are the product of blind natural processes caring nothing about us. What is more, these statements are not presented as personal opinions but as the logical implications of evolutionary science."[33] This is evident in people's zeal to evangelize the world, insisting that others accept naturalism as a matter of moral obligation.

When Christians see the push in this direction, they need to push back, seeing God's fingerprints all over the data. Those missing this are missing a revolution! But what if ID theory detected only intelligence and design, never specifying their nature? Stated differently, what if science accepts certain characteristics of creation, but not the cause behind it all? Does God then exist only as an option?

Design arguments don't answer these questions, since they are aimed mainly at removing misperceptions. But how then *does* one arrive at the God of the Bible? Isn't there some additional evidence? Of course there is! Look at the world around you and see if it fits with the Creator. Look also at the human condition. What fits with it? Finally, look at God's dealings with his people, particularly those of a miraculous nature. These all point to divine causation and a sovereign God.

The question is, when does God become essential? Only when we accept his nature, his purpose, and his words. Seeing origins in this context, creationists have pushed the biblical view for years. Though having shortcomings of their own, they have successfully challenged the naturalistic camp. Calling people back to the Bible while engaging in ever more rigorous science, they have maintained a loyal following.

Today, however, there is a **new** development. The "origins wars" are re-heating! Given the persuasive power of molecular biology in an informational age, the public has become skeptical of evolution – seeing the successful assault on it. Even godless scientists are admitting that anti-evolutionary arguments can be rigorously formulated. As a result, the wearisome references to "science vs. religion" and "Scripture vs. objectivity" are under siege, quelled by solid research. To be blunt about it, evolutionary myths are on the run and the naturalistic model has in effect toppled!

Admittedly, there are still those framing the debate in terms of "Bible-thumpers" vs. "thinking scientists", with particular hatred for "fundamentalists", but even the press has modified its carping, as in *The Wall Street Journal's* characterization of secularists as "anti-theistic" vs. design theorist as "appealing" (October, 1999). Holding the intellectual advantage, Christians can now move *beyond intelligent design*, and we must do so promptly. However, just as it took generations to ignite Darwinism, it takes time to convince the world of *special creation*.

To move forward, we must understand what ID theory really is. It is actually three things: a tool for investigating the universe, a challenge to naturalistic evolution, and a way of understanding initial causes. As Dembski explains it, "Within biology, intelligent design is a theory of biological origins and development. Its fundamental claim is that intelligent causes are necessary to explain the complex, information-rich structures of biology and that these causes are empirically detectable. Intelligent design is therefore not the study of intelligent causes per se but of information pathways induced by intelligent causes. As a result, ID presupposes neither a creator nor miracles. [...] At the same time, it resists speculation about the nature, moral character, or purposes of this intelligence."[34] Much can be said favoring these statements, but they fall short of the Bible's plumb-line. The problem is, when people build arguments on partial premises, they are no longer pursuing Truth. For that, we must compare Scripture with Scripture, not just science with "science".

Why "Beyond" Intelligent Design?

While waiting for an ID seminar, I overheard two university students acclaiming an aged universe. Said one to the other, "You don't suppose they'll tell us that the earth is only a few thousand years old, do you?" Well, they needn't have worried! The age of the universe was out of bounds. Yes, design arguments were presented, but they were tied to some mysterious, inanimate force.

Proponents of design, led by a group of academics and intellectuals, all too often see Planet Earth as billions of years old, not thousands. At the same time, they reject the notion that natural selection can explain intelligence. That, they insist, is the result of a designer, who may or may not be the God of the Bible.

Though being vague about causation, ID theorists have gained support from physicists, astronomers, biologists, physicians, engineers, etc., spawning one university student organization, the "IDEA club" (for Intelligent Design *and* Evolution Awareness). Neo-Darwinists more generally see design theorists as insidious (more so than outright creationists), though the design movement itself asks mainly that it be judged by scientific criteria.

Even with the disclaimers, design theory is gaining momentum. As Dembski explains it, "There is a legitimate intellectual project here." Christians have been quick to pick up on it while evolutionists continue their nagging. Bemoaning how ID theory is used by creationists, Dr. Jerry Coyne (Professor of ecology and evolution, University of Chicago) said, "I would use the words *devilishly clever*. It has an appeal to intellectuals who don't know anything about evolutionary biology, first of all because the proponents have Ph.D.s and second of all because it's not written in the sort of populist, folksy, anti-intellectual style. It's written in the argot of academia." Echoing this, Leonard Krishtalka (Director, Natural History Museum and Biodiversity Research Center, University of Kansas) said recently, "Intelligent design is nothing more than creationism dressed in a cheap tuxedo."

Despite such attacks, and some weaknesses of the ID movement itself, proponents of design are dismantling naturalism. Phillip E. Johnson (author of *Darwin on Trial, Reason in the Balance,* and other books) is a believing Christian and a philosophic theist. Not a defender of "creation science", he cites the need to re-introduce the Creator, though occupying himself mainly with dislodging naturalism. Hugh Ross, a design theorist and author of books on cosmogony, holds to the infallibility of the Word but isn't deeply invested in the *sensus literalis* of Scripture. Michael Behe (author of *Darwin's Black Box*) doesn't look to religion for answers, but says that organisms must have been designed, whether by God or some other agency. William Dembski (author of *Intelligent Design*, *Mere Creation*, and other books) is a believing Christian, willing to take risks for his statements. These are all supporters of the design movement, but their commitment to the Sovereign Lord is wide-ranging. So we must **augment their arguments**. After all, science is not "King", and neither is intelligent design.

Who or what *is* King, then? Divine Causation, Divine Content, and a Divine Being! The Sovereign Lord is the First Intelligence (before all things), the Initial Designer (of all things), and the Primary Cause (for all things). Design theorizing, on the other hand, stumbles at "the way, the truth, and the life" (Jn. 14:6). More specifically, it

- Vacillates regarding the Designer, his attributes, and his purposes
- Equivocates regarding the soul and personhood
- Fails to address the Creator/creature distinction and the antithesis between good and evil
- Does not consistently recognize creation/perfection
- Skirts the arguments for recent creation and a young earth
- Slights the fact that information and order have become garbled over time
- Lacks specificity, being endorsed by an assortment of theorizers
- Has no inherent Christian testimony (or methodology) for re-instating biblical creation
- Demotes God to the level of human comprehension, thereby losing sight of his infinite intelligence, his solitary excellence, and his supreme authority.

Yes, the defeat of Darwinism has elevated the discussion (and the spirit), but that is not enough. Given him whose attributes are on the line, we must state the truth in its entirely. At stake are the sufficiency and authority of the Bible, as in these declarations:

In the beginning was the Word, and the Word was with God, and the Word was God. He was with God in the beginning. Through him all things were made; without him nothing was made that has been made (Jn. 1:1,2).

By faith we understand that the universe was formed at God's command. [...] Anyone who comes to him must believe that he exists and that he rewards those who earnestly seek him" (Heb. 11:3-6).

The one who is in you is greater than the one who is in the world. They are from the world and therefore speak from the viewpoint of the world, and the world listens to them. We, however, are from God, and whoever knows God listens to us; but whoever is not from God does not listen to us. This is how we recognize the Spirit of truth and the spirit of falsehood (1 Jn. 4: 4-6).

Christians should see science and theology for what they are, realizing the pitfalls of assembling limited models into global theories. Believers should also be offering **biblically based models**, showing how the universe fits best with the **Sovereign Lord. The truth is we can continue to beat a dead horse to "death", but there comes a time when we must find a new colt and ride it!** Even were one alone in this effort, that would not render it any less important, for though people might take their pot-shots, the truth will blow them away.

Design arguments have pointed science back to its roots, but they haven't brought us much further along than that. Therefore, we must broaden the debate all the way from undirected causes to supernatural causes, from uniformitarianism to special intervention, from gradualism to fiat, from eons to "days", from pre-determinism to predestination, from coincidence to providence, from natural selection to special agency, from transmutation of species to fixity of kinds, from survival of the fittest to the effects of sin, from natural death to penal death, from animal ancestry to heavenly heritage, from perpetual decay to completed perfection, from upward mobility to downward slope, from opinion and tolerance to truth and light – from *"Paradise Lost"* to *"Paradise Regained"*.

As the youngest of six brothers, sometimes I felt like Joseph, looking up at his brothers from the cistern. Joseph, however, ended up in the palace of Pharaoh! Could it be that we Christians, like Joseph, were given our riches for a purpose? Having both nature and the Word, God does call us to accountability, as in this reminder:

As a masterpiece opens a window into the mind of the artist who made it, so the universe reveals much about its Creator. Indeed, so clearly is God displayed in nature that if all Scripture were lost, we could still know something of his character by carefully studying the works of his hands. From its tiniest details to its most majestic vistas, the whole earth points to the sovereign God of the Bible. Yet the splendor of the earth is only half of God's creation, and to view it by itself is to see it dimly. For mirroring the perfect world of God is the perfect Word of God, which reveals the perfect love of God in Christ, who is the true foundation of all things. Hence, by the brilliant light of his Word, God has graciously illuminated his creation so that all may see and know and enjoy him in it.

("The Art of God", by Ric Ergenbright)[35]

[1] Robert A. Wallace, *Biology, The World of Life,* Scott, Foresman, & Co., 1990, pp. 46-48

[2] Ibid, p. 48

[3] Ibid, p. 48

[4] Charles Thaxton; Walter Bradley, Roger Olsen, *The Mystery of Life's Origin,* Philosophical Library, Inc., New York, NY, 1984, pp. 15-17

[5] Ibid, Forward

[6] Henry Morris, *The Biblical Basis for Modern Science,* Baker Book House, 1984, p. 209

[7] Michael Denton, *Evolution, A Theory in Crisis,* Adler & Adler Publishers, Bethesda, MA, 1985, pp. 262,263

[8] Charles Thaxton, Walter Bradley, Roger Olsen, *The Mystery of Life's Origin,* Philosophical Library, Inc. New York, NY, 1984, pp. 15-17.

[9] Robert A Wallace, *Biology, The World of Life,* Scott, Foresman, & Co., 1990, p.161

[10] Michael Denton, *Evolution, A Theory in Crisis,* Adler & Adler Publishers, Inc., Bethesda, MD, 1985, p. 233.

[11] Ibid, pp. 234-249

[12] Ibid, p. 245

[13] Ibid, p. 250

[14] Michael Behe, *Darwin's Black Box,* The Free Press, New York, NY, 1996, p. 160

[15] Ibid, p. 168

[16] Ibid, pp. 172,173

[17] Michael Denton, Evolution, *A Theory in Crisis,* Adler & Adler Publishers, Inc., Bethesda, MD, 1985, p. 271

[18] Ibid, p. 251

[19] Ibid, p. 250

[20] Michael Behe, Michael, *Darwin's Black Box,* The Free Press, New York, NY, 1996, p. 59

[21] Ibid, p. 64

[22] Ibid, p. 72

[23] Ibid, p. 24

[24] Russell Maatman, *The Impact of Evolutionary Theory: A Christian View,* Dordt College Press, Sioux Center, IA, 1993, p. 110.

[25] Phillip E. Johnson, *Darwin on Trial,* InterVarsity Press, Downers Grove, IL, 1993, p. 39

[26] Jonathan Wells, writing in *Mere Creation,* InterVarsity Press, Downers Grove, IL, 1998, p. 52

[27] Ibid, pp. 57-68

[28] Ibid, p. 57

[29] Nancy Pearcey, writing in *Mere Creation,* InterVarsity Press, Downers Grove, IL, 1998, p. 78

[30] William Dembski, *Mere Creation,* InterVarsity Press, Downers Grove, IL, 1998, p. 15

[31] Ibid, pp. 18,19

[32] Phillip E. Johnson, *Darwin on Trial,* InterVarsity Press, Downers Grove, IL, 1993, p. 8

[33] Ibid, p. 8

[34] William Dembski, *Mere Creation*, InterVarsity Press, Downers Grove, IL, 1998, pp. 16-19

[35] Ric Ergenbright, *The Art of God,* Tyndale House Publishers, Inc., Wheaton, IL, 1999, cover.

READING THE ROCKS
(Chapter 12)

From the Garden to the Grave

At the headwaters of the Jordan River, near the northern border of Israel, there is a special mountain. Its namesake, Mount Hermon of California, is a few miles from the Pacific. "Here God must have stumbled and spilled an extra portion of nature's bounties from his blessing blanket, for here are found giant sequoias and mountain verdure, quiet lake and flowing streams, steep climbs and level promenades, sulfur spring and crystal water, in one of the choicest gardens of God."[1]

As the late Kay Gudnason (long-time Mt. Hermon resident) wrote, "Here, in the quiet of the night and the exhilaration of each new dawn, through calm days and storm, there is surcease from the frenzied trap of traffic and the hectic pace of the world, for here the God-made hush supplants the man-made rush."

On this mountain are ever-moving pines, red-budded madrones, soft-foliaged maples, sweet-scented bay, and oaks of many kinds, along with azaleas, lilac, hazel, manzanita, and ubiquitous ferns crowding each other on the stream. Like the dew of Hermon falling on Mount Zion (Ps. 133), this mountain has three ecosystems related to altitude and climate, all within walking distance of each other. There is a lower-level rain forest with its leafy green foliage, filtered sunshine, and redwoods. There is a more elevated zone with varied tree forms and flowers. And there is a ridge-like summit where ponderosa pines rise commandingly over springy ground and needles. Among these trees, where my wife and I are privileged to live, one is caught up in a world of redwood scent and muted song-birds.

Across a forested canyon are rocks, ridges, limestone, and clays showing the effects of erosion, slippage, and quakes. Here one can find fault lines, fissures, and the remains of a long-lost era, including shark's teeth. Here also the fauna and flora inhabit ecological zones, since God assigned the heights to goats, the crags to rabbits, and the pine trees to storks (Ps. 104). There are interesting things in sediments along the streams as well, including bacteria resembling stromatolites.

Scattered throughout these mountains are fossilized remains like those on the peaks of Africa, Europe, Asia, and the Middle East. These tell of massive upheavals generating billions of casualties. But rocks and fossils don't tell the whole story. We know for a fact that the world started out with some remarkably progressive people. Jabal was "the father of those who lived in tents and raised livestock." His brother, Jubal, "was the father of all who play the harp and flute." Then there was Tubal-Cain, "who forged all kinds of tools out of bronze and iron" (Ge. 4:21-23). Accepting this on faith, we must abandon the cave-man mentality entirely, for if rocks and fossils tell us anything, they do so within a context, from the Garden to the grave.

Paleontologists claim that *the present is key to the past* (as Hutton and Lyle saw it), but in reality *the past is key to the present*, as Scripture presents it. *Facts are tied to assumptions*, so apart from Scripture there is seldom a "brute fact" in origins research. During Noah's day, for instance, palms grew in Montana and dinosaurs roamed the poles. Later, what was once a comfortable biosphere was inundated by water, destroying creatures everywhere. How else would one explain dinosaur bones beneath ice caps and the remains of 9000 rhinoceroses, camels, and wild boars buried together in Agate Springs, Nebraska, many no longer native to that area?

The Noahic Flood entombed organisms in their unique zones, which is why we see ecological zonation in the fossils. The flood arranged them by size, weight, and buoyancy, consistent with the laws of physics, though they were scattering whimsically too, concurrent with fracturing of the earth's crust. But nature's ills were not normal; nor was there anything natural about mass burial!

Unlike in Noah's day, today's degradation is so ubiquitous that creatures are usually eliminated before they can become fossilized. Fossil formation requires speedy action, as evidenced by the thousands of bison lost on the Oregon Trail. Organisms do fossilize, however, when overcome by floods, hurricanes, and earthquakes. But never in history was there fossilization on the scale of that produced by the Great Flood; nor will there be anything like it again since God "swore that the waters of Noah would never again cover the earth" (Isa. 54:9). Said he, "Though the mountains be shaken and the hills removed, yet my unfailing love for you will not be shaken nor will my covenant of peace be removed" (Isa. 54:10).

Today's disasters are considered "natural", but they are cautionary signals heralding end-times when there will be "fearful events and great signs from heaven" (Lk. 21:11). Sadly, these will escalate in number and severity as the Day of the Lord approaches.

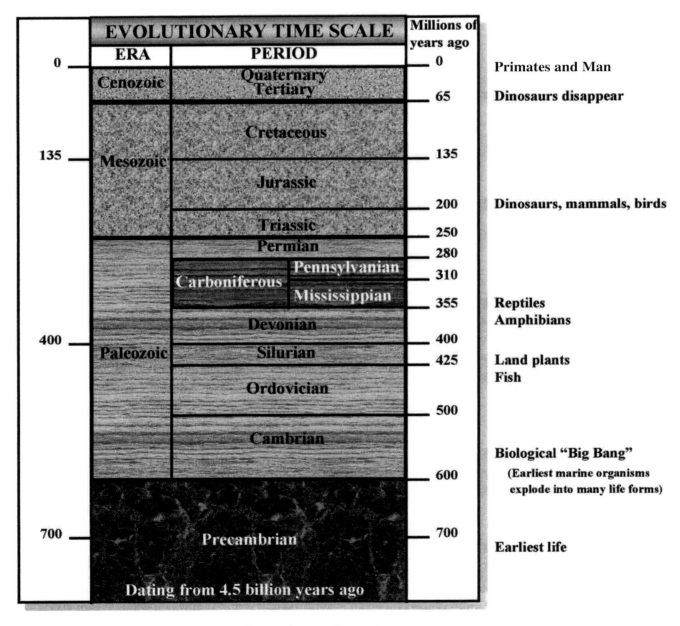

Figure 3: The Geologic Column

Uniformitarian geologists view the fossils as in a column built up over hundreds of millions of years, the older formations buried beneath the younger; the very oldest composed of inorganic materials, mostly crystalline in structure. These theories were introduced by James Hutton, popularized by Sir Charles Lyell, and later adopted by Darwin. Holding to this framework, 19ᵗʰ century geologists began labeling the strata, marking an age for each formation according to **index fossils** (based on the time "required" for each biological organism to have evolved). Simpler fossils were viewed as originating in the lower strata; the more complex (presumably arriving later) being located toward the top. As we shall see, however, the **geologic column** tells us about deposition but not about evolution.

There is geophysical evidence that something of great significance happened in the past. Prior to radiometric dating, the geologic record was divided into relative time units using the index fossils. Contrary to common opinion, the geologic column was devised (before 1860) by catastrophists – not uniformitarians. **Evolutionists** (claiming that successive layers of superimposed sediments were historical happenings, not just hypothetical) saw the strata as proof for their theories. **Creationists**, however, saw the column as squaring with flood geology and biblical chronology, given the following sequence of events:

Day 1: Light and darkness
Day 2: Earth's atmosphere
Day 3: Dry land, seas, plants, and trees
Day 4: Sun, moon, and stars
Day 5: Sea creatures and birds
Day 6: Land animals, creeping things, and humans

> **Comparing the *paired scenarios* of evolution and creation, there is a clash between two perspectives, each firmly held and deeply religious.**

Darwin was unable to say *how* life evolved, but he was convinced that it *did* evolve, thinking the answer would be in the fossils. But what do we know about them? One answer is that there are billions of them – all over the world. Referring to them, Gish wrote, "These formations include the vast Tibetan Plateau, 750,000 square miles of sedimentary deposits many thousands of feet in thickness and now at an elevation of three miles; the Karoo formation in Africa, which has been estimated by Robert Broom to contain the fossils of 800 billion vertebrate animals; the herring fossil bed in the Miocene shales of California, containing evidence that a billion fish died within a four square mile area; and the Cumberland Bone Cave of Maryland, containing fossilized remains of dozens of species of mammals, from bats to mastodons, along with the fossils of some reptiles and birds – including animals which now have accommodated to different climates and habitats from the Arctic region to tropical zones."[2]

Note well that the evolutionary timetable was established at least a century before radiometric dating. And yet the geologic column became the backbone of evolutionary theory (see **Figure 3**). Toward the bottom of that column are three rocky systems so similar that they can be considered together – the Cambrian (600 million years ago), the Ordovician (500 million years ago), and the Silurian (425 million years ago). Within these, the first marine organisms supposedly exploded into many life forms, ranging from land plants to vertebrates. Next in line are the Devonian rocks (400 million years ago) with their preponderance of fish and fishlike forms, including the first amphibians – some now extinct, leaving no representatives in our world. The next higher system (355 million years ago) is the Mississippian which is much like the Devonian, its sharks and reptiles having evolved in a warm, humid climate.

Some entirely new plants are thought to have emerged during the later/cooler/drier Pennsylvanian/Permian period (310-280 million years ago) while glaciation and mountain-building were occurring. Many of these (trees, ferns, and coal-forming plants) are quite different from today's. In the next series there are other surprises: Triassic-Jurassic-Cretacious layers (250-65 million years ago) containing great reptiles, dinosaurs, and trees unlike those in the lower layers: gymnosperms, maples, oaks, and flowering plants. Above these are complicated sediments known as Tertiary/Quaternary, above which are the remains of early humans along with fossilized flora and fauna like those of today. However, a closer look will yield very different answers!

Though widespread in distribution, fossils can be misleading. They change over time, degrading into fragments; at times being removed entirely from the record. Many processes (mechanical, chemical, and radiological) lower their grade, rank, and status. And every system is subject to these processes, though they may not be well understood.

Fossils are arranged in sedimentary beds displaying stratification, inversion, tilting, warping, superimposition, etc. Some see only *local* flooding in these strata, but why would the fossils be everywhere? And why did the world's climates change so suddenly, drastically, and diffusely? Why, if the Flood was local, do we find its after-effects in France, Germany, the Americas, Africa, Asia, Israel, Australia, and globally? The question is, what makes more sense, *many local floods* or *one generalized flood*?

But here is the greater mystery! If creatures were *evolving* during those Paleozoic, Mesozoic, and Cenozoic Eras, shouldn't there be an abundance of *transitional fossils* progressing toward phyla, classes, orders, and families? If simplicity led to complexity, shouldn't we in fact be finding so many intermediates that they would be filling our museums?

Wouldn't there be infinitely more transitions than the completed creatures they became? And shouldn't we be encountering a host of incremental changes, partial and complete, failed and successful (trials and errors) showing proto-organs advancing to organs – not just the abrupt appearance of totally new creatures but also multitudes of intermediates climaxing in sophisticated organisms? Isn't that the idea behind gradualism? Hosts of *evolutionary links?*

Darwin knew that evolution requires links, so how did he account for the fossil record?[3] As a confirmed gradualist, he never lost faith in his theory, but now that we're in the 21st century (and Darwin's links are missing still) geologists are admitting that whole groups of species appear suddenly; not at the end of an evolutionary chain. Darwin knew this, too, seeing that the fossil evidence was the most obvious and severe objection to his theory. Yet he refused to concede his position.

Already in Darwin's day eminent geologists and paleontologists were pointing to *immutability of the species*. Darwin argued that the linkage problem, while serious, was not fatal to his reasoning, stating that the fossil record is imperfect (always hoping that time would be on his side, surfacing more intermediaries over the years). But time has only exacerbated the problem, so gradualism no longer works, not in today's world!
As noted by Gish:

> If evolution produced millions of species, including many thousands of different basic morphologic designs, via intermediates whereby urchins changed into fish, fins changed into legs, scales changed into feathers, forelimbs changed into wings, legs changed into flippers, ape-like skulls changed into human skulls, etc., why can't evolutionists imagine what the intermediates may have looked like? Perhaps Gould and Eldredge have tried. They may have attempted, for example, to imagine what viable, functional intermediates between a land animal and a whale may have looked like. Evolutionists have suggested that some hairy, four-legged mammal, perhaps something that resembled a pig, a cow, a buffalo (or a carnivore of some kind) ventured into the water in search of food or sanctuary. Over eons of time, it is imagined that a tail changed into flukes, the hind legs gradually disappeared, the front legs changed into flippers, nostrils gradually migrated to the top of the head, and the skin was replaced by a heavy coat of blubber – just to name a few of the changes required.[4]

From this we see that evolutionists argue in spite of the evidences, not because of them. Claiming that transitions aren't so important after all, many are holding to old-fashioned ideas, so gradualism is still the dominant theme in texts and documentaries. Yet it is because of the evidences themselves that creationists have been dismantling Darwinism.

Gould at least acknowledged the fossil problem in two areas: 1) *Stasis:* the lack of directional change (fossils look the same when they "disappear" as when they first "appear"), and 2) *Abrupt appearance:* the sudden arrival of fully-formed species overlapping in time with their alleged ancestors and descendants. Others see the fossils as a reflection of "mosaic evolution" and "stabilizing selection". Mosaic evolution means that soft body parts were evolving invisibly while the fossilized parts remained the same, showing no biological transitions although they were in fact occurring. Stabilizing selection means that natural choice prevented change, eliminating innovations for millions of years despite conditions that should have encouraged adaptive innovation. In either case, there would need to be magical jumps as in Gould's "punctuated equilibrium."[5] But these are all jumps into Wonderland!

Clinging to their old orthodoxy, Darwinists say that the record *has* provided transitional forms after all. The Academy of Sciences claims this too, alleging so many intermediates between fish and amphibians, amphibians and reptiles, reptiles and mammals, and even along the primate line, that it is often difficult to identify the line to which a specific genus or species belongs.[6] Despite this optimism, however, the Academy is in error and every objective paleontologist knows it.

As mentioned in *Darwin's Leap of Faith*, "We are now about 120 years after Darwin and the knowledge of the fossil record has been greatly expanded. We now have a quarter of a million fossil species but the situation hasn't changed much. The record of evolution is still surprisingly jerky, and ironically we have even fewer examples of evolutionary transition now than in Darwin's time. The truth is, the fossil record is composed entirely of *gaps*."[7] (See also *The Cambrian Explosion*, Chap. 13.)

Cracks in the Column

The trees of the Lord are well watered. […] There the birds make their nests;
the stork has its home in the pine trees. The high mountains belong to the wild goats;
the crags are a refuge for the coneys (Ps. 104:16-19).

The discovery of *Archaeopteryx*, an extinct bird with reptilian features, satisfied many that a transition had been found, especially when placed alongside other presumably transitional forms: *Pikaia* among the chordates, *Baragwanathia* among the lycopods, *Ichthyostega* among the amphibians, *Purgatorius* among primates, *Pakicetus* among whales, and *Proconsul* among the hominoids.[8] But none of these is convincing, not even the so-called "stratomorphic intermediates": Anthracosaurs (between amphibians and reptiles), Phenacodeontids (between horses and their supposed ancestors), and mammal-like reptiles – none of which have *intermediate structures*.[9]

The fact is, all organisms are locked into their kinds from the outset, displaying neither evolving morphologies nor proto-organs. Even the down-covered tyrannosaurs supposedly linking reptiles with birds (announced by the Chinese Academy of Geological Sciences and the American Museum of Natural History) show no evolutionary ancestry. As reported in the January 25, 2001 issue of *USA Today*, they are yet another hoax. The Bible tells us birds were created on Day 5 and Dinosaurs on Day 6, so (more than a century post-Darwin) evolutionists are still stuck with intergenerational gaps, which isn't at all surprising to creationists!

In addition to the ubiquitous absence of transitions, the geologic column has other problems, in part because it was fabricated from a combination of partial remains from many sites. G.R. Morton claims that the complete column actually exists in basins around the world, but this is disputed by Woodmorappe (on the basis of columnar thinness, fossil evidences, etc.). Even Grand Canyon, one of the best examples, has fewer than half the systems required for such a column, and reworking them is no more convincing.

Complete or not, the column is jinxed! When each of its supporting arguments is thoroughly examined, the end result is totally unimpressive given the reliance on index fossils, transitions, exceptions, and eons. While dating **rocks from fossils** and **fossils from rocks** may strike some as fitting with inductive reasoning, this method is as shaky as the tenets from which it was built. To make the layers fit Darwin's time-scale, geologists have come up with tongue-twisters like "unconformities", "nonconformities", "paraconformities", and "disconformities", but these tell us nothing about eons. The only way to have non-depositional (erosional) demarcations between the strata is to disclaim geologic continuity, a mindset as circular as the index fossils themselves (given the insistence on gradualism, or smoothness).[10] Gradualism is the step-by-step superimposition of sediments (stratigraphic succession) involving lengthy timetables for those drawn-out "eras" *required by evolution*.

One could go on to discuss the coexistence of dinosaur tracks with human footprints (as in the beds of Paluxy, Texas) and cave art portraying dragons (in the grottos of France), but the evolutionary time scale has more serious problems still, seeing that we haven't yet considered its inability to explain fossil-bearing mountain tops, fluvial plains, terraced rivers, incised meanders, vast ice-sheets, and the widespread dispersal of bones, all of which are readily explained by *catastrophism* and *zonation*.

During Noah's day, the great springs of the deep burst forth and the skies were opened wide for forty days and nights. All the high mountains under the heavens were covered, and waters inundated the earth for 150 days. As a result, everything that had the breath of life in its nostrils died (Ge. 7: 11-24). Should such a tragedy occur today, wouldn't marine life be buried in the lowest sediments (save for upward thrusting, volcanization, and generalized chaos)? Wouldn't land animal be entombed higher (though the churning deeps could produce exceptions here as well)? Wouldn't quicker creatures (mammals and birds) retreat to higher grounds still? And wouldn't humans with superior cerebral capacity end up in the highest sediments of all, just as we see in the strata?

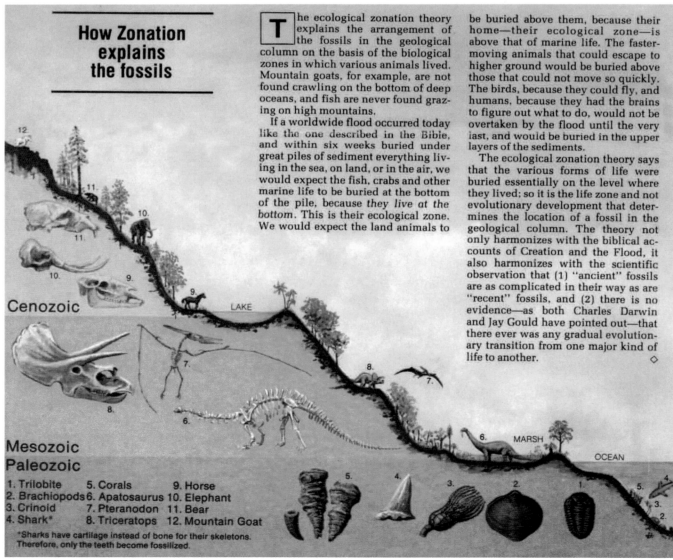

How Zonation explains the fossils

The ecological zonation theory explains the arrangement of the fossils in the geological column on the basis of the biological zones in which various animals lived. Mountain goats, for example, are not found crawling on the bottom of deep oceans, and fish are never found grazing on high mountains.

If a worldwide flood occurred today like the one described in the Bible, and within six weeks buried under great piles of sediment everything living in the sea, on land, or in the air, we would expect the fish, crabs and other marine life to be buried at the bottom of the pile, because *they live at the bottom*. This is their ecological zone. We would expect the land animals to

be buried above them, because their home—their ecological zone—is above that of marine life. The faster-moving animals that could escape to higher ground would be buried above those that could not move so quickly. The birds, because they could fly, and humans, because they had the brains to figure out what to do, would not be overtaken by the flood until the very last, and would be buried in the upper layers of the sediments.

The ecological zonation theory says that the various forms of life were buried essentially on the level where they lived; so it is the life zone and not evolutionary development that determines the location of a fossil in the geological column. The theory not only harmonizes with the biblical accounts of Creation and the Flood, it also harmonizes with the scientific observation that (1) "ancient" fossils are as complicated in their way as are "recent" fossils, and (2) there is no evidence—as both Charles Darwin and Jay Gould have pointed out—that there ever was any gradual evolutionary transition from one major kind of life to another.   ◇

Cenozoic

Mesozoic
Paleozoic

1. Trilobite   5. Corals   9. Horse
2. Brachiopods 6. Apatosaurus 10. Elephant
3. Crinoid   7. Pteranodon   11. Bear
4. Shark*   8. Triceratops   12. Mountain Goat

*Sharks have cartilage instead of bone for their skeletons. Therefore, only the teeth become fossilized.

Figure 4: (© Signs of the Times, 9/'82, reprinted by permission)

Truth is, the results of such a deluge would be very much like what we see in Grand Canyon today where viewing the strata is like a walk from the bottom of the ocean across tidal zones and on into the uplands, not at all like a walk through evolutionary time![11]

There are also evidences related to land plants, trilobites, and misplaced fossils, as in these comments by Parker and Morris :

> Evolutionists believe that land plants didn't appear until over 100 million years after the Cambrian trilobites died out. Yet over sixty genera of woody plants, spores, pollen, and wood itself have been recovered from the lowest "trilobite rock" (Cambrian) throughout the world. [...] Most evolutionists still believe that land plants didn't evolve until much later. The creationist says, "we think the land plants and the Cambrian trilobites lived at the same time in different ecological zones". Normally, these sea animals and land plants would not be preserved together for ecological reasons, but a few plant specimens escaping decay could occasionally be entombed with trilobites in ocean sediment, and that's what we see.
>
> Footprints of man and dinosaurs together also represent "misplaced fossils". Misplaced fossils are common enough that evolutionists have a vocabulary to deal with them. A specimen found "too low" in the geologic column (before it was supposed to have evolved) is called a "stratigraphic leak", and a specimen found "too high" is called a "re-worked specimen".[12]

Trilobites were from the sea and dinosaurs from the land, so common sense tells us that trilobites, were they alive today, would still not be found among land animals and trees. Why not? Because God created each according to its kind, designing them for their particular locales – padded paws for ice and prehensile appendages for branches – which is why polar bears occupy icebergs and orangutans the forests. God then destroyed them, arranging their remains in understandable ways, so the **Paleozoic** trilobites, brachiopods, crinoids, and corals are found most often in the lowest deposits, below the Apastosaurus, Pteranodon, and Triceratops of the **Mesozoic** – these being below the **Cenozoic** horse, elephant, bear, and mountain goat, none of them showing transitional forms. The fact is, the column makes sense only within the framework of Scripture. "Creation wins hands down, and so does the Flood," said Gish. "There is simply no contest!"[13]

The Bible needs no vindication of course, but there is parallel evidence from Mount St. Helens. Within hours of its eruption, hurricane-velocity flows produced a 25-foot block of layering, superimposed over earlier air-fall debris. Overlying these layers were thinner, but massive, mud-flow deposits. And what does this look like today? A miniature Grand Canyon (on a scale of 1:40), its laminar layers resembling those of the geologic column but formed within *months*, not *eons*.

The bottom line? If Mount St. Helens didn't come from eons, neither did Grand Canyon. As we know from Genesis 6:5, Grand Canyon formed because "the Lord saw how great man's wickedness on the earth had become and that every inclination of the thoughts of his heart was only evil all the time". Consequently, "every living thing on the face of the earth was wiped out" (Ge. 7:23)! The remains of that disaster are a testimony to God, not evolution.

Chronometric Dating

Adam lived 930 years, and then he died (Ge. 5:5).
Methuselah lived 969 years, and then he died (Ge. 5:27).

Adam was 130 years old when Seth was born, and he had sons and daughters for years afterward. Methuselah had children after becoming the father of Lamech, at 187 years of age. Such proclivity is unheard of today, even with stem cells and transplants. How could Methuselah have lived so long? Was he perhaps an adolescent in his 80's? What would his teeth and brows have looked like after 900 years? Was he stoop-shouldered and hunch-backed, given his age and nutrition?

How should we view history? Did the sun's shadow actually reverse by ten steps, as in Isaiah 38:8, or is this merely a story? Who monitored the newborn stars? Did they radiate and die like ours? Were the rocks of Eden radioactive? If so, did they contain parent atoms only, or radioactive daughters as well? How consistent was their decay over time, and what can our indicators tell us about them? How should we decide these questions? Certainly not by disrespecting science or scientists, though they admittedly do make mistakes. Wisdom implies respect for the scriptures, objectivity in science, and a critical appraisal of what each of these can tell us about origins. But many don't take these things seriously.

To see how chronometric dating works in principle, *one could examine a well-preserved clam embedded in limestone*.[14] To date it , we might consider carbon-14, the radioactive constituent in all living organisms. However, carbon-14, with its short half-life, is accurate to only several thousand years. Moreover, since fossils are *rocky* and carbon-14 cannot be used to date *rock*, we would need other methods to date this particular clam.

Knowing also that certain rocks cannot be dated by any radiometric method, we could compare this clam with fossils used to date rocks (e.g., trilobites dating the Cambrian). If a similar fossil from a list of "index fossils" existed 300 million years ago, we could date our clam and its mineral surroundings from about that age. However, we would need to ask ourselves first, "How were the index fossils dated?"

Driving all old-earth assumptions is the need for *time*. Even before radioactivity was discovered (in the late 1800s), the complexity of biological organisms was evident, so age estimates were growing longer. Index fossils were therefore placed in an artificial context where the "older" were seen as in the lower strata and the "younger" in the higher, always allowing plenty of time for the assumed transformations. With that as the backdrop, rocks were then dated from fossils and fossils from rocks.

Understanding the vagaries of such methods, *suppose we wanted to date rocks above or below this clam*, like the hardened material from the earth's mantle. Radioactivity is like a clock, so scientists are able to date certain rocks (e.g., recent lavas) by the decay of their components. Examining comparable ones, we could perhaps derive a mathematical age for our sample, knowing something about initial conditions, decay rates, atomic ratios, and half-lives, assuming also that this material started out with parent substances only. Radioactive parents decay into daughter substances, and increasing ratios of daughters are produced with time. Accordingly, the ratio of daughters to parents might determine the age of a sample. A ratio of zero would indicate no age at all; any higher ratio would mean an older age. The existence of daughters only (no parent elements) would mean an age-ratio of infinity.

Granites and basalts contain radioactive elements, but because of heat during the formation of igneous rocks they would contain no fossils (fossils occur mostly in sedimentary rock). Realizing this, we could grind our rock into a powder, isolating its minerals for computer-analysis. Methods for this would vary, depending on the sample, but they would commonly involve lead-uranium, potassium-argon, strontium-rubidium, or one of the more esoteric isotope combinations. Using any one of these methods, we could measure the decay of parents into daughters, whether daughters existed initially or were added later. Comparison assays could then be made, but the results would vary with the *assumptions*.

Each radioactive element has its own half-life, the length of time for half of it to decay. The half-life for potassium 40, for example, is 1.3 billion years. It exists in most geologic materials and decays into argon (an inert gas). Using potassium-argon (or methods like it), scientists have come up with lengthy geological ages. They say also that their techniques are accurate to within a few percentage points, that they agree amongst themselves, and that there are few anomalous readings.

For the rocky material under consideration, the all-important question is this: Where was it found and what are the characteristics of any near-by fossils? If it came from below a "300 million year old clam", it must be older than the clam itself (barring unusual circumstances). If additional assays indicated a significantly later date, only those methods consistent with the time parameters of the fossil bed would be accepted. We see then that radiometry is based on *old-earth assumptions*, and the guesses driving them never seem to die!

To function like a clock, chronometers would need the following: 1) an observable geophysical process with measurable, quantitative descriptors, 2) a well-characterized past history, and 3) a known rate of change over time. Given these, one could trust chronometers if the following were also true: 1) the initial state is known, 2) it is known that the initial state changed over time, 3) the pattern of change is clearly discernible, and 4) there has been no contamination of the data by changing decay rates or the intrusion of foreign substances, either of which would invalidate the results.

To satisfy these requirements, one would need more information than is usually available, so the assumption of radio-consistency over thousands of millennia has to stretch one's imagination to the limit. Decay byproducts (e.g., argon, radon, helium) are mobile, so deformation, pressure, and heating of rocks can affect their isotopes. Water can transport their contents as well, leaching and re-depositing them, resetting the hands of the clock. Neutrinos can also interact with atomic nuclei, so any hyper-density of them could have sped up radio-decay, making rocks look older than they actually are.

Knowing the limitations of chronometric dating, we can assume radio-consistency, but many factors can invalidate the results. As for agreement among the various tests, geologists claim that the percentage of anomalies is very low, but there are actually *many* such anomalies. As mentioned by geologist Steven Austin, "A careful study of the isotopic abundances of three important geologic units of Grand Canyon shows that *no* coherent picture of 'age' emerges. [...] If we embrace the popular assumptions of radioisotope dating for Grand Canyon rocks, we can make a case for the *youngest* rocks being deeply buried within the Precambrian strata and the *oldest* rocks being on the surface among the Quaternary strata. Such an interpretation is, of course, contrary to the fundamental superimposition of Grand Canyon rocks worked out by geologists!"[15]

But when several chronometers all point to the same age, wouldn't this convergence be self-confirming? Not at all! Some may be convinced by such comparisons, but we simply haven't enough information to come to these conclusions.[16] Scientifically speaking, we must know the informational content of our assertions and whether or not they can be substantiated, and that's not as easy as it might seem! Why accept even one such method when they all share the same deficiencies? Isn't this the reason behind observable, verifiable processes in the first place?

Not having the key data, isn't it obvious that we need a fresh appraisal of the methods and greater openness to alternatives? Having used radioisotopes myself in surgery, I can say quite frankly that there are exacting standards for testing, involving basal conditions, decay rates, ratios, sensitivity, dilution, contamination, background noise, etc. The concern is that radiometric dating (driven by bias) skirts these very requirements. "The problem", says Austin, "lies not in the techniques used to determine the abundances of isotopes, but in the assumptions used to make the interpretation of great age."[17]

Were you or I to have a brain scan under similar circumstances, we could be in serious trouble! Instead of radio-consistency, there are wide ranging discordances, as listed in Woodmorappe's ten pages of divergent age-values for igneous and metamorphic rocks (see *Studies in Flood Geology*).[18] Methodological flaws are based on 1) selective acceptance of isotopic data, 2) attempts to explain away discrepant data, and 3) artificial imposition of time-values based on old-earth guesses. Except for certain lavas, the true history of rocks will therefore always be in question since no scientist has lived long enough to observe them over the years.

Recent Creation?

Geologists at the Danish Center for Earth System Science reported in April, 2000, that low oxygen levels in the earliest atmosphere prevented the burst of biological organisms until late in geological history. They based this on the presumed connection between past oxygen concentrations and sedimentary sulfates (containing oxygen), claiming that these sulfates came from bacteria. Observing bacteria near hydrothermal vents, they then concluded that significant oxygen levels did not accumulate until the late Proterozoic Era, 700 million years ago. For a split second one might buy this, except for the usual disclaimers: "probably", "presumably", and "perhaps".

Employing similarly flawed methods, scientists have come up with results far afield from the known ages of certain substances. Examples are these: 1) Wood growing from living trees, dated by carbon-14 at ten thousand years of age, 2) living snails dated at 2,300 years using the same method, 3) 200 year old lava flows dated at 3 billion years, 4) recently-formed lavas at Mount St. Helens yielding dates in excess of two million years, and 5) fifty year old lava flows at Mt. Ngauruhoe, New Zealand, dated at 3.5 million years. Even within a single sample there can be wild fluctuations – e.g., moon rocks dated anywhere from 2 million to 28 billion years.[19] And researchers have observed similar discordances all along!

To eliminate the problem of initial conditions, geologists use discordia curves, but isochron assays of suites of rocks (supposedly of the same age) are based on *fundamental uncertainties*, so we're left with strata that may simulate *eons* or *no age at all*. Primordial neutrinos, as already noted, could have reset many atomic clocks, including those of potassium-argon and uranium-lead, distorting the age of the earth.

As an added observation, while radiometric chronometers may be interesting exercises, they can never negate the Bible. By the end of the creation week, Earth's rocks were only six days old (having been of zero-age at their inception), so why ridicule the notion that a multibillion year history should be viewed with suspicion? The evidences can be placed more credibly within a young-earth model, as shown by some gifted geologists. Though not to defend all their arguments, they have stated effectively that none of today's methods can substantiate those prolonged ages of naturalism. While their research endeavors may lag at times behind those of their evolutionary colleagues, that isn't surprising considering the relative size and funding of the two parties.[20]

In actual practice, radiometric dating hasn't worked very well, and it has been regularly criticized. So, as J. D. Morris observes, "we may be witnessing the demise of a failed theory." Keep in mind that creation and evolution are separate views of history – neither of which is occurring today. Stressing this, creationists have focused on methodological errors, but they are now focusing on original conditions (isotopic history). The force behind this is the "Rate Group" (for **R**adioisotopes and the **A**ge of **T**he **E**arth). Heading their efforts are leading scientists in geology, geochemistry, and physics, sponsored by the Institute for Creation Research and the Creation Research Society.

Although the jury is still out (and will be for some time), intense radiation may have existed during the first few days of creation, occurring at a level that would be catastrophic today. During and right after the Flood, any number of disturbances could have given rocks the appearance of age, invalidating isotopic dating generally. Unusual influences might have included cosmic explosions, neutrino and/or gamma ray fluxes, declining magnetic fields, and catastrophic tectonics. These possibilities may have problems of their own, including the biological hazards of radiation, heat generation, the doctrinal implications of perfection and decay, the quirks of geophysical catastrophes, etc., but "accelerated decay" (including as an explanation for shortened life spans) is at least up for discussion (see *Radioisotopes and the Age of the Earth* by Vardiman, Snelling, and Chaffin, I.C.R., 2000).

Where then did the geologic column originate? From tumultuous incidents in the past, impacting Earth's mantle, crust, and core. Right from the beginning, there must have been rearrangement and shuffling of molten, watery layers. The word "creation" means "to make habitable", and to make Eden habitable, igneous rocks formed from the upward flow of magma, carrying with them radioactive parents and daughters – or else incorporating daughters from the mix, giving rocks an apparent age when they had none at all. Another possibility is that the earliest minerals were not radioactive at all, becoming so only after the Fall. Later on, the Flood's fossils (most of them similar to the creatures of today) became lodged within pancakes laid down by incredible geological forces. Granting certain exceptions, the lowermost layers would have formed before the higher, but there is no evidence for lengthy ages either *within* or *between* them.

The bottom line? Admitting to uncertainties is better than glossing them over! Whether resulting from *inheritance, entropy, or catastrophe*, radio-decay is not as reliable as was thought, which may explain why man-made artifacts (a thimble, bell, gold chain, spoon, vase, screw, coin, doll, hammer, nails, etc.) were found embedded in layers said to be hundreds of millions of years old.[21]

But while today's chronometers may be crumbling, one thing is still rock solid: *the account of Moses*.

Every word of God is flawless ...
Do not add to his words, or he will rebuke you and prove you a liar.

(Pr. 30:5-6)

[1] Kay Gudnason, *Rings in the Redwoods*, Big Trees Press, Felton, CA, 1972, p. 283

[2] Duane T. Gish, *Evolution, The Fossils Say NO!* ICR Publishing Company, San Diego, CA, 1973, p. 40

[3] Phillip E. Johnson, *Darwin On Trial*, InterVarsity Press, Downers Grove, IL, 1993, pp. 46-47

[4] Duane T. Gish, *Creation Scientists Answer Their Critics*, ICR, El Cajon, CA, 1993, pp. 136,137

[5] Phillip E. Johnson, *Darwin On Trial*, InterVarsity Press, Downers Grove, IL, 1993, p. 53

[6] As quoted from The National Center for Science Education, Inc. *Voices for Evolution*, p. 56 – see Ankerberg & Weldon's *Darwin's Leap of Faith*, Harvest House Publishers, Eugene, OR, 1998, p. 211

[7] John Ankerberg and John Weldon, *Darwin's Leap of Faith*, Harvest House Publishers, Eugene, OR, 1998, pp. 212-213

[8] Ibid, p. 219

[9] Ibid, p. 219

[10] Henry M. Morris and Gary E. Parker, *What is Creation Science?* Creation-Life Publishers, San Diego, CA, 1983, p. 198

[11] Ibid, p. 131

[12] Ibid, p. 131,132

[13] Duane T. Gish, *Creation Scientists Answer Their Critics*, ICR, El Cajon, CA, 1993, p. 112

[14] This section on dating clams is an application from *The Young Earth*, Master Books, Colorado Springs, CO, 1994, Chapter 1, (*What Do the Rocks Say?*)

[15] Steven A. Austin, *Grand Canyon, Monument to Catastrophe*, Institute for Creation Research, Santee, CA, 1994, p. 128-129

[16] Russell Maatman, *The Impact of Evolutionary Theory, A Christian View*, Dordt College Press, 1993, p. 58-59

[17] Steven A. Austin, *Grand Canyon, Monument to Catastrophe*, IRS, Santee, CA, 1994, p. 129

[18] John Woodmorappe, *Studies in Flood Geology*, Creation Research Society Quarterly, Vol. 16, 1978

[19] John Ankerberg & John Weldon, *Darwin's Leap of Faith*, Harvest House Publishers, Eugene, OR, 1998, p. 293

[20] Ibid, p. 290

[21] Joe White & Nocholas Comninellis, *Darwin's Demise*, Master Books, Green Forest, AR, 2001, p. 93

MUTABLE ENTITIES
(Chapter 13)

Surprise! The Trilobites!

The evolutionary paradigm assumes that life began in the Cambrian (Mesozoic Era) and continued climbing until finally, at the top, humans emerged. But the clock is way off! If evolution is true, the lower layers would contain mostly primitive life forms. Higher up, there would be gradual changes from simple to complex, with transitional forms en route. The creation model, in contrast, predicts the sudden, explosive appearance of highly complex, widely diverse life forms, as in the surprising appearance of trilobites in the Cambrian.

Trilobites are extinct. Labeled as marine creatures and often regarded as primitive, they were in fact among the most complex of invertebrates. They "appear" suddenly in the deepest sediments, having been discovered in higher layers also in what appeared to be the fossilized footprints of a man's sandal (discovered in Utah in 1968, by William Meister).

Resembling arthropods, trilobites are classified with lobsters, crabs, scorpions, spiders, and insects. In the geological strata, they are the lowermost multicellular life forms displaying hard parts. Their shells are divided into three sections (or lobes) – the head, thorax, and tail – *tri* for three and ***lobite*** for lobes. They had advanced organ systems, including a circulatory system, jointed legs, antennae, muscles, gills, and an intricate nervous system. Trilobites' eyes incorporated some of the most sophisticated optics ever found in organisms, involving Abbe's Sine Law, Fermat's Principle, and Snell's Law of Refraction. They consisted of multiple lenses, each correcting for spherical aberration, allowing them to see undistorted images under water.[1]

Trilobites are anything but primitive. They appear suddenly in the record, fully formed, totally functional, and without ancestry. In the layers beneath them, there are no precursors, countering evolutionary theory itself. From the naturalistic perspective, there is no explanation for their origin. Such remarkably elaborate creatures, appearing so abruptly, could have come only from the fiat creation of a brilliant Designer.

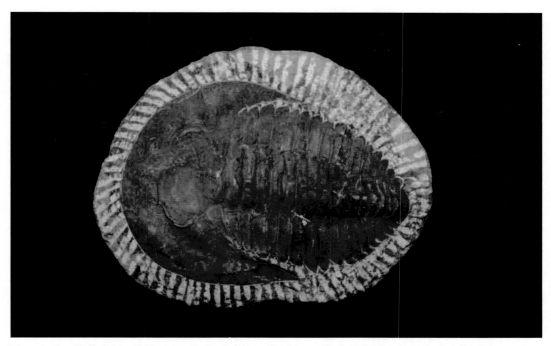

Figure 5: Trilobite (1/2 actual size) from the so-called "Early Cambrian", Morocco.

Cambrian Explosion

Geologists tell us that the rocks at the bottom of the geologic column began forming 600 million years ago. In this thick Cambrian layer there are billions of complicated invertebrates: sponges, snails, clams, brachiopods, jellyfish, trilobites, worms, sea urchins, sea cucumbers, sea lilies, etc. They supposedly evolved from single-celled organisms over a relatively brief period of time on the evolutionary calendar.[2] However, they are all without forerunners, as if entering the highway of life without an on-ramp!

Slightly higher are the vertebrates, and beneath the Cambrian is the fossil-rare Precambrian. Its rocks are derived from vulcansim, magma, mountain building, etc. This stratum is thousands of feet thick and perfectly suitable for the preservation of fossils, but it shows no trace of precursors for the dramatic explosion of almost every life form just one layer up. What we find instead is a huge gap between non-living matter and life itself. Given also the discontinuity between single-celled organisms and invertebrates, we have a gap "so immense and indisputable that any further discussion of the fossil record becomes superfluous."[3] Thus, Darwin's phylogenetic tree is broken at the root, but just as severely as at its trunk and branches (between invertebrates and vertebrates in the immediately adjacent Ordovician period).

Cambrian fossils have "modern" body parts but no proto-organs. But why would sophisticated organisms have sprung forth so suddenly? Because, according to evolutionists, at this time in history atmospheric oxygen had finally reached the threshold for life, permitting the explosive branching of new life forms. Yet metal-oxides can be found two billion years earlier, if one holds to the notion of "billions". And even with all the oxygen in the world the problem remains the same: There is no pathway for new phyla and classes.

The Cambrian explosion is pictured as **"The Biological Big Bang"**. Its most striking feature is the sudden burst of general body plans out of nowhere, each creature having its distinctive blueprint from the time of its first arrival, like the abrupt appearance of a forest (as creationists see it), rather than the gradual arrival of a tree (as evolutionists see it). Animal history is thus an explosion, followed by quiescence, after which no new taxonomic types arrived, fitting perfectly with created "kinds" in the beginning.[4]

Right from the start there was a "written plan" for every organism, its **"Blauplan"**. Quoting from Wallace's *Evolutionary Biology*, Paul Nelson writes: "The *Blauplan* of an organism can be thought of as the arrangement of genetic switches that control the course of the embryonic and subsequent development of the individual, and such control must operate properly both in time generally and sequentially in the separately differentiated tissues. Selection, both natural and artificial, that leads to morphological change and other developmental modification does so by altering the settings and triggerings of these switches. The extreme difficulty (when attempting to transform one organism into another but still functioning one) lies in the difficulty in resetting a number of the many controlling switches in a manner that still allows for the individual's orderly (somatic) development."[5]

The hitch is, there is genetic "bicoid" controlling the development of body parts, but it comes from *parental DNA*, having had to come from somewhere. Without it there is no pathway for morphologic change, no matter how long the time-frame. Simply put, if DNA doesn't provide the program for new body-plans, they couldn't arrive. As Nelson sees it, "No answer is forthcoming from neo-Darwinism or from the filtering mesh of our biological knowledge taken broadly. [...] Rather, we have stumbled into a landscape of paradoxes. Key embryonic regulators, apparently similar at the genetic level, are employed in building very different morphological endpoints. [...] Flies and mice are – well – flies and mice."[6] They become what they are because of their forbears' bicoid initiating new body parts, and it's never the reverse.

The Biological Bang, *Time Magazine*'s cover story of a few years ago, presents an enigma for Darwinists. Though realizing this, they refuse to move out of their evolutionary paradigm, always hoping for an answer yet fearing that there won't be one. Even having no fossils at all, the problem would persist, for it is has to do with how animals are built. Why is this so unsettling? Because Darwin said that evolution begins with intra-populational variation and ends with all the varying phyla, orders, families, genera, and species. Lacking a transfer mechanism, however, there is an insurmountable leap from unicellular organisms to the remarkably complex phyla. And seeing that the number of phyla is increasing as paleontologists continue searching, the problem of body plans is accelerating (since there is no informational pathway for them).

The "lowly" roundworm (*C. elegans*) has only exacerbated the evolutionary predicament. Scientists know its sequences, but what seemed simple to Watson and Crick is no longer so. To make a protein, the cell needs help from hormones and enzymes, and it needs to know when to turn them on and off. Even supposedly simple worms have byzantine patterns of words with sprawls of sequences providing instructions for their cells. So, although the details are not fully understood, the earthworm is lowly no more, considering its recipe for life. As Watson remarked, recalling when DNA was first unraveled, "The great and wonderful thing about DNA back then was that it seemed so simple. Initially everyone liked DNA. It's not that we dislike it now, but its frightening trying to figure out what you do with all that complexity. My brain can't handle it."[7]

The name "elegans" is fitting indeed. Every roundworm begins with an egg, the oocyte, containing the full complement of maternal genes. Once fertilized, it becomes a single-celled zygote. From the fused genetic material in that zygote, new worms are built by cell division, a process immutable from one generation to the next. There is always a cell lineage for specialized tissues, including a nervous system, musculature, etc., with the goal of becoming a complete worm. Cell division serves no purpose, however, unless it results in creatures with functionality. For such to exist, all the lineages must unite into a final body plan. That plan boasts a mouth, a pharynx, a clump-like brain, a circulatory system, a crop, a gizzard, paired nephridia, an intestinal canal, propulsive setae, and reproductive organs. Each adult worm therefore has the complexity of a finely-tuned machine!

Even the simplest organism has its characteristic **blauplan**. For that, there must be paired genetic contributions, maternal and paternal in most cases, and new body plans must move away from "mom and dad". But moving out requires *specialized cells* dedicated to the formation of *novel structures* (cells not needed for routine morphogenesis). The problem is, the zygote has already *had* its marching orders, so there is no pathway for such novelty.

As with any marching band, forward movement means organization. No new orders, no new structures – no new structures, no new organisms! So what is natural selection based on? Nothing at all! Not only are there no undesignated cells, there aren't any new structures to aim for. In street language, natural selection can't "code for the road". There is no map, no route, and no vehicle! As mentioned, this isn't new to evolutionists, their having addressed the problem in terms of *teleological evolution* – evolution with an end-point. Neo-Darwinists need such an end point desperately, but they haven't delivered it – no matter how hard they have tried.

Knowing more now than Darwin ever did, scientists are realizing that something has to give. Even were a male pelican to hatch from a rattlesnake's egg, a matching female would be required at exactly the right time and place! According to Nelson, "Golden ages of evolution are postulated (e.g., the Cambrian explosion) in the absence of any mechanistic understanding, to accommodate the demands of a philosophy of nature that holds, in the face of abundant disconfirming evidence, that complex things come into existence by undirected mutation and selection from simpler things. And yet, however unlikely they may be, these golden ages of macroevolution are preferred by neo-Darwinians to taking at face value the limits of organismal structure and function – for those limits imply the primary discontinuity of organisms one from another".[8]

This is seen most clearly at the juncture between invertebrates and vertebrates, since nobody has found a mechanism for creatures with soft inner parts and hard outer parts to develop hard inner parts and soft outer parts. The likelihood that accidental mistakes could produce even a single new fundamental life pattern, coordinated at every step, is infinitely remote, let alone the appearance of fifty new phyla and over 300 new body plans all at once. To accept this is to believe (as Gould did) in magic! Christians need not cling to magic, however, since God's Word eliminates that necessity.

Our Mutable Globe

In Job 38, God asked his servant, "Who shut up the sea behind doors when it burst forth from the womb, when I made the clouds its garment? Have you journeyed to the springs of the sea or walked in the recesses of the deep? Who can tip over the water jars of the heavens when the dust becomes hard and the clods of earth stick together?" Job knew about God's fury, for there was a time when "all the springs of the great deep burst forth and the floodgates of the heavens were opened" (Ge. 7:11). But when the waters receded, Noah and the animals found their way to distant climes, much as God had guided them into the Ark earlier.

All the while that Planet Earth was being deluged from above, water and lava spouted out from below, creating basaltic volcanoes and immense oceanic rifts. This continued for forty days and nights, thrusting the layers upward and re-orienting their magnetism. Temperatures were oscillating so severely that polar ice would have quick-frozen millions of animals. Enormous pockets of plants were trapped under thousands of feet of water and silt, producing coal, oil, and gas. For years to come, as glacial activity advanced and abated, sediments at the continental shelves spread over the oceanic floors.

As for the skies, some think that the world's primeval vapor envelope declined considerably after the Flood. Though only a model, a dense canopy perhaps protected Paradise from harmful radiation, facilitating the growth of dinosaurs. Whether due to hyperbaric oxygenation, the greenhouse effect, or a combination of factors, dinosaurs grew to gigantic proportions. One such long-necked animal, 80 to 100 feet in length and weighing about 70 tons, lived on a lush coastal plain, now the Sahara. Scientists recently unearthed its remains and named it "Paralititan", placing it in the family *Artgentinosaurus* (Sauropods). But these seem to have died out shortly after Noah's day.

Following the Flood, rains, winds, and cold affected large parts of the world, although equatorial air eventually warmed most of it. In cycles and seasons, vast ice sheets began to thaw, and many antediluvian animals (e.g. the dinosaurs) could no longer survive. Others thrived only marginally. Humans got along well, however, although they remained mostly in the fertile crescent of the Mesopotamia Valley.

Then another great disaster struck. Because of the rising cacophony of sin, God punished humanity at Babel, though not this time with another flood (honoring his rainbow promise). Confusing people's tongues, he created a world of chaos, both psychological and social. Originally of one language, humans were thrown into turmoil by their garbled speech, so they scattered over the earth, God himself dispersing them (Ge. 11:1-8). At about that same time, the earth may have split into continents, a concept even unbelievers will accept.

Triggered by the puzzle-like fit between South America's eastern coast and Africa's western coast, Alfred Wegener published a paper in 1912, proposing the theory of ***continental drift***. Said he, if one could push today's continents into a single land mass, the fit would be nearly perfect. Wegener then coordinated this jigsaw-like puzzle with geologic and climatological data, claiming that all the continents were joined together some 200 million years ago into one enormous land mass which he called "Pangaea". During the ensuing millennia, according to him, Pangaea broke apart and the individual continents drifted toward their present location.

Note the naturalistic twist in Wallace's review of this (italics added):

> Geologists have long maintained that the earth's surface is a restless crust, constantly changing, sinking, and rising because of incredible unrelenting forces beneath it. These constant changes are now known to involve large, distinct segments of the crust known as plates. At certain edges of these masses, immense ridges are being thrust up, while other edges sink lower. Where plates are heaved together, the buckling at the edges has produced vast mountain ranges. When such ridges appear in the ocean floor, water is displaced and the oceans expand. An understanding of continental drift (plate tectonics) is vital to the study of the distribution of life on the planet today. It helps to explain the presence of tropical fossils in Antarctica, e.g., and the unusual animal life in Australia and South America. ***Continental drift provided just the sort of separation of sub-populations that would permit widespread speciation forming the basis for widely diverging groups of primitive organisms.***[9]

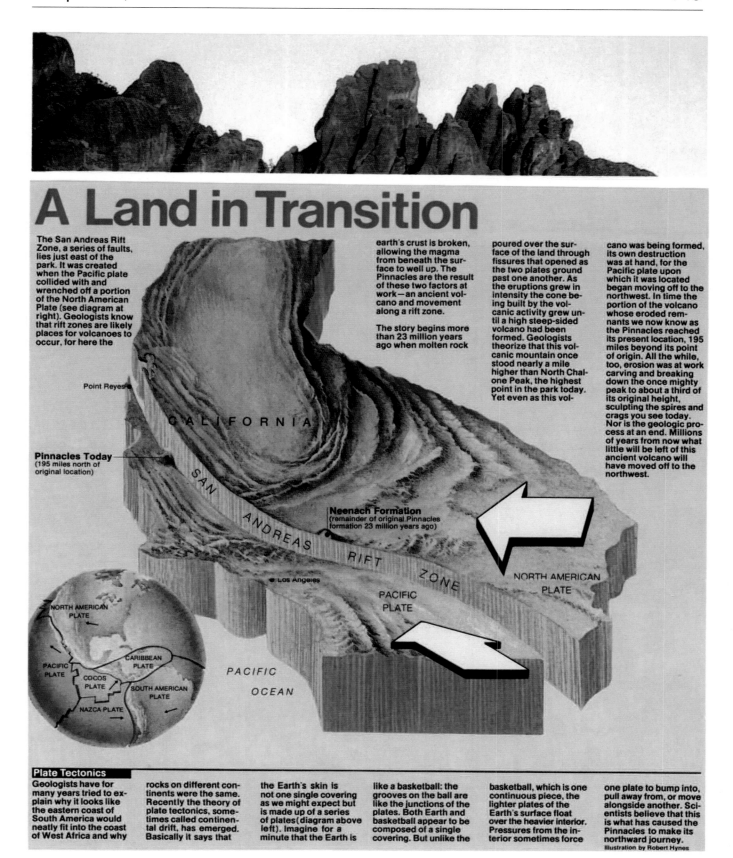

A Land in Transition

The San Andreas Rift Zone, a series of faults, lies just east of the park. It was created when the Pacific plate collided with and wrenched off a portion of the North American Plate (see diagram at right). Geologists know that rift zones are likely places for volcanoes to occur, for here the earth's crust is broken, allowing the magma from beneath the surface to well up. The Pinnacles are the result of these two factors at work—an ancient volcano and movement along a rift zone.

The story begins more than 23 million years ago when molten rock poured over the surface of the land through fissures that opened as the two plates ground past one another. As the eruptions grew in intensity the cone being built by the volcanic activity grew until a high steep-sided volcano had been formed. Geologists theorize that this volcanic mountain once stood nearly a mile higher than North Chalone Peak, the highest point in the park today. Yet even as this volcano was being formed, its own destruction was at hand, for the Pacific plate upon which it was located began moving off to the northwest. In time the portion of the volcano whose eroded remnants we now know as the Pinnacles reached its present location, 195 miles beyond its point of origin. All the while, too, erosion was at work carving and breaking down the once mighty peak to about a third of its original height, sculpting the spires and crags you see today. Nor is the geologic process at an end. Millions of years from now what little will be left of this ancient volcano will have moved off to the northwest.

Point Reyes

CALIFORNIA

Pinnacles Today
(195 miles north of original location)

SAN ANDREAS RIFT ZONE

Neenach Formation
(remainder of original Pinnacles formation 23 million years ago)

Los Angeles

NORTH AMERICAN PLATE

PACIFIC PLATE

PACIFIC OCEAN

NORTH AMERICAN PLATE
PACIFIC PLATE
CARIBBEAN PLATE
COCOS PLATE
SOUTH AMERICAN PLATE
NAZCA PLATE

Plate Tectonics

Geologists have for many years tried to explain why it looks like the eastern coast of South America would neatly fit into the coast of West Africa and why rocks on different continents were the same. Recently the theory of plate tectonics, sometimes called continental drift, has emerged. Basically it says that the Earth's skin is not one single covering as we might expect but is made up of a series of plates (diagram above left). Imagine for a minute that the Earth is like a basketball: the grooves on the ball are like the junctions of the plates. Both Earth and basketball appear to be composed of a single covering. But unlike the basketball, which is one continuous piece, the lighter plates of the Earth's surface float over the heavier interior. Pressures from the interior sometimes force one plate to bump into, pull away from, or move alongside another. Scientists believe that this is what has caused the Pinnacles to make its northward journey.
Illustration by Robert Hynes

Figure 6: Pinnacles National Monument, demonstrating plate tectonics and fault lines.
Note the imaginary 23 million years (from National Park Service Brochure, 2001)

Continental division is implied in the magnetism of lavas since their north-south polarity is seemingly reoriented. Partitioning also solves the problem of creatures occupying every continent of the globe. The Bible offers little insight into this, although it does tell us about a Semite named Peleg, a man who lived a few generations after Noah when "the earth was divided" (Ge. 10:25). Now, before laughing out loud, let me say that this could relate to any of the following: 1) division of the languages, 2) division of the inhabitants of the land, 3) division of the lines of descent, and/or 4) division of the continents.

If this was truly a geophysical division, the world must have been in turmoil during the immediate pre-Abramic generations. As for the division itself, it must have been more like a *sprint* than a *drift*. There is no real indication that it produced new animal species, however, or that biological transformations resulted from its reproductively isolated sub-populations. Nor is there any basis for this division occurring during the Triassic. But what might it have been like, living during this time? Oakland's Family Radio president writes:

> Continental division must have been exceedingly traumatic. The earth began to shake and buildings began to fall. Relentlessly, great masses of continental size began to slide over the ocean floor. At the forward edge of these masses, mountain building began to occur with dramatic suddenness. Land masses of sedimentary rock were twisted and folded and overturned. Like a toy, the earth shuddered for the second time in 2,000 years under stresses too huge for our minds to comprehend. And man was spread apart and isolated. [...] The animals moved with the part of the fragmented continent on which they happened to be living. Most of mankind lived in or near the Mesopotamia Valley and they remained on the same continent which became known as Africa and Asia. But the nomads who migrated away from the population centers moved with the continental pieces where they lived.[10]

When the dust finally settled, our globe would have looked much as it does now, with its faults, fissures, geysers, vents, plates, and caves. The animals must have scattered themselves throughout their newly-separated continents, displaying great variety by virtue of their genetic capability, though not because of upward mobility. The dinosaurs would have been affected too, most likely because of fall-out debris and climatic changes.

Global Catastrophes

Global flooding and **continental sprint** do seem to be reasonable explanations for what we see in our world today. Our oceans are wider, deeper, and more dispersed than they once were. Ice caps cover what were once semitropical regions, and canyons and rifts are everywhere. Earth's strata are strangely tilted, their shattered remains remarkably contorted. Both the hard and soft parts of animals are fossilized in the sediments, and stores of hydrocarbons are locked within deep-seated pockets. Where water once flowed, deserts now exist, and the mountains are filled with oceanic fossils. These all have explanations, as do the attenuation of life and the extinction of dinosaurs. How utterly amazing! And all from the hand of God!

People should not try to place all the geophysical evidences within the context one or two great catastrophes, but the globe makes little sense without at least a universal flood. Had it not been **global**, God would not have left such a clear description of it as this:

- The waters rose and covered the mountains to a depth of more than twenty feet (Ge. 7:20).
- Every living thing that moved on the earth perished – birds, livestock, wild animals, all creatures that swarm over the earth, and all mankind (Ge. 7:21).
- Only Noah was left, and those with him in the ark (Ge. 7:23).
- The waters flooded the earth for a hundred and fifty days (Ge. 7:24).
- At your rebuke the waters fled. [...] Never again will they cover the earth (Ps. 104:7-10).
- I will establish my covenant with you: Never again will all life be cut off by the waters of a flood; never again will there be a flood to destroy the earth (Ge. 9:11).

It takes only a few texts to nail down universality. Had the waters not inundated people everywhere, why would only Noah and his family have survived? Why would animals have been placed in the Ark in the first place, had they been able to survive elsewhere on Earth? How would one characterize the borders of a *local* flood? What would be the meaning of a rainbow covenant, had the flood not been universal? Had Noah's Flood not been global, why would everything on earth have perished? And what could God have meant, saying ***all*** the springs of the deep were opened?

Still, there are those who refuse to accept global flooding. Why? Because they see the evidences as fitting within the context of a lesser flood. Christians fall into this trap also, as in geologist Davis Young's, *The Biblical Flood*[11] and physicist Alan Hayward's, *Creation and Evolution*.[12] Referring to theorists like them (claiming lesser flooding), Whitcomb wrote, "In asserting that the Book of Genesis is wrong about a global catastrophe, they are underestimating the God of creation, the God of miracle, and the God of judgment."[13] But no matter their resistance, catastrophism is still the best explanation, though we may not be able to explain everything having to do with deltas, silting, glaciers, migrations, the size of the Ark, etc. – all of which are legitimate concerns, but involving premises of their own.

Scientists were already telling Darwin that everything points to a major hydrologic catastrophe. This was the prevailing mind-set amongst nineteenth century geologists. Catastrophism was also advocated by Cuvier, the father of paleontology. "Cuvier believed that the geological record shows a pattern of catastrophic events involving mass extinction, followed by periods of creation in which new forms of life appeared without any trace of evolutionary development."[14] His model was not that of Genesis, but he did understand that minor catastrophes can never explain the fossils.

Cuvier's proposals were followed by those of Lyell, who saw the earth's strata as "the result of slow workings over immense time; everyday forces working gradually but not catastrophically.[15] Knowing the nature of fossilization, however, only catastrophism can explain Earth's relics. Even the claim that coral reefs are extremely aged can be shown, on solid scientific grounds, to be in error. Reef formation is said to require millions of years, yet a five foot growth was found on the bow of a recently sunken ship.

The truth is, flooding is settled by two realities: God's Word and gravity. If water covered all the high mountains, nothing would have stopped its flow over the whole earth. With the flood model, one can almost sense the rifting oceans, freezing Arctics, and thrusting ridges. Huge pockets of organisms were fossilized beneath thousands of feet of water and silt, further compressed by mountain building. The dynamism for this could have come only from God. Only he could have raised the muddy waters so dramatically that, before solidifying, the rocks were pushed upward to great heights. While still plastic, they neither split nor shattered but were bent and twisted like pages in a thick magazine, just as we see them today.[16]

How about humans? Early on, they were not yet plentiful, which explains the scarcity of their remains in the so-called Cenozoic. After the deluge, God scattered the tribes over the earth. Dispersed and isolated, they wrote stories about a monstrous flood, many of them still in existence in Mesopotamia, India, and China. But how could such a global consensus have arisen, had there not been a global flood? What but such an event would have inspired these ancient epics?

Even the newly-formed relationships between humans and animals imply universality, as in these edicts to Noah: "The fear and dread of you will fall upon all the beasts of the earth and all the birds of the air, upon every creature that moves along the ground, and upon all the fish of the sea; they are given into your hands" (Ge. 9:2); "everything that lives and moves will be food for you" (Ge. 9:3), and "whoever sheds the blood of man, by man shall his blood be shed" (Ge. 9:6). Because of these declarations we now have a biosphere of fear, a world with new rules impacting the globe and its inhabitants as universally as the Flood itself. Added to that, two-thirds of our globe is still covered with water, so the deluge remains visible everywhere, even in the fossilized seedlings along Lake Loveland's shores (see Figure 7).

Figure 7: Fossilized seedlings (1/2 actual size) from Lake Loveland, Colorado, indicating *rapid* lithification.

Isn't it remarkable how plainly the Flood fits with history and the findings? As Ken Ham is fond of saying, Earth's strata speak of "billions of dead things, burried in rock layers, laid down by waters, all over the world." Upon serious reflection, evolutionists can see this too, given their inability to explain the evidences otherwise.

Since the earth's crust can no longer be explained by slow processes, gradualism is passing off the scene and catastrophism is staging a come-back. Commenting on this reversal of thought, P. Johnson quipped, "It is as disappointing to Darwinist expectations as is the record of sudden appearance followed by stasis."[17] Clearly, there are evidences for which there are no gradualistic explanations at all, including the following:

- *Fossil graveyards:* Logic points to aqueous catastrophism as the rationale for these vast graveyards with their tossed and crushed remains, more being uncovered even after centuries of remarkably productive fossil-finding.
- *Polystrate fossils:* Logic tells us that fossilized trees crossing multiple strata indicate rapid entombment, not sediments accumulating around them over the ages.
- *Ephemeral markings:* Logic tells us that ripple marks, rain prints, worm trails, and bird tracks suggest instantaneous burial and rapid lithification.
- *Preservation of soft parts:* Logic tells us that scavengers, erosion, and decay would have removed soft parts from the record, except for water burial and quick entombment.
- *Stratification:* Logic points to the strata as having formed rapidly by way of dynamic processes.
- *Alluvial valleys:* Logic tells us that modern rivers flow through valleys that once carried far more water than now.
- *Incised meanders:* Logic indicates that meandering streams (coursing through rocky hills) were formed when the beds were still pliable.
- *Desert rocks:* Logic says pebbles and boulders were deposited by rushing waters where there is no water today.
- *Dinosaurs:* Logic tells us that cold-blooded reptiles (with voracious appetites) would not have lived at the frozen poles where their remains are now located.
- *Fish:* Logic testifies that fish were stranded within massive mud deposits where they died by the trillions.
- *Climates:* Logic tells us that today's hydrological-climatological cycle is not that of Adam's day.

Logic alone isn't the final answer, since we are not to lean on our own understanding (Pr. 3:5), but the evidences fit naturally with global inundation and hydrologic sorting – albeit continental division and zonation would have produced some interesting deposits, too.

During the process of inductive reasoning, the more hypotheses the better, at least early on. Having sifted through all the possibilities, however, "Occam's Razor" declares that simple explanations are usually better than needlessly complicated ones. Furthermore, the **unknown** is explained by the **known**, not by the **unnecessary multiplication of hypotheses**. It all comes down to a simple question: Are we reading the evidences biblically? When research is so inclined, science regains the respectability it so fervently craves!

Time, Eternity, and Chronometric Dating

Einstein shook the world when he defined time as just another dimension, claiming it could be warped and stretched like taffy. The riddle of time has been with us for centuries, prompting physicist Bryce DeWitt to couple general relativity and quantum mechanics into a single theory. How did he do it? By removing time entirely from the equations, all but a slight of hand having no basis in reality.

The most natural explanation is that time began with the illumination of Planet Earth on Day 1 – not with the sun, moon, and stars since they were not present until Day 4. Seeing time as arriving in this way is the height of child-like faith, like David's looking up at Goliath. Many are confused by this, refusing to believe that Planet Earth existed before both time and light when the globe was "formless and empty" (Ge. 1:2).

Earthlings struggle with two incompatible views of time, one beginning with the first day of creation, the other with the Bang, ten to twenty billion years ago. The problem is, when people reject Genesis, their concepts of time and eternity are easily garbled.

If time is mutable, it can be variably defined. Einstein wrestled with this, as did Davies in his *About Time – Einstein's Unfinished Revolution*. God's ways are not ours, though, so time and eternity must be tied to an accurate representation of his Word. This is not always appreciated, so note again that the *Westminster Confession* (Ch. 4) states, "It pleased God to create the world and all things therein, whether visible or invisible, *in the space of six days*, and all very good." This is the plainest reading of Scripture, as recognized by Christendom over the centuries.

Time as we know it provides the framework for everything else. It is measured in days, weeks, years, etc., not giga-years and eons. In Genesis, the terms "night" and "day" are defined as periods of darkness and light, which would be totally pointless if "evening and morning" were not parts of a normal day. The problem is, some are so taken with the **cosmic egg** that they see only **it** as being time-related. Grappling with an unintelligible point in history, they ignore the fact that dating techniques (based on retro-calculated light and radioactivity) are dependent on changes observable over time as God defined it – a framework which he alone could provide.

Age-indicators are a function of light, so when time is in question (variable in definition), cosmic and geophysical dating can be thrown into a cocked hat offering little insight into eternity's interface with the temporal. Keep in mind that God is **beyond time**, which is perhaps why volumes have been written about time, eternity, and age-dating. Remember also that biblical creation (Earth predating stars) and cosmic evolution (stars predating Earth) are two separate views of history, neither of which is occurring today. Finally, bear in mind that Day 1 was unique, lacking light at the outset.

To evolutionary cosmologists the universe appears ancient, but Einstein's theory may afford another explanation. Relativity says time is affected by gravity. In outer space, where there is little gravity, light may be traveling faster than closer in (where it slows down), so today we see light from stars billions of light years away though it left them only thousands of years ago.

To uniformitarian geologists, rocks have been decaying since time began. However, as we have already seen, natural processes don't always act at fixed rates. But one thing is certain, nobody can harmonize the eons of evolution with the days of creation. So why applaud evolutionary scientists (and/or theologians) at their weaker moments?

Even were science as essential to the truth as some think, few understand its whims. And how much *more* would science need to tell them before they would accept God's Word, were science actually the arbiter of truth? The fact is, God gave us an accurate accounting of beginnings and we should rejoice weekly in our celebration of that. He told us also about what is good – indeed "very good" – about beauty, order, and harmony – things that give him pleasure. Rocks and fossils, however, speak of death and destruction, so our claims about them should match history.

Science, properly conducted, supports the Bible to its smallest detail. Admittedly, the data can be interpreted variably, supporting either billions of years or only a few thousand, but contradictory views can be settled when we study God's Word. Yet the reliance on radiometric testing has been so absolute that all other methods of inquiry are assigned inferior status when they disagree. Even so, *special creation* has grown in stature, given the recent advances in science plus the realization that the *information alone* doesn't mandate one's belief system. There is thus every reason to challenge today's dating techniques.

Seeing time as beginning with light, as in Genesis, we can be confident that God managed the interface between time and eternity within a single day. Planet Earth arrived during a day of ordinary length when light first appeared, and that is the *highest view of the Confessions*, accenting the primacy of Scripture.

The Bible tells us everything we need to know about origins, but here is the mystery: It tells us nothing about *God's* origin. He himself has neither beginning nor end. Nonetheless, through his Son he reached down to us time-conditioned creatures. The reason he bound himself to time is because he loved us from eternity, and therefore we can have an eternity with him, when time shall be no more!

Meanwhile, be wary of spins! The last thing we need is another book filled with human error!

Also, while waiting for science to catch up with the Bible, shouldn't we stop teaching evolution in our schools? The answer is obvious, isn't it? Seeing evolution's ontological swamps and teleological deserts, we must stop teaching *it!* But never should we stop teaching *about it*. As a matter of fact, we should be teaching a lot more about it than many want taught!

> In the last days scoffers will come, scoffing and following their own evil desires. They will say, "Where is this coming he promised? Ever since our fathers died, everything goes on as it has since the beginning of creation". But they deliberately forget that long ago by God's word the heavens existed and the earth was formed out of water and by water. By these waters also the world of that time was destroyed. By the same word, the present heavens and earth are reserved for fire, being kept for the day of judgment and the destruction of ungodly men (2 Pe. 3:3-8).

[1] The description of trilobites is from Andrew Snelling, *In Six Days*, Master Books, Green Forest, AR, 2001, pp. 293-295

[2] Duane T. Gish, *Creation Scientists Answer Their Critics,* ICR, El Cajon, CA, 1993, p. 115

[3] Ibid, p. 115

[4] Phillip E. Johnson, *Darwin on Trial,* InterVarsity Press, Downers Grove, IL, 1993, p. 55

[5] Paul A Nelson, *Mere Creation,* InterVarsity Press, Downers Grove, IL, 1998, p.160

[6] Ibid, p. 159

[7] *Time Magazine Article,* "Secrets of the Gene", Vol. 196, Oct., 1999, p. 54

[8] Paul A. Nelson, *Mere Creation,* InterVarsity Press, Downers Grove, IL, 1998, p. 168

[9] Robert A. Wallace, *Biology, The World of Life,* Scott, Foresman and Co., Glenview, IL, 1990, p. 209

[10] Harold Camping, *Adam When?* Family Stations, Inc., Oakland, CA, 1974, pp. 255, 256

[11] Davis A. Young, *The Biblical Flood,* Wm. Eerdmans Publishing Co., Grand Rapids, MI, 1995

[12] Alan Hayward, *Creation and Evolution,* Bethany House Publishers, Minneapolis, MN, 1985

[13] John C. Whitcomb, *The World That Perished,* Baker Book House, Grand Rapids, MI, 1981, pp. 17,18

[14] Phillip E. Johnson, *Darwin on Trial,* InterVarsity Press, Downers Grove, IL, 1993, p. 45

[15] Ibid, p. 45

[16] John C. Whitcomb, *The Early Earth,* Baker Book House, Grand Rapids, MI, 1986, p. 80

[17] Phillip E. Johnson, *Darwin on Trial,* Inter Varsity Press, Downers Grove, IL, 1993, p. 57.

OXYMORONIC MYTHS
(Chapter 14)

Trembling at God's Word

Has not my hand made all things and so they came into being?
But this is the one I esteem: he who is humble and contrite in spirit,
and who trembles at my word (Isa. 66:2).

Facing his foes, an unbelieving king is rumored to have said, "rather an army of atheists than one believer with a Bible!" Darwin must have felt that way too! Today, however, rather than trembling at God's Word, people "say it like they see it". But what are they saying and how do they see it?

Was Darwin right, claiming that Moses was wrong, or are the *neo*-Darwinists right, claiming that Darwin was wrong? Could it be that **both** Darwinists and neo-Darwinists are wrong because naturalism is wrong? Portraying God as a disinterested robot reduces him to the level of an android pre-programming the universe like a computer whiz might have done it. Having withdrawn from his handiwork, how could he be the God of the Bible? Who would tremble at *his* Word? Could we even communicate with him, let alone look to him for answers?

As mentioned in the introduction to this book, no matter one's view of beginnings, the arguments can be stated in five categories: *cosmic origins, geophysical origins, biological origins, human origins, and societal origins.* As for their fit with creation, think again about our first parents. After God made Eve, he "brought her to the man" (Ge. 2:22). Did you catch that? God brought these two together, uniting them in marriage. How unlike their being at the center of the universe, as Darwin saw it, which ends up only degrading both marriage and God!

Did Adam become "truly man" through the spiritual mutation of Cro-Magnon man? This might be conceivable without Chapter 1 of Genesis, but now we have God's invisible qualities (his eternal power and divine nature) to reckon with – and the sanctity of life, that portion of our being which is subject to regeneration and unexplainable by animalism. Animals may eat, sleep, and even play like people, but humans have a dimension beyond that.

Truth does not hinge on science alone. We know this because the Bible is self-explanatory, and also because of the insurmountable barriers to evolution. At issue are the nature and extent of biblical authority as well as the scope of science. A good theory might fit some of the facts, and a better theory more of them, but evolutionary theory fits none of them at all. It fails empirically, but it fails more broadly because it cannot account for the sweep of history.[1] Moreover, it is failing increasingly with time, so it is sheer arrogance for Dawkins and Dennett to charge creationists with being "stupid, wicked, or insane" for denying the insufficiency of undirected natural processes. Or, to compare creationism with arguing for a flat earth.[2]

How could this immensely complex macrocosm have come from something so feeble and so far removed from hard science as to be comical? Why would *that* have any following at all except for the psycho-religious vacuum of unbelievers? Calling that science is hardly intellectual prowess, its most noxious feature being its low view of the Bible.

Rules of Science

See to it that no one takes you captive through hollow and deceptive philosophy,
which depends on human tradition and the basic principles of this world …
(Col. 2:8)

Returning to the **naturalistic chronology of origins** (from Chapter 3), why not go with it? Because science isn't so cut and dried as that; nor is it as unshackled from faith as some might like it to be. Empiricism is only one method for determining the truth, so origins scientists must allow for God's uniqueness. They must submit to the Bible too, or else they will be constraining God (as if that were possible). Science, after all, is not the exclusive repository for knowledge!

What can scientists tell us about supernatural events? Nothing at all, so they dismiss them as impossibilities. But guesses aren't facts, no matter how educated they might be or how firmly one might hold to them. Otherwise the Galapagos Islands would be co-equal with the Bible and theologians would have to submit regularly to science's superiority.

Science is changeable. The only sure thing is that its theories will frequently be discarded and replaced. Though it was assumed for years that no intelligent person could question evolution, criticisms of it are entering into the mainstream. Today, more than at any time in the past century, there is a shift toward special creation. Intellectuals are taking notice too, disgruntled as they are with gradualism. Believing scientists are living "as strangers here, in reverent fear" (1 Pe. 1:17), seeing orderliness and rationality as supernaturally inspired. From this came the realization that design and purpose are at the heart of the universe, shaping it rather than being antithetical to it.

Orderliness does not fit with chance. Nor would a rational Creator impose randomness on resistive material. Right from the beginning, God had a plan. Science is merely the application of its rationality, based on the fact that the universe came from the ordered hand of God.

The initial motivation for science was simple enough, "to glorify the Creator". Stressing this, Nancy Pearcey writes, "Scientists living between 1500 and 1800 inhabited a very different universe from that of the scientist living today. The early scientist was most likely to be a Christian believer". In that setting, faith was the ally of science, not its enemy. "That should not have been so hard to figure out", says Pearcey. "After all, modern science arose within a culture permeated with Christian faith."[3]

That is the view to which many are returning today, insisting again on order and rules. Are these fresh-sprung creationists abandoning the intellectual arena? Not at all! Why be tied to pre-Copernican cosmology? Nobody needs antiquated ideas! But neither should we be tethered to the outmoded (evolutionary) assumptions of the past. Look at the world around you! It is as non-evolutionary as Genesis itself! Realizing this, creationists are conducting their work in faithfulness to God and in keeping with the rules. The *guiding rule* is that there can be *no animosity between God's two revelations*, converging as they do into a *single body of truth*. The only real threat to inquiry is unbelief, accompanied by arrogance and sloppiness.

Science has been right about many things, but it has also been wrong. Scientists make mistakes, both honest and dishonest, at times presenting false evidence for their favorite theories. Myths like the "peppered moth" are persuasive and not easily removed from textbooks, so one must be vigilant. When science ignores its own rules, whether intentionally or unintentionally, it cannot be pitted against Scripture; nor should we modify our Bibles to fit with it. This is not the kind of science that has proven itself of worth in our daily lives, as in the surgical arena. But where science *has* followed the rules, it has established enough for us to understand that the universe fits best with the God of *special creation*.

Science is built on principles, but there is a gap at the dawn of history where intelligence stumbles. Knowing nothing about singularities, what are scientists to do? Too often, they simply dig in and lash out at creationists. But who has the greater freedom? Believing scientists, of course! Though they too must live with the rules, why be tied to the dead guesses of the past?

Freed to engage in real science, creationists are strengthening research at the forefront, though people don't always grasp this. Referring to that, David Hall (Covenant Theological Seminary) writes, "If evangelicals fine-tune their message to fit a waning scientific cosmology just as secularists themselves are beginning to realize its indefensibility, we will not provide the best possible testimony to eternal truth."[4]

One of the strangest ideas ever is that order and complexity could have arrived without a Creator! Evolutionists don't even see him as real or praiseworthy. Others of a theistic bent, though perhaps well intentioned, seem to value their autonomy more than God. Could it be that the pillar and foundation of truth was meant to keep them on track (1 Ti. 3:15)? There is, after all, an error-free authority. Jesus referred to it more than 200 times, accenting the historicity of Genesis.

Imagine the power that assembled entire galaxies with no raw material at all! Imagine also the creativity of him who dreamed up all the creatures in the world, packing them with so much information that it would crash the fanciest computers. Yet the Bible presents these truths so clearly that even a child can understand them.

One problem is that scientists differ. They can also be side-tracked. Even the rules change, so science must remain critical of itself. The evolutionary world is not good at that, however, having little policing of itself – so Christianity is vital to science's ranks.

An Intensifying Battle

Rather than being at war with each other, science and Christians should be friends, seeing that modern day advances owe their genius to Christianity. Today, there is an intensifying battle over "religion". Evolutionists bristle when people equate their naturalistic notions with religion, not wanting science and religion joined under any circumstance. As Gould wrote in his *Rock of Ages*, "I do not see how science and religion could be unified, or even synthesized, under any common scheme of explanation or analysis."[5]

Hoping to resolve this, Gould offered his "contemporary principle", "NOMA" ("nonoverlapping magisteria"), proposing it as a "blessedly simple and entirely conventional resolution that allows science and religion to coexist peacefully in a position of respectful noninterference". Science would then define the natural world and religion the moral, honoring their separate spheres of influence. It would follow then that nature could offer no moral instruction at all. According to Gould:

> If your particular form of religion demands a belief that the earth can only be about ten thousand years old (because you choose to read Genesis as a literal text, whatever such a claim might mean), then you stand in violation of NOMA – for you have tried to impose a dogmatic, idiosyncratic reading of a text upon a factual issue lying within the magisterium of science and well resolved with a radically different finding of several billion years of antiquity.

> The fallacies of such fundamentalist extremism can be easily identified. But what about a more subtle violation of NOMA commonly encountered among people whose concept of God demands a loving deity, personally concerned with the lives of his creatures – and not just an invisible and imperious clock-winder? Such people often take a further step by insisting that their God mark his existence (and his care) by particular factual imprints upon nature that may run contrary to the findings of science. [miracles] Now, science has no quarrel whatever with anyone's belief in such a personalized concept of divine power, but NOMA does preclude the additional claim that such a God must arrange the facts of nature in a certain set and predetermined way.[6]

What was Gould saying here? Simply this: "Nature is all there is, all that was, and all that ever will be", as Sagan said it. How very shallow! While one might long for science and religion to be at peace, Gould saw only his religious naturalism as making that possible. But is this a "blessedly simple solution", or could it be spiritual warfare bordering on anarchy? Was Gould attacking only those refusing his progressive ideas, or was he attacking a particular kind of extremism?

To be sure, fundamentalists take some irrational leaps in their reaction to liberalism, even making irrationality a principle, so we must know what we mean by liberalism and fundamentalism. Contrasting them, Os Guinness wrote, "Liberalism, from the rise of Higher Criticism onwards, has not understood Christianity on its own premises. Instead, its distinguishing feature has been the attempt to baptize biblical theology in whatever naturalistic secular philosophical presuppositions were current." "However", says Guinness, "extreme fundamentalists are equally irrational, though for different reasons. [...] This failure to understand not only results in a failure to communicate but stiffens into an intellectual stance that is at best non-rational and at worst incredible or absurd. We need only prick its finger in order for it to bleed to death."[7]

Was Gould lashing out at that kind of fundamentalism? Yes, but he was also taking a swipe at believers – and their Bible. And who are the transgressors? Those holding to the fundamentals of the faith!

What Gould wanted was a world where his ideas could trump the Almighty's, unencumbered by a single verse from Scripture! But how condescending to lump all believers together with extremists! Yet Gould was not without a faith of his own. So strong was his faith in naturalism that he saw only *it* as **knowledge**. To him, biblical creation was the approach of mental dwarfs, amounting to **belief** but not **reality**. This distinction was important to Gould since only scientific rationality could be objectively valid to him, and only his brand. Faith is then only for the "believer", and it should never be passed off as knowledge, or even valid.[8]

But this outlaws the mind of God! Reacting to that view, Phillip Johnson writes, "Truth as such is not a particularly important concept in naturalistic philosophy [...] 'truth' suggests an unchanging absolute, whereas scientific knowledge is a dynamic concept. What was knowledge in the past is not knowledge today, and the knowledge of the future will surely be far superior to what we have now. Only naturalism itself and the unique validity of science as the path to knowledge are absolutes. There can be no criterion for truth outside of scientific knowledge; no mind of God to which we have access."[9]

The disquieting thing about Gould's philosophy is that it will never rest until it has dominated the world. And how has Christianity responded to it? Says Johnson, "One might have supposed that Christian intellectuals (along with religious Jews) would be eager to find its weak spots. Instead, the prevailing view among Christian and Jewish professors has been that Darwinism – 'evolution', as they tend to call it – is unbeatable and that it can be interpreted to be consistent with Christian belief."[10]

This has resulted in "naturalistic theism", a compromise holding that naturalism can flourish within theism. Naturalism, however, has already decided that biblical considerations are inadmissible, being "non-scientific", so naturalistic theism subjects creation to the same old philosophy. Whatever role God played in *it* is superfluous, if not invisible, and that is atheism!

What is the issue here? Simply put, **genuine science** vs. **a philosophy opposed to Christianity**!

As Colson and Pearcey describe it, "Evolution, as typically presented in textbooks and museums, confuses the two – presenting as 'science' what is actually naturalistic philosophy. Indeed, many secular scientists insist that only naturalistic explanations qualify as science. But why should we let secularists make the definitions? Let's be clear on the distinction between empirical science and philosophy, and then let's answer science with science and philosophy with philosophy. This becomes all the more imperative when we see what we're up against. The moment a Christian questions evolution, he or she is labeled a backwoods Bible-thumper, an ignorant reactionary who is trying to halt the progress of science."[11]

To break that stereotype, we must understand what the debate is all about, and then we must "pursue an unbiased examination of the evidences, following them wherever they may lead". Underlying this is the tension of science vs. pseudo-science, faith vs. "faith", religion vs. "religion", world view vs. world view, Christianity vs. paganism. Framed in this way, the controversy is clear, but the battle intensifies!

Evolutionary Science (Oxymoronic Absurdity)

Paleontologists recently discovered something they had despaired of finding: the heart of a dinosaur – four-chambered at that – suggesting that dinosaurs were warm-blooded, their hearts more like those of birds than reptiles. Many see this as bolstering the case for dinosaurs becoming birds, but the leap from cold to warm-blooded animals isn't at all convincing. Besides, warm-blooded animals of this size could never have lived at the poles!

For well over a century, scientists have tried to explain peacocks, whales, giraffes, hummingbirds, and humans on the basis of their inborn potential, environmental fit, adaptational need, etc. Why have they been so unsuccessful at this? Because "evolutionary science" is a contradictory term. There is "evolution" and there is "science" but there is no such thing as "evolutionary science", at least not in the macro- or meaningful sense.

Evolution can't be imposed on science in any sustainable way, nor can it be forced on theology. There is "theism" and there is "evolution" but there is no such thing as "theistic evolution" since "kinds" reproduce kinds, based on the information within them. Why is it so hard to find mutational progression in the universe? Because it isn't there! Common characteristics don't mean a common ancestry, yet people continue to push this nonsense, claiming that literal creation is a story that exists only in the minds of irrational anti-intellectuals. Who cares about narrow-minded Christians? Why be tied to a god who isn't even around?

Holding to this, evolutionists have told the world that Genesis is wrong, though *chance* is an abandonment of *logic* and abandoned logic produces only tension. Evolution is at odds with the Creator, replacing him with a lie, for "the fool says in his heart that there is no God" (Ps. 14:1). God is not so easily displaced, however, since he has relinquished neither his attributes nor his Word.

Jesus referred to creation, de-creation, and re-creation as fiat accomplishments, doctrinally related, so nothing can be interpreted as favoring naturalism, no matter how scientific it seem. Many have turned their backs on these doctrines, favoring randomness and chance. Why have they fought so hard for these myths? Because they love darkness and hate the light. The question is, "Who is our Master and whom shall we serve?" This is the age-old question that needs to be answered. But science is not the best teacher, though some might see it as such. Like all paradigms, science can drift into the hands of one who is clever indeed!

Give Satan the throne and he'll take it! What is so vexing about him is that his methods have found their way into the hearts of believers. Science tells them what *is*, so Genesis can no longer mean what it *says*. This has affected the entire world, all the way from churches and synagogues to colleges and universities, most of which no longer accept God's Word as **written**. Satan's manipulation is a reversal of everything that science knows to be true. The Bible, on the other hand, is trustworthy, and nothing in science can overthrow it. Why would it be so surprising to find that an all-knowing God made things functional and whole right from the beginning, showing every sign of recent creation?

All other positions are hobbling, but if there is one thing that society holds to be absolute, it is the freedom of science. If I tamper with that, I'm an imbecile. Why? Because the whole rationalistic universe collapses with fixed authority – and post-modernists want none of that! This is a huge mistake, however, making no sense either philosophically or theologically. As Luke wrote, "When the Son of Man comes, will he find faith on the earth" (Lk. 18:8)? Or, only fraudulent science?

Genuine science is rooted in *faith and reason*, not some *fairy-tale*. "Evolutionary science", on the other hand, is a renunciation of both. Why then do people insist on it? The answer is, to assure their standing and maintain their credentials. Also, because they are in awe of magic. But magic isn't science, so why not just say, "I don't believe in genuine science?"

Theistic Evolution (Oxymoronic Crossbreed)

Oxymoronic myths are an assault on all Scripture, not just "traditional belief". One such myth is *"theistic evolution"*, the theory of those committed to evolution except where it conflicts with the Bible *as they see it*. Those holding to this are theists, since they accept God, but they are also evolutionists. The main difference between them and their unbelieving counterparts is that they see God as guiding the process while their colleagues attribute it to time and chance.

As theistic evolutionists see it, the Bible is right in pointing to God as the Creator, but science is equally correct in its "billions of years". It follows that creation days are illusory, which is neither *theistic* nor *evolutionary.* But isn't theistic evolution at least a possibility, seeing that the word "let" (as in "let there be") occurs throughout the account, and God never mentioned the formula for his creativity? The answer is, not when *"bara"* is introduced into the picture.

The Hebrew, *bara*, implies the making of things uniquely. As Boice wrote, "In Genesis 1:21, it speaks of the creation of conscious life (of animals as opposed to plants) and in Genesis 1:27 it speaks of the creation of man in God's image. At each of these points there is the introduction into creation of something strikingly new; something that did not and could not have evolved from things in existence previously."[12] Yes, some still insist on evolutionary processes, but the correct rendering of *bara* makes that impossible. God's goodness doesn't allow it and neither does his perfection. *Bara* is incompatible with cruel, wasteful, misguided processes. If *bara* tells us anything at all, it cannot be evolutionary, nor does it fit with the violent heritage of a common ancestry.

Not only is theistic evolution *oxymoronic* (the words being mutually exclusive), it accomplishes nothing as an intellectual exercise. As Boice said, "The theistic evolutionist who is really a *biblical* theist has become a creationist though he does not describe himself by that word."[13] Given that reality, some substitute the word "science" for "evolution", but "theistic science" fares no better than "theistic evolution", since its bent is equally unfaithful to both science and Scripture. The fact is, there is no justification for Christian evolution. Jesus never taught it and it isn't in Genesis! Nor can it be found by the scientific method.

As for bridging the gap between theism and science, Howard Van Till's "categorical complementarity" doesn't span it.[14] While it is true that neither theology nor science can provide a complete picture of creation, the designation of these two as separate and complementary categories grants more autonomy to science than it rightfully possesses, since science is only a human endeavor.

Even Van Till's "creationomic science" doesn't link science with Scripture, since it is merely *camouflaged theistic evolution.* According to Dembski, the problem isn't so much with what the word *evolution* is doing there but with what *theistic* is doing there. "Theistic evolution takes the Darwinian picture of the biological world and baptizes it, identifying this picture with the way God created life. When boiled down to its scientific content, theistic evolution is no different from atheistic evolution – treating only undirected natural processes in the origin and development of life."[15]

Theistic evolution places theism and evolution in an odd tension. If God created things through evolutionary means, he made it seem as if they were without purpose, making him the master of stealth who cannot be detected empirically. Another concern is that such theories are never done deals. Speculative and fluid, they settle nothing since nobody was present when things first appeared.

The fact is, were one able to rewind the clock, there are still only two possibilities: *either* the universe evolved according to its own laws and processes *or* it arrived supernaturally. Faced with these two choices, Van Till writes, "We are simply offered two packages of answers and the demand that we choose one or the other. [...] This is a crucial error. It commits us to mixing up specific answers to questions of internal affairs (cosmic properties, behavior, and history) with specific answers to questions on matters of external relationships (cosmic status, origin, governance, value, and purpose). To demand a choice between only two packages of answers to distinct and separable questions is to commit the fallacy of many questions" (as in Occam's Razor).[16]

To correct that, Van Till offers an evolutionary hybrid, knowing that God must be brought into the discussion somewhere. But his crossbreed (theistic evolution) is at ease with suffering and death, and isn't it also the fallacy of at least one too many questions, or options? God never limited himself to ordinary providence *after* creation, so why hold him to it *during* it? That would link him with eons of suffering, foreign to his Person. Would he then not be a capricious and hateful God, and that without cause?

The God of Genesis is not like that, so the options still boil down to only two: special creation vs. naturalistic evolution, not some crossbreed! Both are beyond proof, but which of them speaks to the soul? Accepting Reformed hermeneutics, we're left with only one choice. Seeing that all the indisputable facts fit best with the verbatim account of creation, wouldn't we be better off admitting that everything came about **supernaturally**?

Having said that, what should our approach be? Openness to all truth, certainly, but not the openness allowing science to sit in judgment on Genesis. Rather, we must bring every thought into subjection to God's Word.[17] But, though confessing this, Christians can be woefully naive. Referring to their naiveté, Phillip Johnson writes, "The main point of theistic evolution is to preserve the peace with the mainstream of the scientific community. Theistic evolutionists therefore unwittingly serve the purposes of scientific naturalists, by helping persuade the religious community to lower its guard against the incursion of naturalism."[18]

If there is any humor in this, it is that Darwinists find it harder to accept evolutionary theists (bringing evolution into their theology while arguing the separation of science and religion) than to live with creationists (who make no such attempt at all). As Dembski puts it, "The Darwinian establishment views theistic evolution as a weak-kneed sycophant that desperately wants the respectability that comes along with being a full-blooded Darwinist but refuses to follow the logic of Darwinism through to the end. It takes courage to give up the belief that life on earth has a purpose. It takes courage to live without an afterlife. Theistic evolutionists lack the stomach to face the ultimate meaninglessness of life, and this failure of courage makes them contemptible in the eyes of full-blooded Darwinists."[19]

Why would Christians concoct such a crossbreed? One possibility is that, though having had godly mentors, they abandoned their moorings. Though starting out with faces aglow, they faded when confronting the world. Could it be that they wilted because they were given the right answers, never having asked the right questions?

As De Koster commented, "Deluded by the ease with which the Bible can seemingly be set aside, the theistic evolutionist ardently advocates living with one foot on each of two highways, striding down the 'broad way' in the company of the latest heroes of 'science' while climbing up the 'narrow way' in company of the Jesus of popular evangelism. The Bible disowns that."[20]

Fading Fashion

Many have inflated expectations as to what science can deliver because they are dedicated to intellectual fashion. Like perpetual teenagers, they accept what they're told, and the majority rules. Pressure is then applied, urging them to "get on with it". Believers need never be intimidated by them, however. Nor should they be swayed when Van Till surmises, "The answer will be found by empirical study; not by philosophical or theological dictation", his having said also, "My guess is that a fully satisfactory description for the processes of biological evolution will eventually be worked out."[21] Were one to accept this, creation might be a profound "story" but it could still be hopelessly outdated and ambiguous.

For Van Till, the words of Moses are the packaging in which the message is wrapped.[22] This lays the groundwork for a thoroughly humanistic philosophy in which the events of creation are merely illustrative. And what about the content? It is easily lost with the *wrapper*, for Van Till claims that the biblical materials may better be seen as "artistic illustrations" than as "journalistic reports of specific past events."[23]

What are we left with then? A good vehicle and some attractive packaging but no reliable message.

Risky methodology? Definitely so! One would think that some have an inside line to the Author, segmenting his Word into what is divine and what isn't. Why wouldn't the wrapper be authoritative, too? For as Paul wrote, "*all* Scripture is God-breathed and is useful for teaching, rebuking, correcting, and training in righteousness" (2 Ti. 3:16,17). To think otherwise is to embrace concordism (man's thoughts equal with God's) and/or higher criticism.

People combine theism with evolutionism, but there is no such mix. In the creation record there is **genuine history**, not some intermediate position. Theistic evolutionists see this to an extent, but they are strangely dyslexic about it, being so opposed to literalism that they will discard what they had hoped to emphasize, namely Creation's Creator! This might be laughable, but it is part of a more serious problem: The Word without wisdom! Perfect God without perfection! Holding to this is no more fashionable than design without a Designer, and it can no longer be defended either logically or theologically.

Those calling creationists ignorant or inept are balking at God's Word. They see it as trustworthy only when it conveys to them some "teaching". Who or what can then determine its message? Van Till's answer is this: "We may confidently expect that we will see the message all the more clearly when we make proper use of critical tools."[24] The question is, "Who is the keeper of these marvelous tools?" Any guru would suggest that only science can decide which biblical accounts are of lesser status than others, allowing theists to be reputable in their professional communities, albeit in the hippodrome of hypocrisy!

Devil's Poison

Of all scenarios, the literal account is the winner, but *theistic evolutionists* question it, holding as they do to lengthy ages, biological ascendancy, and death before sin. But what could be the difference between their ideas and *outright evolution*, except for the granting of a severely limited creator?

The proof of God's omnipotence is in Revelation 21 where the curse is undone "and there will be no more death, mourning, crying, or pain." How unlike Satan's poisoned world! The curse has twisted things badly, which is why believers prize the Word of God so highly, but "the time will come when men will not put up with sound doctrine. Instead, to suit their own desires, they will gather around them a great number of teachers to say what their itching ears want to hear. They will turn their ears away from the truth and turn aside to myths" (2 Ti. 4:3-4). In this scenario, science and Satan are the winners and insentient matter ends up supreme every time!

In England, there has been a push toward eliminating the teaching of creation in private Christian schools. This flap isn't about education, it's about power! If Satan had his way, he would ban the Bible and gag its author, being particularly intent on eliminating the first few chapters of Genesis. Consider carefully these contrasting views, by DeKoster and Berghoef:[25]

> **Genesis:** "In the Beginning, God", the Father Almighty.
> **Evolution:** In the beginning, Bang.
> **Theistic evolution:** In the beginning, the Bang plus God, who is used to set off the Bang and sustain what follows it, but is forbidden to interfere with evolutionary processes.

> **Genesis:** Man is made an adult, in God's image.
> **Evolution:** Denies making of man as an adult and has no conception of a divine image.
> **Theistic evolution:** Denies making of man as an adult and has no way of violating the "principle of uniformity" to fit a divine image on the evolutionary process.

> **Genesis:** God breathes into adult man's nostrils to make him "a living soul".
> **Evolution:** Ignores.
> **Theistic evolution:** Would like to believe that somewhere in the evolutionary process God made some animal "human", but cannot accept such intrusion on the order of nature.

Genesis: God makes Eve out of Adam's rib, thus ensuring an integrity of human flesh and blood for Jesus' incarnation.
Evolution: Denies.
Theistic evolution: Denies.

Genesis: God sanctifies human marriage in words confirmed by Jesus, and as a model of the relation between Christ and the Church, by having made Eve of Adam's flesh.
Evolution: Denies and erodes marriage and the family.
Theistic evolution: Provides no foundation in creation for the sanctity of marriage, nor for its being a model for the relation of Christ and the Church.

Genesis: God made all things, man included, "very good", thus making man responsible for his own misbehavior.
Evolution: Has no provision for man's ever being "very good".
Theistic evolution: Has no provision for man's every being "very good".

Genesis: God separates his acts of creation into discrete and separate segments.
Evolution: Development moves without interruption from species to species.
Theistic evolution: Development moves without interruption from species to species.

Genesis: Man falls from his created perfection through an act of disobedience, and thus plunges all mankind into guilt and depravity.
Evolution: No provision for a Fall because no provision for a created perfection from which to fall.
Theistic evolution: Same as evolution.

Genesis: Death enters history as consequence of man's Fall, and is an urgent call to repentance.
Evolution: Naturalizes death.
Theistic evolution: Same as evolution.

Were it not for the truths of Genesis, "our first parents would have been so low, being on the same level as animals, that they could not have fallen further, being already on the ground."[26] So said Drs. T. Plantinga and C. Venema. But Pierre Teilhard de Chardin had a solution to this. This Catholic priest, a theistic evolutionist, believed in the "perfectibility of man", a doctrine which has ominous implications all the way from reprobation to restoration, and doesn't begin to address the weakness of human theorizing.

Evolutionary Enigmas

Within a ten mile radius from my home there is a bio-diversity unparalleled in the world. The whole world is, in fact, filled with unimaginable things. In Madagascar, scientists have unearthed the most spectacular of dinosaur remains. But what could be more mystifying than finding both *Homo-* and *hominid* fossils at the same dig, as in South Africa's "Valley of the Mummies"? And if humans truly came from *A. Robustus*, why did these hominids disappear?

Obviously, the fossils have hit a snag! Paleontologists haven't yet abandoned their ancestral charts, but they admit that vertical progression would require an army of cells capable of generating new information; not just the pre-programmed cells found in everyday organisms. "Junk genes" are seen as a ray of evolutionary hope, but (as noted already) there seem to be fewer and fewer such meaningless modules as we learn more about them. Were it otherwise, we should be finding all kinds of mutants in the fossils!

Quoting the *N.Y. Times* regarding the plausibility of evolution, Nicholas Wade wrote in the *Denver Post* (July 16, 2000), "The dates have become increasingly awkward. Instead of there being a billion or so years for the first cells to emerge from a warm broth of chemicals, life seems to pop up instantly after the last of the titanic asteroid impacts that routinely sterilized the infant planet. The chemistry of the first life is a nightmare to explain. No one has yet devised a plausible explanation to show how the earliest chemicals might have constructed themselves from the inorganic chemicals likely to have been around on the early Earth. Thus the spontaneous assembly of small RNA molecules on the primitive earth would have been a near miracle."

Admittedly, the evidences can be confusing, but they aren't the mystery to believers that they are to their atheistic counterparts. As Wade sums it up, "The fossil evidence fades out at 3.5 billion years ago. The phylogenetic evidence is for the moment blurred by horizontal gene transfer. The best efforts of chemists to reconstruct molecules typical of life in the laboratory have shown only that it is a problem of fiendish difficulty." Along with the new genetics have come advances in cosmology, theoretical physics, geology, and biology, but these only further accentuate the unyielding problem of the evolutionary origin of life. Consequently, there is now a turn of events where the bulk of the information is supporting special creation, all the way from strings to wings.

God's Revelation vs. Man's Reason

Oliver Wendell Holmes, a highly regarded law scholar, surgeon, researcher, poet, and teacher, met regularly (as a member of the elite Saturday Club) with men like Emerson and Longfellow. During the mid-1800's, serving as Professor of Anatomy at Harvard, he held up a skeleton. Turning to his class, he remarked, "These, gentlemen, are the bones on which Providence destined mankind to sit and view the works of creation."

Satan wants people to think that God's providence is phony and puny. Claiming this, his most useful weapon is criticism of the Bible. When theists accept this, they end up like their atheistic counterparts. Whether using "logic" to prove or disprove God's Word, "reasoning" then dismembers Scripture, segmenting it into acceptable and unacceptable portions. What the text says can then no longer be true since it is controlled by the intellect, not by itself.

Embracing only evolutionary scenarios, many are trying to confirm their myths with more research and money, so an estimated ten billion dollars are poured into this annually. But when John opened his Gospel with, "In the beginning was the Word", he used the Greek *"logos"* (reason) to describe the force behind the universe. In doing so, he was transforming rationality in a radical new way saying, "***The Logos*** became flesh and made his dwelling among us" (Jn. 1:14).

Why "Logos"? Logos can be variously translated as "word", "reason", and "wisdom". Translate it as you wish, but what John said about Jesus is of enormous importance. Christ the Creator took on human flesh, placing him within reach of humanity! Understood in this way, impersonal rationality was redefined in terms of a Personal Being. Alternatively, when Christ's personhood is replaced with poison (whether by rationalism, romanticism, pragmatism, existentialism, modernism, or postmodernism), his work is lost as well. The result? Truth is replaced by "enlightenment" and we're headed for the New Age!

Not only is truth a matter of Christ's Person, it is also a matter of hermeneutics. Keep in mind that:
- The universe attests to the Bible.
- Man's reason is sometimes true, but God's revelation is always true.
- Human theories are frequently guesses, but God was actually there.
- Naturalism omits sovereignty; uniformitarianism constrains it.
- A pearl of great price is worth special handling.

God reveals himself through science, but there is a limit to theorizing. Granted, truth should be rational, but it isn't always verifiable. Arguing that empiricism can save the day elevates it to the role of Savior, and once we nail this down we should be able to see that ***salvation is tied to creation***. Also, we can be freed from academic isolation and individualism, since the Christian view is more than an isolated belief system with a smattering of doctrine thrown in.

Truth involves the domination of ***reason*** by ***revelation***, as in these comparisons:
- **Biblical Creationism** holds that the evidences are to be tested by Scripture since the Bible is *true*.
- **Modernism** holds that Scripture is to be tested by the evidences since the Bible is *provisionally true*.
- **Post-modernism** holds that Scripture is to be *rejected* by the evidences since the Bible is *false*.

Truth, after all, is a matter of *self-revelation.* People may accept the testimony of men, but God's testimony is final – all the way from guilt, to grace, to gratitude – from sin, to salvation, to service. Nonetheless, people have said "God is dead and Darwin lives", which is why Schaeffer insisted that holding a strong view of Scripture (or not holding it) is the watershed of the evangelical world. Said he, "If we don't have a foundation, we won't know how to respond to false doctrine." For that, remember that *the grammatico-historical method* involves *genuine history*, including people, animals, heavenly bodies, and time-frames.

Ray of Hope

Fallen people, distorted from birth, can't even imagine history. One has only to read the ramblings of theistic evolutionists to see that their "god of the gaps" (stripped of his divinity except where science has no answer of its own) could act only at certain points in history. This is an insult to the Creator, detouring around his abilities. Ceationists can detour too, of course, having blemishes of their own, but there is an emerging group of scholars returning science to its roots. Clearing away the evolutionary smoke, they are re-connecting super-clusters, radioisotopes, and genes with the Bible. As new information pours in, it is checked for its fit with the Creator.

Creationists are beating off erroneous concepts, even those deeply cherished, but their strongest contribution is that of re-instating the Creator. Though their efforts have been called trivial, nonsensical, and even part of a well-planned movement destroying science, Dembski has a simple reply: "If we're generating such strong visceral responses, we must be doing something right." Creationists are in fact winning the day hands down, pointing out that a multitude of conclusions drawn from a dearth of information (erroneous at that) is not science.

What a thrill that science, properly conducted, is affirming God's Word to its every detail! Many are confessing that extra biblical information is relevant only to the extent that it harmonizes with God's Word. Yet, despite the converging evidences for special creation, people are still holding to ideas as out of touch with reality as they are out of sync with the Bible. Clinging to outmoded paganism, they are ushering in the pathos of our generation, where students can hear about Darwin but not about Christ. How did we arrive at this dreary point? By accepting a chain without links, denying the information supporting creation!

As for the evolutionary gaps, here is a summary of them: Source, intelligence, design, information, plans, pathways, chronology, sequence, matter, antimatter, star and galaxy formation, complexity, functionality, "kinds", transitions, trees, trails, parents, sentience, spirituality, conscience, morality, eternity, hope, and joy!

Even were one able to fill in these gigantic voids, there is still the question of the evolutionary timetable. The problem is, it doesn't work! Not for geophysics, not for paleontology, not for biology, and not for humanity! Why all the emphasis on redshifting and radiation when these have so little to do with the age of the universe? Why the adulation of Mother Earth and Father Time when time is "neither an ally nor an engine of creation, but rather an ogre of death and destruction"?[27]

As Donald DeYoung noted, even the birth of stars has never been totally observed. "Notice that the entire life of a star is an aging process: main sequence – red giant – white dwarf. Instead of stellar evolution, it might better be called stellar decay, degradation, or degeneration. [...] The principles of physics demand special conditions for star formation and also a long period of time. A cloud of hydrogen gas must be compressed to a sufficiently small size so that gravity dominates. [...] In space, however, almost every gas cloud is light-years in size, hundreds of times greater than the critical size needed for a stable star. As a result, outward pressures cause these clouds to spread out farther, not contract."[28]

Despite the yearning for a naturalistic heritage, evolution didn't happen, isn't happening, and can't happen. Why? Because nature is *down-grading*, not *up-grading*, and even natural selection can't solve that problem! People may ask, "Don't we see selection and adaptation in nature?" Well, of course we do, in the elimination of weak and anomalous creatures no longer available for reproduction. This doesn't lead to new species, however, since natural selection is *conservatory*, not *evolutionary*. Survival of the fittest doesn't work either, because the best don't become better, at least not on their own. Nor can time and chance solve the problem any more than the lottery's alleviating poverty.

So why is evolution still "the law of life"? Well, it isn't! As Philip Hughes observed more than fifty years ago, "Those who *opposed* the evolutionary doctrine of inevitable progress were, in fact, a hundred years ahead of their time." Peking and Nebraska Man were labeled "millions of years old" on the basis of evidences so flawed that evolutionists themselves rejected them. Given the swarm of equally flawed "evidences", Genesis comes through as remarkably reliable. There is also the matter of superior organisms. To arrive at them through evolutionary processes would require at least the following:

> An open system
> Energy influx
> Pre-adaptational need
> A purposeful plan
> Change mechanisms

The problem is, even having the first two of these, the last three are non-existent in the biosphere. Without pre-adaptational need there can be no adaptation, without a plan there can be no forward movement, without a coding/decoding mechanism there can be no change. Also, seeing that design can't be denied, and design requires a designer, evolutionists are facing yet another dilemma: To grant design they must acknowledge God, but to call design an accident they must deny reality. So what do evolutionists do? Replace Truth with trickery, partiality, and lies! Commenting on this, a wise man once said, "I read Darwin to make me angry and the Bible to make me smart."

As an aside, the "New Age" is not new at all; it is merely a replay of first century Gnosticism, the idea that reason, not faith, is the key to life's mysteries. Paul warned Timothy about the opposing ideas of what is falsely called "knowledge" (1 Ti. 6:20). Though Paul knew nothing about modern science, he did know about teachers in the strongholds of learning – teaching *about* creation but not about it as *Truth*. The good news, however, is that once we eliminate their myths, our logic, grammar, and rhetoric will fall into place.

The bottom line? God is either sovereign, dealing with the universe as with a blank slate, or man is on the throne. Since even the glory days of science can't envision the latter, believers have both the right and the duty to insist on supernatural causation, looking to *God's revelation* – not *man's reason*. The compromise is to hold equally to both premises, defying logic. The result? Half-truths granting structure but not sovereignty – accepting the "who and why" of creation but not the "how and when" of it.

Truth is, we need more than *design*; we need an *interpreter*! After all, knowledge without wisdom is as dangerous as an airplane without a rudder!

> *God moves in a mysterious way, his wonders to perform.*
> *He plants his footsteps in the sea and rides upon the storm.*
> *Deep in unfathomable mines of never-failing skill,*
> *He treasures up his bright designs and works his sovereign will.*
> *Blind unbelief is sure to err and scan his work in vain;*
> *God is his own interpreter and he will make it plain.*

> *(William Cowper, 1772)*

[1] William A. Dembski, *Mere Creation,* InterVarsity Press, Downers Grove, IL, 1998, p. 22
[2] Ibid, p. 22
[3] Nancy Pearcey, *Bible-Science Newsletter, How Christianity Gave Rise to the Scientific Outlook,* Jan. 1989, pp. 6,7
[4] David W. Hall, *Did God Create in Six Days?,* Southern Presbyterian Press, Taylors, SC, 1999, pp. 268,269
[5] Stephen Jay Gould, *Rock of Ages,* The Ballantine Publishing Group, New York, NY., 1999
[6] Ibid, pp. 93,94
[7] Os Guinness, *The Dust of Death,* InerVarsity Press, Downers Grove, IL, 1973, pp. 322-324
[8] Phillip E. Johnson, *Objections Sustained,* InterVarsity Press, Downers Grove, IL, 1998, p. 28
[9] Ibid, p. 29
[10] Ibid, p. 30
[11] Charles Colson and Nancy Pearcey, *How Now Shall We Live?,* Tyndale House Publishers, Inc., Wheaton, IL, 1999, p. 55
[12] James Montgomery Boice, *Genesis, An Expository Commentary,* The Zondervan Corporation, Grand Rapids, MI, 1982, p. 45
[13] Ibid, p. 47
[14] See Van Till's discussion, *The Fourth Day,* Wm. B. Eerdmans Publishing Co., 1989, pp. 202-203
[15] Ibid, pp. 20
[16] See Van Till's discussion, *The Fourth Day,* Wm. B. Eerdmans Publishing Co., 1989, pp 218,219
[17] James Montgomery Boice, *Genesis, An Expository Commentary,* The Zondervan Corporation, Grand Rapids, MI, 1982, p. 48
[18] Phillip E. Johnson, *Objections Sustained,* InterVarsity Press, Downers Grove, IL, 1998, p. 32
[19] William A. Dembski, *Mere Creation,* InterVarsity Press, Downers Grove, IL, 1998, pp. 21,22
[20] Lester DeKoster, *The Reformed Witness, Theistic Evolution, The Unchanging Issue,* June, 1993, p. 8
[21] See Van Till's discussion, *The Fourth Day,* Wm. B. Eerdmans Publishing Co., 1989, pp. 188, 208
[22] Ibid, pp 84-85
[23] Ibid, p. 247
[24] Ibid, p. 12
[25] Material in this section is a distillation from De Koster and Berghoef's *The Great Divide, The Plan of Redemption,* Christian Library Press, Inc., Grand Rapids, MI, 1988, pp.172,173
[26] Theodore Plantinga and Cornelis Venema, *Evolution, Original Sin, and our Creeds, The Outlook,* Reformed Fellowship, Inc., Grand Rapids, MI, 1991, pp. 7-13.
[27] Jeremy Walter, *In Six Days,* (edited by John F. Ashton), Master Books, Green Forest, AR, p. 18.
[28] Donald B. DeYoung, *Astronomy and the Bible*, Baker Books, Grand Rapids, MI, 2000, pp. 83-86.

THE HUMANISTIC VOID
(Chapter 15)

Crisis of Truth

Of all personages in the world, Jesus Christ is the most popular, but many slight him as Creator. The result is a crisis of truth in both the secular and evangelical camps of the world. The symptoms may differ, but the disease is common and the cause clear. It consists of a doctrinal deficit at the core of what people believe, influencing how they behave.

Throw out the *first chapter of Genesis* and you will throw out the ***remainder of the Bible***! The results are:

- **Man rather than God:** To the lost the Bible is veiled, but to the redeemed it is a fountain of wisdom.
- **Tolerance rather than truth:** The world says there is no certainty, so tolerance reigns and truth is up for grabs. Only biblical truth can adjudicate the argument.
- **Fancy rather than faith:** Inspired by dreams, rather than vision, many are trying to convince others, hoping their ideas will prevail. But Christ came to dispel their myths.
- **Closed minds rather than open minds:** The academic community, averse to God, considers open-mindedness the height of virtue, but only as academia defines the term. True open-mindedness is the mind of Christ.
- **Stories rather than expository study:** People with faulty theology and bad science are obsessed with stories. Some won't accept God's Word as his *word*, so there is a crisis regarding its sufficiency. Subjectivity is substituted for revelation because people refuse infallibility. Perhaps they should read the Bible more carefully to see that it isn't anecdotal, but a chart and a compass.
- **Nature rather than character:** Philosophic naturalists, knowing that their fancies are fading, have a narcissistic bent toward self-adulation. At every turn there is adoration of man, but God will surrender his glory to no one.
- **Pleasure rather than praise:** People worship nature and themselves, but the *Heidelberg Catechism* says the chief end of man is to "glorify God and enjoy him forever". Life should therefore be a sacrifice of praise, but the average person is too "sophisticated" for that.
- **Silence rather than salt:** Naturalism silences God. Christians must therefore regain their saltiness – and their voices.

The loss of truth is seldom a blow-out; it's more like a slow leak. People have fed on fiction for so long that they have little truth to pass on to the next generation. But this will not be evident until another generation passes, depending upon the rate of extinction of what little truth is left. The problem is, novels create a following but they cannot create a foundation (or a culture).

Teachable Minds

The eyes of the Lord keep watch over knowledge, but he frustrates the words of the unfaithful (Pr. 22:12).

Those who manipulate truth are harder to reach with biblical creation than those who have never considered it. In the opinion of DeKoster, "Today, the temptation is the court of public esteem. What flies? Is the fad evolutionary theory? The 'church' finds room by way of a compromise. [...] Just a little touch here (are the 'days' long periods of time?) and another there (did God give his Image to gradually evolving creatures?) with a whiff of hermeneutic (it's all interpretation anyhow, isn't it?), and evolution is presented for baptism. Evolutionary theory impresses the gullible by lending an aura of 'scientific' authority to deprecation of the Word. Theistic evolution baptizes that infidelity."[1]

Many never learn the facts because of a failure to attend sufficiently to God's Word. As Packer stated in his *Knowing God*, there are two prerequisites for true knowledge. "We must learn to reverence God, and we must learn to receive God's Word". Said he, "not until we have become humble and teachable – standing in awe of God's holiness and sovereignty, acknowledging our own littleness, distrusting our own thoughts, willing to have our minds turned upside down – can divine wisdom become ours."[2] Consider also these insights from Packer's *"Knowing Christianity"*:

> God is not bound by any of the limitations of space or time that apply to us, his creatures, in our body-anchored experience. [...] He has a plan for the history of the universe, and in executing it he governs and controls all created realities. Without violating the nature of things, and without at any stage infringing upon human free will, God acts in, with, and through his creatures to do everything that he wishes to do exactly as he wishes to do it. By this sovereign, overruling action he achieves his goals.[3]

Sovereignty implies authority, the kind of exclusivity that God alone exercises over every square millimeter of the universe. With that as the framework, Christians need to reclaim every sphere of learning. At issue are God's glory and our submission to it. Accepting his Lordship over every particle, drop, and wave in the universe (including our personhood), we are to honor him in everything we're engaged in. Some may scoff at this, but that does not remove God's controlling interest from the universe.

The Father's dominion is over everything imaginable, so we have no right to separate religion from science, or God would lose his *place*. Nor may we argue that science and religion are co-equal, or God would lose his *authority*. People are inclined toward intellectualizing things into isolated domains, but God has claimed them all for himself, so there are really no secular spheres at all. With that in mind, we are to represent him in science, art, literature, etc. But there is a caution also; we are not to resist his authority, for God is not in awe of persons – not even the Pope with his peculiar championing of evolution.

How could our body-anchored experiences be especially noteworthy except when permeated with the Word and the Spirit? Having God's Word in our hearts, ready on our lips, is pleasing to him (Pr. 22:18). But speaking Truth takes time, study, and prayer – plus the conviction that God's words are an honest record of history. Ignoring this, we can be easily swayed. Being "wretched, poor, lame, and blind", like the Laodiceans of Revelation 3, isn't it amazing how much we *don't* know about the universe? Yet, small though we are in God's eyes, we are significant in his mind, as long as we're teachable.

Great Intellectual Void

The tongue of the wise commends knowledge, but the mouth of the fool gushes folly (Pr. 15:2).

In the Gospel of John we read, "The Word became flesh and made his dwelling among us. We have seen his glory; the glory of the One and Only, who came from the Father, full of grace and truth" (Jn. 1:14). Paul spoke of this at Mars Hill, addressing the Neo-Platonists of the Areopagus (Ac. 17). Centuries earlier, Athens was at its peak, but by Paul's time it had many gods, holding that supreme good is in personal happiness and the moment. Consistent with human nature, these ideas had degenerated into sensuality. How the Athenians needed Christ!

When Christ (***The Logos***) appeared, he was greater than Plato's Republic, by far! Not only did he reclaim the spiritual realm, he rescued the intellectual world as well, and one day he will restore design and order. Greco-Roman culture was fully capable of detecting design and order, but it never did so in any sustained way – not until after Mars Hill, that is.

Once The Logos came into view, reasoning acquired meaning and purpose. Over time, however, scientists began to explain things materialistically, and people of faith argued amongst themselves, forgetting the real enemy. The church retreated from its heritage, also, so neither it nor society had the same interests as those of the early Christians. As a result, we now have overwhelming darkness where any form of irrationality can be peddled as long as the vendor has an academic degree of some kind.

In a *New York Times* poll (March, 2000) 70 percent of Americans said that God was involved in creation, but he used evolutionary means. This poll showed that there is broad support for evolution in the public schools, which for many doesn't represent a conflict with their religion. However, people have been listening to the evolutionary elite, not the Lord of the universe, and their quixotic melding of incompatible views is the height of irrationality.

Commenting on that, evolutionary biologist David Haig (Harvard University) said, "It is logically inconsistent both to believe in the theory of evolution (that humans descended from animals) and to believe the opposite (that they were created)." Wagging his finger at theistic evolutionists, this unbelieving scientist was criticizing those who see evolution as an ordained process.

That Christians would handle the Bible so recklessly is unbelievable. There is no more reason to attack God in Genesis than to attack him elsewhere in Scripture. This carries over into society, contributing to the irrationality of our day where newspapers present humanism on one page and horoscopes on another.

Given this state of affairs, we're drowning in signs and wonders, unscientific at best and demonic at worst, and there is little retreat from this paganism. Neither is there much hope, however, since our culture goes on mindlessly demolishing logic, wisdom, and the concept of "university". Is it any wonder then that so few know how to die well, having never considered the Logos?

Great Spiritual Void

During the Flood, the world was destroyed by an outpouring of God's wrath. Because his wrath is burning still, the world will be destroyed again, along with the heavens – only this time by fire. In 2 Peter 3:10 we read: "The day of the Lord will come like a thief. The heavens will disappear with a roar; the elements will be destroyed by fire, and the earth and everything in it will be laid bare". Unbelievers are fascinated by this (check the best-seller lists), but they see it only through their own eyes.

As envisioned by Ferris (*The Whole Shebang*), cosmic destiny will be decided by a tug-of-war between two opposing forces. "If the gravitational force is strong enough to bring expansion to a halt, the universe will collapse, ultimately dissolving into a fireball – a Big Crunch that amounts to the Big Bang in reverse. If it's not, and expansion wins out, then the universe will grow unpleasantly dark and cold."[4] Of these two alternatives, telescopic observations suggest that the fate of the cosmos will not be a fiery cataclysm, but a gradual descent into eternal frigid darkness. Says Ferris, "When the hydrogen and helium run low, old stars will sputter out without any new ones to take their place, and the universe will gradually fade to black." However, the Bible tells us that this is a myth.

Why do people embrace these fabrications? Because they don't want God in their lives. As Solomon warned, "Where there is no revelation, the people cast off restraint" (Pr. 29:18). No Creator, no judge – no judge, no law – no law, no responsibility! If the universe is random and without reason; if behavior is erratic and the future uncertain; if man is an animal and life is a riddle, then everything is autonomous and ungovernable. There is then no meaning or value to anything! Everything is ill-fated and we can do nothing about it. Religion is then a hodgepodge and there is no commitment, except to science, which alone can point the way.

Echoing this, the two great lies of the 21st century are these: truth is relative and life is purposeless. Why crowd our lives with spiritual things? If God is an inconvenience and man is on the throne, why not live for the moment? Why not pleasure, seeing we live only once? Why not lust? Why can't we decide for ourselves? In the final analysis, nobody is to blame, no matter what. Yet God is blamed for everything!

That is the unbelieving world-view in a capsule, and it's a poison pill if there ever was one. Yet this has become the religion of the day, and people are enslaved to it despite its secularism and hedonism. It leads ultimately to *orthodox atheism*, embodying any of three theological views: Rationalism, New-Ageism, and Humanism.

Humanist Manifesto I appeared over seventy years ago. This anti-Christian paper from supposedly "scholarly minds" offered a developing viewpoint driven by "increased knowledge and expanding experience in various fields of human activity". Rather than affirming God's sovereignty, *religious humanism* endorses some frankly shocking principles, among them the following:

- The universe is self-existing and not created.
- Man, as a part of nature, has emerged as a result of a continuous process.
- The traditional dualism of mind and body must be rejected [failing to mention the soul].
- Man's religious culture and civilization, as clearly depicted by anthropology and history, are the product of a gradual development due to his interaction with the natural environment and with his social heritage.
- The nature of the universe, as depicted by modern science, makes unacceptable any supernatural or cosmic guarantees of human values. The way to determine the existence and value of any and all realities is through intelligent inquiry, and by the assessment of their relations to human needs. Religion must formulate its hopes and plans in the light of the scientific spirit and method.
- Nothing human is alien to religion. The distinction between sacred and secular can no longer be maintained.
- The complete realization of human personality is the end of man's life, seeking its fulfillment here and now.
- In the place of old attitudes, worship, and prayer, religious emotions should be expressed in a heightened sense of personal life and in a cooperative effort toward social well-being.
- There will be no uniquely religious emotions and attitudes of the kind associated with belief in the supernatural.
- Man will learn to face the crises of life in terms of his knowledge, naturalness, and probability, discouraging sentimental and unreal hopes, and wishful thinking.
- Religion must work increasingly for joy in living and the satisfactions of life.
- Religious institutions, their ritualistic forms, ecclesiastical methods, and communal activities must be reconstituted [dissolved?] as rapidly as experience allows, in order to function effectively in the modern world.

Humanist Manifesto II appeared in 1973, again claiming that traditional theism (faith in a prayer-hearing God) is an unproven and outmoded faith. According to this newer version, salvation is "harmful", diverting people toward false hopes of heaven hereafter. These ideas were proposed in *The Humanist* (Jan./Feb., 1977) as an "affirmative and hopeful vision for the twenty-first century", as follows:

> For many years it has been well established scientifically that all known forms of life including human beings, have developed by a lengthy process of evolution. It is also verifiable today that the very primitive forms of life, ancestral to these earliest living things, in growing more complex, became ever more diverse and increasingly different from one another. Humans and the other highly organized types of today constitute the present twig-end of that tree. The human twig and that of the apes sprang from the same ape-like progenitor branch. [...] There are no alternative theories to the principle of evolution, with its "tree of life" pattern, that any competent biologist of today takes seriously. [...] Creationism is not scientific; it is a purely religious view held by some religious sects and persons strongly opposed by other religious sects. Evolution is the only presently known strictly scientific and non-religious explanation for the existence and diversity of living organisms. It is therefore the only view which should be expounded in public school courses on science.

The discussion continues with over 180 signatories to the second declaration, most having professorial status, some even claiming to be Christian! But surely we know more now than we did in the '70s! Or do we? Christ never mentioned humanism by name, but he did say, "By your words you will be acquitted and by your words you will be condemned" (Mt. 12:37). Need we say more regarding the power of words and the impotency of humanism?

Positive Presence of Unity

At the door to our home is a greeting: ***"Shalom!"*** To the ancient Hebrews it meant "hello", "good-bye", "God with you", "peace", etc. Israel's shalom, however, was only a truce – the cessation of hostilities, not the positive presence of unity. It was replaced by singing angels. Bethlehem's peace was superior to the old shalom because of the person and work of Christ. But unity is not something we inherit from animals! How do we acquire it then? Not by saying confidently, "Here's how you get it." We do that habitually, shaking off our shackles only to be bound by others.

Paul said, "May the God who gives endurance and encouragement give you a spirit of unity among yourselves as you follow Christ Jesus" (Ro. 15:5). We see then that unity is from God, but spiritually dead people can't grasp this. The result is a fragmentation of knowledge, learning, culture, and fellowship, affecting them and the whole world.

Hearts that have been to Calvary are united, not fragmented. As Jonathan Edwards said, "By being united with Christ, we have a more glorious union with (and enjoyment of) God the Father than we otherwise could". This is what unity is all about. The more we're joined with Christ, the more we reflect him! In this mysterious synthesis, we lose much of our authority, but Jesus comes to the rescue, ruling our hearts and minds, and giving us peace.

Unity is so precious that we should be willing to give up almost anything for it. Except Truth! So here are some questions. Have today's oxymoronic myths produced the positive presence of unity? Have they brought harmony to our classrooms, our churches, our seminaries, and our homes? Have they united students and teachers in a bond of peace? Rhetorical questions, you say? No doubt about it! However, if there is discomfort in them, shouldn't we be testing the spirits to see whether they are from God (1 Jn. 4:1)? How else could we Christians influence the world except by being of one mind, one spirit, and one voice, grounded in the Word?

Unlike Christ's shalom, unbelievers are never truly united with believers, so Christians can't expect to be at peace with them. Nor should we count on a cessation of hostilities, since there is yet another aspect to unity. The same Christ Jesus who said, "Peace I leave with you; my peace I give to you" (Jn. 14:27) also said, "Do not suppose that I have come to bring peace to the earth. I did not come to bring peace, but a sword" (Mt. 10:34). Believers can have "the peace of God which transcends all understanding" (Php. 4:7), but unbelievers have only a sword (and a dull one at that)! The reprobate mind is always at war, and the battle will only intensify. But we shouldn't surrender to it, nor should we negotiate a settlement with it, fusing faith with fancy. For oxymoronic hybrids are not only unstable, they're an abandonment of the faith.

Faith is unity, and unity is other-worldly. Therefore, we can't expect to be at peace with fables – not in the classroom, not in the media, and not in any other area. As long as people insist on toying with Scripture, there will be no harmony at all, so we might as well prepare for the inevitable. Truth is an offense to unbelievers, so we must take a stand, even on creation. The fact is, there are major issues that surface *because* we are faithful.

Conflicts are not what we desire, but they will come. In dealing with them, we have this advice from Paul: "Be strong in the Lord and in his mighty power. Put on the full armor of God so that you can take your stand against the devil's schemes. For our struggle is not against flesh and blood, but against the rulers, against the authorities, against the powers of this dark world and against the spiritual forces of evil" (Eph. 6:10-12). This armor (the belt of truth, the sword of the Spirit, the shield of faith, etc.) is not compromising. It holds certain truths to be self evident because of God's *self-revelation*.

Biblical World-view

Stop and think about that! The Bible always assumes, never argues, the Creator's existence. Everything had a beginning, but God has always *been* – and he has *been* what he *still is*. As for his works, he may reveal his fullness or only a glimpse, but he has shown us enough to shut our mouths, for the earth is filled with the knowledge of the glory of the Lord. "Does the clay say to the potter, 'what are you making' (Isa. 45:9)?" "Shall what is formed say to him who formed it, 'Why did you make me like this' (Ro. 9:21)?" Neither may we question God's creativeness, for we have been entrusted with his words (Ro. 3:2). Yet people assign certain things to objectivity and others to metaphysics, ignoring him who knows the past and the future better than we can ever know the present.

Have you considered the Sovereign Lord lately? Isn't he still in charge? Where would you be if God removed his hand from you for just one nanosecond? Why are you still breathing? What regulates the temperature in your body? The answer is, the genius of God and his grace! God planned things so well that "nothing can befall us without the will of our Heavenly Father. (*Heidelberg Catechism*, Q/A 1). His purpose? That we would love and serve him forever.

Whether our lives are hectic or heroic, God is in them all, numbering our days and giving them worth. Nothing can happen without his permission. So superintending is his providence that he causes our hearts to beat, our synapses to fire, and our personalities to rejoice. Why then would we have any hesitation about committing our lives to him?

But we're still dependent creatures. We have a dependent certainty, not always knowing the truth. Though having regenerated hearts, we have fallen brains producing dissonance within us. In our quest for answers, like a drunken mount we keep falling off the other side of the horse. Though having a degree of certainty, there is still that Creator/creature distinction that keeps us dependent upon God. What certainty we have is because we are anchored in Christ, but doesn't that imply some absolutes also? Of course it does, for although we are recipients of nobility, what we do with it has eternal consequences.

Unbelievers have no such connection at all, which is why they are so disconnected from reality. Blinded by their "independence", they blur the Creator/creature distinction even further, as in fish emblems with legs. One sees this also in matriarchy and witchcraft, since the natural mind is darkened (it's corruption pervasive), the problem being that some can no longer see their creatureliness, let alone make their way to the heights from which they have fallen!

Adam's days were numbered when Satan said "do". God had said "don't", but Adam said, "I will decide". From then on Adam began to die, and he became a marshmallow, hiding in the brush. Now he saw things differently. As for his epistemology, how could he *know* that he knew the truth? Was he still a creature of God? All these issues! Ethics, morality, and religion! How should he respond to his Master? Should he come out from behind the bushes? Could he trust his Maker, or should he go with his senses? Did life still have meaning, or would he have to live existentially? Having fallen so far, Adam must have wondered, "What is truth? Am I a fluke of nature? Some cosmic accident?"

In one split second, sin changed everything, so today we have all kinds of issues coming at us. Post-modernists argue that we cannot put these into syllogisms (inferential thoughts invoking the Divine), either inductively or deductively, since truth is not a real concept to the fallen mind. But they end up asking foolish questions: Why God? Why not rebellion? Why not promiscuity, abortion, and euthanasia? These are all illogical queries, of course, since the premise for logic is intelligence, order, and design. More importantly, logic and reason make sense only because God *is*, and because he *is* who he *says* he is. How else could we find the answers to life?

As Kuyper put it, "God is sovereign over every square inch of earth and every second of time." That should silence us, binding us to the Logos rather than the culture of the day. Given Kuyper's words, isn't it clear that the biblical view has a bias allowing no neutrality in morals, ethics, and truth? This might be a slanted view, but so is the world's. Unlike that view, however, Christians can be committed to a perspective that has no need to close off the truth, or the Source. Best of all, we can have life eternal, love, joy, peace, hope, and all the other fruits of the Spirit, providing we're grounded in Truth and bathed in blood.

Reclaiming the University

Darwin argued that one shouldn't expect to see evolution occurring since that would take eons of time. But neo-Darwinists say that evolutionary leaps would take no time at all. Being of at least average intelligence, what am I missing? The answer is *meaningful change*! It doesn't happen! Not in spurts! Not in eons! Not at all! If it *is* happening, shouldn't we be seeing it happening *somewhere*? Shouldn't the real world and that of academia be the *same*?

Why have human/baboon transplants (xenografts) been all but abandoned? Why must we remove all pigishness from porcine heart valves before implanting them into humans? Why irradiate bovine bone, destroying cow cells before implanting them into humans? Because of the "accelerated rejection phenomenon", the hostile encounter between incompatible tissues. Correspondingly, animal implants have given way to synthetics. No matter how carefully we match various species, there are unbridgeable barriers between them. Baboons remain baboons! Pigs remain pigs! Cows remain cows, and humans remain human, whether because of phyla-differences, "knock-out genes", or something else. Except in fictional documentaries, apes never become humans, putting evolution on the run!

Truth is, there is no fairy-god-mother for evolutionists and there isn't one for *theistic* evolutionists either, so people might as well stop claiming the impossible. So fearfully and wonderfully are we made that it tugs at the heart, producing fear even in rebels. Why else would evolutionists be running away from creationists? To be sure, evolutionists have been losing the debates regularly, but shouldn't people of opposing viewpoints be having a dialogue? What are people so afraid of? Could it be the realization that we finally know something about what it takes to build an animal? Or, is it the sanctity embedded in the human soul? No matter one's suppression of *that*, it is inescapable, for God has written it within our being.

The soul is not easily ignored; it is restless until it rests with God. Secularists won't discuss this, nor will they entertain the supernatural. Why not? Because of fear! Fear of losing their colleagues, their respect, their positions, and their grants! Those bucking the trend are treated as outcasts, mocking the openness of learning. To see how this came about, let's begin with Aristotle and the "university". Aristotle encouraged students to dissect worms, but the gentlemen of his day wouldn't dirty their hands, maintaining that there was no purpose in it. In coming years, however, the material universe was ennobled by people of faith and duty, those defining the concept of "university" from the perspective of a Universal Knowledge Source.

During the first millennium AD, people were formulating their doctrines through Councils, Confessions, etc. During the second millennium, there was an intellectual schism, persisting today, due to divergent views on truth. During our millennium, therefore, shouldn't we be repairing the breach, seeing the all-out war over beginnings? This is a battle between believers and unbelievers, between teachers and students, between majorities and minorities – a clash without precedent – one without justification within the concept of "university" (where truth should reign supreme). Truth has been banished! God can still exist in the seminary (though he's losing out there too), but he has been banned from the laboratory. And he can't be mentioned in the classroom except as some "has-been". Given the materialistic take-over in the halls of learning, he is confined to private thinking – no longer welcome in academia. The fact is, Satan has his stronghold in the university, for he has "blinded their eyes and deadened their hearts" (Jn. 12:40).

To recover what built the university in the first place, we must overcome manipulation and fear. Isn't it obvious that the respect of academia and research is contingent on calling something *wrong* when it is *wrong?* Besides, we can do better science knowing its limitations (like the boundaries of fruit-flies). Once people admit this, they can stop worrying about their dying selves and begin saying, "Thy will be done."

Why succumb to the world? Why give creation a twist, based on guesses? Science can neither prove nor disprove evolution any more than it can prove or disprove creation. There are no eyewitnesses for either, yet many discoveries have occurred in today's world convincing even the scholarly of six-day creation. Not only is that interpretation again thinkable, it has become fashionable; thousands of scientists have endorsed it, causing many to revise their positions – but others to squelch the truth.

In a recent book, *In Six Days, Why Fifty Scientists Choose to Believe in Creation,*[5] one can read the testimonies of fifty scientists (university professors and researchers around the globe in Australia, the US, the UK, Canada, South Africa, and Germany) – astrophysicists, geologists, chemists, zoologists, botanists, biologists, and mathematicians – few of them scientific creationists as such. All are convinced of six-day creation because of evidences like the lack of fossil forerunners (there should have been billions of them), ambiguous redshifting (distorting the age of the universe), the conservation of baryon number (stating that particles from energy occur in equal numbers of matter/anti-matter pairs, countering the Bang's extreme dominance of matter over anti-matter), the zircons in Precambrian granite (huge helium concentrations begging the question as to which is more trustworthy, the diffusion of a noble gas in a crystalline lattice, or the radioactive decay of isotopes), etc. But rather than tripping over million dollar words, what was the conclusion? Said they, "Taking the Bible seriously, we must admit that the days of Genesis 1 were **normal days**, there being no scientific need for reinterpreting God's Word."

Why not The Source, then, seeing that we can learn more from God than by swapping DNA modules? Why not sharpen the debate and restore objectivity? Is it too much to hope that our universities will come to their senses? Reclaiming them is worth the effort, since there are still things to be learned about origins, whether in our colleges and universities, or in our seminaries. We live in a world with many freedoms, including academic freedom, but we must stand up for them. So why not support the movement?

Addressing the World

See one, do one, teach one is the mantra of surgery, but it doesn't work for creation. If only we could *see* and *do* creation, we could teach it more convincingly. For those resisting what they know to be true, we read in Romans, "What may be known about God is plain to them because God has made it plain. For, since the creation of the world, God's invisible qualities – his eternal power and divine nature – have been clearly seen, being understood from what has been made, so that men are without excuse" (Ro. 1:18-21). Paul is telling us in these verses that the truth is self-evident.

Do unbelievers know about God? Yes, he has placed that within them as part of his image. Everyone is born with an imprinted conscience, however rudimentary. God speaks so clearly through Creation that they know *him* by *it*.

How do unbelievers know about him? God is like humidity, everywhere present. People have an understanding of him already, but some allow Satan to blind them. Ephesians 4 describes unbelievers as "futile in their thinking; darkened in their understanding, and separated from God, having lost all sensitivity". The emphasis is on what people have *lost*, so they must have had something to surrender initially, namely *Truth*.

What do unbelievers do with their knowledge of God? They suppress it, not because they don't know the truth, but because they want their autonomy.

The Christian faith has long endured the chipping away at authority which is the hallmark of modern academia. But church and campus have never seemed as estranged as with the advent of postmodernism – the notion that there is *no universal truth*, merely competing narratives jockeying for supremacy. So said David Van Biema in *Time*, December 17, 2001.

Post-modernists, unable to see what's happening to them, are in active rebellion, so blinded that they no longer care about Truth. This places them in defiance of everything absolute and eternal. It also makes God indecisive and disposable, rather than sovereign and supreme. How could anyone win arguments with such people? The answer is, we shouldn't even try. We have but to show them the way, since they have deep needs and hurts. We should never be arrogant and we shouldn't argue endlessly. Rather, we must speak the truth in love, upholding everyone in our prayers. After all, lights need not be noisy, they need only to shine!

Post-modernism is antagonistic to the truth, longing to obliterate it, so remember the *antithesis*. Believers will be an offense, but the issue is disbelief (flowing from sin) and only Christ can change that. Man has an ontological problem, for sin has changed his "being", and this can be as real for Christians as for unbelievers. Humanity is no longer innocent before God, and it isn't just a matter of degree. So completely have we fallen that we can no longer distinguish normality. We have a hole in the heart, a defect so sweeping that we shall have to take that into account.

Must we therefore abandon all rationality, leaning on faith alone? Not at all! No matter how great the Fall, it can still be undone, though not by saying, "I'm in control." Instead, we must listen to him who says, "I will help you". Man's mind is thereby renewed as it comes under the authority of God's Word (Ro. 12:2) – not that of competing narratives jockeying for space.

What is Truth then? It is grounded in metaphysics (biblical reality), epistemology (biblical wisdom), and ethics (biblical morality), as attained through the still, small voice of the Spirit. Think of it in this way: Reality is based on God's sovereignty; wisdom on his Word; morality on the full counsel of God. These are all rooted in God's image as reflected in believers. Ultimate knowledge is therefore attainable only through God's self-disclosure, for even Adam had to be told the truth. How else could he have gotten it straight? Not from science and not from society, but from the Word of God! And that's what people need!

Faced with the issues of life, do we really need more information? Not to the extent that some think, since it's not an informational problem. Besides, information has a way of getting people into trouble, as with genetic manipulation, "safe sex", "smart missiles", etc. Even managing the environment has only polluted the world further, angering a lot of people. And modifying human behavior doesn't work either, since people can't agree on the problem.

How about some revised assumptions? Better theories? People latch onto these as if truth depended on them, but they end up with a kind of neutrality endorsing nothing, since their beliefs are based on "evidences" and these are cloaked with uncertainty. So they make up their minds, relinquishing Truth. Believers, on the other hand, know they cannot unravel certain things on their own. Seeing that reason is not neutral at all, they would rather be molded by God than by humanistic speculation.

Even with a theistic slant, **humanism** is always **dehumanizing**. It has its roots in Babel: man's monuments and towers to his own pride and glory! As someone once said, "The word 'ego' comes from **e**dging **G**od **o**ut". In the church we get caught up in this too, with our fancy cars, expensive clothing, and symbols of self- aggrandizement. Why does this happen? Because we're sinners, preoccupied with our own pursuits rather than God's.

Humanism is as much a shaping of the mind as any overt brainwashing. It leads to idolatry, and idolatry leads to immorality. If children are animals, how shall we discipline them? Should we say, "Be like your ancestors, the apes?" What is it that makes them **special**? If they aren't image bearers, who or what will confer morality on them? Will their teaching be biblical, or legislated?

If the past gives us any indication, we're in *Code Red* already. Many are experiencing sorrow because their children have no spiritual capital. Rather than leaving them to entropic decay, rotting in the woods, here are some proverbs from Solomon.

- He who obeys instruction guards his life, but he who is contemptuous of his ways will die.
- The rod of correction imparts wisdom, but a child left to himself disgraces his mother.
- Discipline your son, and he will give you peace; he will bring delight to your soul.
- Listen to advice and accept instruction, and in the end you will be wise.
- He who gets wisdom loves his own soul; he who cherishes understanding prospers.

Garbling the Adam/Ape distinction has impacted our culture severely! The world has spawned a generation of individuals with little faith and less morality. The "me" generation with its blunted spirituality harbors immense hostility toward the God of history. Believers are therefore facing a rerun of Noah's day! But we're also experiencing the best of times. Many are coming to faith, and even the unregenerate are serving God's purposes, albeit in a dark and mysterious way.

Looking into the future, the battle is joined but Truth is the casualty. Children of the '80s are taking over the leadership, but how will they lead and who will help them? Will Truth prevail or will it succumb to total darkness?

When Truth fails it is only a matter of time until the whole facade collapses. One would think that since the information revolution is here, nothing could stop it, but naturalistic totalitarianism is trying its best. No matter the suppression, however, Christians can rejoice. Why? Because Christ will see us through the darkness. Though we too can have problems, faith is our strength, as it was for Christ's disciples. When people saw the faith of Peter and John, realizing that they were unschooled men, they were astonished and took note that these men had been with Jesus (Ac. 4:13).

Like them, we're wise in helping people toward belief. Some might see that as foolishness, but faith is the test, so don't let anyone extinguish your flame! Like a rider on a mount in the middle of the night, have the Spirit in your heart and fire in your eyes!

Listen, my friend. Listen! Turn over the enclaves of your resistance. In this day of spiritual famine, knowing whom you trust and why, stand tall as a child of God and you will find the peace that passes understanding!

Be faithful, even to the point of death,
and I will give you the crown of life.
(Rev. 2:10)

[1] Lester DeKoster, *The Reformed Witness, Theistic Evolution, The Unchanging Issue*, June, 1993. P. 8
[2] J. I. Packer, *Knowing God,* InterVarsity Press, Downers Grove, IL, 1993, p.101
[3] J. I. Packer, *Knowing Christianity,* Harold Shaw Publishers, Wheaton, Illinois, 1995, p. 46
[4] Timothy Ferris, *How Will the Universe End?, Time Magazine,* April 10, 2000, p. 108
[5] John F. Ashton, *In Six Days, Why Fifty Scientists Choose to Believe in Creation* Master Books, 2000

TO THE PRAISE OF GOD'S GLORY
(Chapter 16)

Wisdom's Call

Why do geese fly south for the winter? Why do eagles nest in the heights? How did caterpillars learn to spin their cocoons? Creationists know that God built this into them! Accordingly, the skies are bluer, the birds are cheerier, and the flowers are brighter for believers than for anyone else, since we see them as gifts from the Maker.

Truth is a gift also. "In the past God spoke to our forefathers through the prophets at many times and in various ways, but in these last days he has spoken to us by his Son, whom he appointed heir of all things, and through whom he made the universe. The Son is the radiance of God's glory and the exact representation of his being, sustaining all things by his powerful word" (Heb. 1: 1-3). Creation and providence are clearly the products of Christ's wisdom, leaving no ambiguity regarding the Designer's intelligence. Here is Solomon's version of it:

> I, wisdom, dwell together with prudence; I possess knowledge and discretion. [...] The Lord brought me forth as the first of his works, before his deeds of old; I was appointed from eternity, from the beginning, before the world began. When there were no oceans, I was given birth, when there were no springs abounding with water; before the mountains were settled in place, before the hills, I was given birth, before he made the earth or its fields or any of the dust of the world. I was there when he set the heavens in place, when he marked out the horizon on the face of the deep, when he established the clouds above and fixed securely the fountains of the deep, when he gave the sea its boundary so the waters would not overstep his command, and when he marked out the foundations of the earth. Then I was the craftsman at his side. I was filled with delight day after day, rejoicing always in his presence, rejoicing in his whole world and delighting in mankind. Now, then, my sons, listen to me; blessed are those who keep my ways. Listen to my instruction and be wise; do not ignore it. Blessed is the man who listens to me, watching daily at my doors, waiting at my doorway. For whoever finds me finds *life* and receives favor from the Lord. But whoever fails to find me harms himself – all who hate me love *death* (Pr. 8:12-36).

Those denying wisdom's call can appreciate only a tiny portion of God's Creation. Trivializing the struggle for survival, they see it as normal. Sin, however, changed things drastically, so we must abandon the idea that nature has always been as it is. Things that are harmful today (e.g. tuberculosis bacilli) may have been helpful in the past, and even less dangerous things (worms, lice, rats) still show the purposes of God.

Death, however, has always been abnormal, having reigned from Adam. In this way death came to all men (Ro. 5:12-14). Job saw it "lying naked before God" (Job 26:6). But one day there will be no more death (Rev. 21:4), for he who holds its power (Heb. 2:14) has already destroyed it (2 Ti. 1:10). The last enemy is death itself (1 Co. 15:26), and it will be swallowed up forever (Is. 25:8) by him who holds the keys of death and Hades (Rev. 1:18). The soul will continue into eternity, however, rendering significance to every aspect of life. One day there will be an end to wisdom's call, and it could be at any moment!

Models of Origins

God made everything in a state of completed perfection, by sovereign acts of his will, during six sequential days. When all the arguments are in, this model will prevail since the others don't make sense. People refusing this should go read their Bibles. Interestingly, *scientists* (*not theologians*) seem to be the most instrumental in pointing this out, beating off evolutionary dogma in the process. Theologians, with few exceptions, have been behind the power curve on this.

Creation and evolution cannot both be right since they are mutually exclusive views. Both make predictions which can be compared, but evolutionary theory lacks a foundation, a mechanism, and a workable model. Many are confused by this, stating the argument in terms of Christianity vs. science. Even in the church, some are sounding an uncertain trumpet, making their testimony easily ignored.

The key is a proper understanding of Scripture. No longer bullied by *"science"*, the literal view becomes classy again, leaving its second-class status behind. The door is then open for a clear confession by science and theology, reaffirming the words of Genesis. The touchstone is not ***old earth*** vs. ***young earth*** cosmology, but Wisdom Himself. All models rest on his attributes.

Granting this, presenting the literal account as a testable model is an exciting venture. Employing models capable of making predictions, Christians can influence the scientific community, addressing legitimate concerns that creationists' claims (to be taken seriously) should be offered in testable forms whenever possible. Understand though that ***earth*** and ***life*** sciences lend themselves better to testing than does ***cosmic*** science, given the vagaries of time, space, and early conditions.

The ***biblical model*** would require at least the following:

- Creation days of ordinary length, since God called the light "day" and the darkness "night" (Ge. 1:5)
- Purposeful planning, incorporating intelligence, design, and order
- A relatively young universe appearing during a week of ordinary length
- Chronology and sequence as in Genesis 1
- Early complexity with life-forms appearing promptly
- Functional maturity displaying completed perfection
- Initial immortality for all sentient life
- Immutability of "kinds"
- Humanity starting out with moral rectitude (true knowledge, righteousness, and holiness)
- Meaningful history, beginning and ending with obedience

Admittedly, the six-day model is incompatible with the naturalistic chronology in Chapter 3. However, one has but to scan the scientific literature to realize that the naturalistic view is crumbling. Here are some examples:

- Based on Hubble's unexpected data, scientists are again saying that the universe appeared instantly (from energy in a vacuum), suggesting *ex nihilo* creativity.
- Hubble's findings are shrinking the age of pulsars and nebulae, and some "black holes" are turning out to be galaxies.
- The Hubble telescope shows galaxy formation occurring much earlier than in the standard Bang's scenario.
- Super-clusters (clustered galaxies) are too large, too fast moving, and too "old" to fit with the Bang.
- Cosmologies are again locating the earth at (or near) the center of the universe, raising once more the question of geocentricity. The Bible doesn't require this, but it could be an alternative to the cosmological principle, fitting also with the isotropy of the universe.
- Modern science is discovering that our sun, rather than being an "ordinary star" is a very special star.
- There is mounting mathematical evidence that the gases forming the sun could not have swept today's massive planets into the solar system (fitting with Earth's arriving independently.)
- Differences among various planets (with or without rings) are major and unexplainable by Big Bang cosmogony.
- Scientists suspect that the moon's basaltic flows could not be more than several thousand years old.
- Life depends on the carbon atom, but carbon formation would have required highly improbable happenings: the collision of helium atoms at just the right time and velocity to produce beryllium, and the collision of beryllium and helium at just the right time and velocity to produce carbon atoms, not just a few of them but zillions.
- Carbonaceous substances (kerogens, graphite, apatite, etc.), known to have come from recent biological activity, have been dated at 3.9 billion years.
- Polonium Halos (remnants of radioactivity in granites) indicate a relatively young earth.
- There is still no geologic evidence for pre-biotic soup.
- Blue-green algae could never have arrived under the hostile conditions of naturalism's early earth.
- Fossils in the Burgess Shales in Canada (supposedly from the Mid-Cambrian) reveal that life was more varied and complex in the distant past than it is today, showing no trace of ascendancy.
- The diversity of flowering angiosperms remains to be explained. As Darwin himself admitted, the lack of precursors (primitive plants) is an "abominable mystery".

- Human evolution over millions of years would have meant mountains of bones leading to modern man. Also, today's populations should be exploding if humans traced back a hundred thousand years.
- Douglas Futuyma cites vestigial organs (appendices in humans, pelvic vestiges in pythons, rudimentary eyes in cave animals) as proof that evolution occurred, but vestigial organs seem to have functionality after all.
- *Sahelanthropus tchadensis*, the latest hominid find (supposedly dating to 7 million years) is again and as always without ancestral links.
- DNA suggests that *Neanderthals* were human, though suffering from genetic drift. Also, rickets seems to have deformed their bones.
- Genomic research has failed to bridge the gap between instinct and intellect. The great divide is obviously not between genes and chromosomes, but between animalism and spirituality.

Now that genomes for humans and certain animals have been determined, the race is on with plants. Though early in the game, scientists have already discovered so much complexity and specificity in plants that the uniformitarian chronology in Chapter 3 is again derailed. Given this and the above, six day creation is currently the most robust of all models. It also fits best with the ***anthropic principle***. In other words, the fine-tuning of the universe demands an explanation, and it supports ***creation***, not ***evolution***.

But brace yourself for another revolution (though it may not come about for a generation or two). While Big Bang cosmogony has been dominant for thirty years, it is overdue for revision. The Bang's balloon analogy has caught on, but this is a balloon that has clearly burst! Cosmologists haven't yet figured out what will replace it, but they know it is falling apart! Saving the Bang would in fact require a leap like Gould's punctuated equilibrium!

In biology and physics a ***quantum leap*** means jumping to a higher level without stopping (indeed, without even traveling through) anywhere in between. In the uniformitarian paradigm that is impossible, but with God it is routine. Not surprisingly, such leaps fit beautifully with divine agency, divine concurrence, and divine intervention. They fit also with molecular and cellular biology, whereas that same information contradicts evolution. ***And now that a reasonable, testable case has been made for the supernatural origin of life, all other areas are opened to the literal account***, including cosmic origins, geological origins, human origins, sentience, rationality, and spirituality.

Sequencing of fossil DNA cannot negate the Bible, for God's workmanship is not a matter of science alone. As we have seen, many "evidences" are interpretive at best and dishonest at worst. Those questioning this think it impossible to find room within six days for everything that occurred there, but the frontiers of science are changing that, and theology is catching on (see Ligonier Ministries' *Tabletalk*, July, 2001)! And, yes, evolutionists may see this as "devilishly clever", but it can be to the praise of God's glory! Creation, after all, speaks of God's ***nearness and purpose***, not ***isolation and chance***.

Children of the King

The mountain where I live is very special. Compared with the Himalayas, the Pyrenees, and the Alps, Mount Hermon is a ***holy*** place where many have met their Creator, Savior, and Lord! In this cause and effect world we may think that our blessings are from our own efforts, but God provided them from eternity past. The mind-boggling thing is that he envisioned us from before the world as holy and blameless people. We couldn't have figured this out on our own, so he revealed it to us through the riches of his grace.

Those missing this are missing the A.B.C.s of Christianity – **A**cknowledgment, **B**elief, and **C**onfession – based on God's character and name. The name, "Yahweh" (Jehovah), was considered by the early Hebrews as too holy to be spoken or written. It implies four things: 1) holiness and righteousness, 2) love and mercy, 3) self-existence, and 4) Personhood. "Sabaoth" refers to the Lord of Hosts governing the vast array of the heavenly bodies (Ge. 2:1). In Genesis 32:1, it refers to the hosts of angels, and in the Book of Exodus it refers to the throng of God's people. Combining "Yahweh" with "Sabaoth", we see that God exists in the ***eternal present*** where he owns, controls, and rules everything (from the material to the ethereal).

God also longs for a relationship with his people, based on *a robe, a mansion, and a crown*. Unlike the evolutionary joke, Paul referred to God's kinship with believers in these words:

> Praise be to the God and Father of our Lord Jesus Christ, who has blessed us in the heavenly realms with every spiritual blessing in Christ. For he chose us in him before the creation of the world to be holy and blameless in his sight. In love he predestined us to be adopted as his sons through Jesus Christ, in accordance with his pleasure and will – to the praise of his glorious grace, which he has freely given us in the One he loves. In him we have redemption through his blood, the forgiveness of sins, in accordance with the riches of God's grace that he lavished on us with all wisdom and understanding. And he made known to us the mystery of his will according to his good pleasure, which he purposed in Christ, to be put into effect when the times will have reached their fulfillment – to bring all things in heaven and on earth together under one head, even Christ. In him we were also chosen, having been predestined according to the plan of him who works out everything in conformity with the purpose of his will, in order that we, who were the first to hope in Christ, might be for the praise of his glory. And you also were included in Christ when you heard the word of truth, the gospel of your salvation. Having believed, you were marked in him with a seal, the promised Holy Spirit, who is a deposit guaranteeing our inheritance until the redemption of those who are God's possession – to the praise of his glory (Eph. 1:3-15).

This is one of Paul's most sublime writings, in which he is taking us into the heavenly realms, showing us God's purpose and grace. Grace has been described as "God's riches at Christ's expense"! My future is sealed with the guarantee of God's Spirit, so now I can live to the praise of his glory! Here is the hope of the Christian, since Christ clothed himself in frailty to cover our sins! Isn't it sad that this is reprehensible to so many, even in the church?

As someone once said, "The purpose of theology is doxology", and the same could be said of science. In other words, a proper understanding of nature and the Word always results in praise! There is more to God's riches, however. Seeing in nature some glimpses from Eden, it holds the power to catch my breath. When I see the dew on Mount Hermon, the snow on Big Bear, the moon over the Pacific – when I awaken to the desert sun with my grandchildren – that is when I experience the stillness of fellowship.

Nature, however, isn't synonymous with God. But who would have known this simply by saying some mantra or worshiping a cow? Who would have known the Creator by bowing down to the stars or being awed by DNA? These will all disappear, and what will happen to Pantheism then? How could its mantras add luster to Christ when they throw him to the wind?

Why did God give me so much more than that? Why all this beauty, joy, and fellowship? For one reason: To lead me to his glory! When I enjoy my Creator, it blesses him too. Imagine that! God blesses me and I can bless him! What's more, he is planning a bride for his Son, having selecting me for his crown! Oh, the lavishness of it all! When Christ makes up his jewels, believers will add luster to him. We ourselves can't brighten him, but he will make us like many-faceted diamonds, and Yahweh Sabaoth will be glorified through us from eternity to eternity!

How blessed are we who call our Father "Abba" (Heavenly "Daddy")! Christ, however, didn't call out from the Cross, "Abba Father", but rather, "My God, my God." Why? Because God forsook *him* for *us*, and no longer is it sacrilegious to call him "Yahweh". "The Spirit himself testifies with our spirit that we are God's children. Now if we are children, then we are heirs – heirs of God and co-heirs with Christ, if indeed we share in his sufferings in order that we may also share in his glory" (Ro. 8:16,17). The fact is, we are not just heirs, but co-heirs, since God's glory is inherited by *us*! The Christian's inheritance will be God himself, and we shall be with him forever (Ps. 73)!

Not only that, but the servants of Christ are in for a surprise! Luke wrote, "I tell you the truth, Christ will dress himself to serve, will have us recline at the table, and will come and wait on them" (Lk. 12: 37). Did you catch that? *Christ* will wait on *us!* In stark contrast, Hell is separation from the God-head forever. Redeeming grace can prevent that, however. And how can I be so sure about that? Because Jesus told his disciples, "Heaven and earth will pass away, but the Word of God will never pass away (Mt. 24:35). "Oh, the depth of the riches of the wisdom of God! How unsearchable are his judgments and his paths beyond tracing out! [...] Who has ever given to God that God should repay him? [...] To him be the glory forever" (Ro. 11:33-36)!

"Be Still and Know"

Mary's cousin, Elizabeth, said, "Why am I so favored that the mother of my Lord should come to me?"   Mary replied:

> My soul glorifies the Lord and my spirit rejoices in God my Savior, for he has been mindful of the humble state of his servant. From now on all generations will call me blessed, for the Mighty One has done great things for me. Holy is his name. His mercy extends to those who fear him, from generation to generation. He has performed mighty deeds with his arm; he has scattered those who are proud in their inmost thoughts. He has brought down rulers from their thrones but has lifted up the humble. He has filled the hungry with good things but has sent the rich away empty. He has helped his servant Israel, remembering to be merciful to Abraham and his descendants forever even as he said to our fathers (Lk. 1:46-56).

Reflecting on these words, I see Mary as a maiden of wisdom, honoring her Lord from an early age. Worshiping God in the beauty of his holiness, she said what she said, but she didn't shout it. She might not have been the greatest cheerleader at "Hebrew High", but she was filled with her Savior. Hers were the poetic words of a humble Jewish girl who spoke spontaneously, providing us with the picture of an obedient person. Though knowing that she would give birth to the long-expected Messiah, Mary was self-effacing, for she rejoiced in what her Savior would do *for* her. Expressing her wonder, she remained submissive. And when she stopped speaking there must have been total silence, for she rejoiced in Christ, not in herself. How unlike the Pharisees of old, who lengthened their tassels to be seen by the crowd.

The psalmist wrote, "Be still and know that I am God" (Ps. 46:10). Like him, Mary was struggling with mystery, unable to grasp the incarnation. What she knew affected her so profoundly that she worshiped God in the fullness of her person. Wouldn't it be wonderful if today's scholars would turn to him in the same way? Many have lengthened their tassels, priding themselves in their intellects. Perhaps we should say to them, "Confronted with *the Logos*, what is the locus of *your* intelligence? Do you really want to bully those bringing God into the equation? Don't you know that conceit kills learning, as does fear? And how about your soul?"

Standing at the threshold of a new era, the study of the cosmos has barely begun. Hubble's Space Telescope is one of the grandest ventures ever, but in coming years NASA will be developing its Next Generation Space Telescope to learn more about how galaxies were assembled. With a mirror ten times the size of Hubble's, the NGST (orbiting the sun) will offer resolutions beyond any ever attempted. And in decades to come, another probe (the "Terrestrial Planet Finder") is slated for roll-out. Unlike its predecessors, it will be a cold space telescope with many components, each larger than Hubble's, producing sharper images by far.

In terms of their sophistication, these projects are like the lunar lander! Speaking of that, if the photos from space did nothing else, they demonstrated the insignificance of humans on the grand scale of things. When I see pictures from the moon, I ask myself, "Where am I on Earth's globe?" You couldn't find me, that's how small I am! King David must have felt that way too, for he said, "When I consider your heavens, the work of your fingers, the moon and the stars which you have set in place, what is man that you are mindful of him?" (Ps. 8:3-4) Yet out of the vastness of God's universe, he noticed me – *and you* – out of his own free will, and for no other reason. Therefore, be still and know!

Radiating the Son

Who was Mary? A teen-aged girl in a day when women were considered uneducable, a nobody in the grand scheme of things and hardly relevant to the march of history. She wasn't the Queen of Sheba and she wasn't Pharaoh's daughter either. Had it not been for her Son, she would have died unnoticed except for a few close friends and her immediate family. Yet, in her humble state she acclaimed God as the Author and Historian of everything – the one who had noticed her and all humanity. In response to God's great mercy, Mary wanted to please her Master.

Have you thought of what pleases God? What makes him happy? Those who know and honor him, of course! As a believer, have you stopped to think that, because you are Christ's, God is delighted? It cost him *everything* to come down the stairway of the stars to a feeding trough, and yet he was obedient to the Cross! Oh, the marvels of his grace, for he looked on all that he had made and all that he had treasured and he was satisfied. The redeemed will therefore be "Exibit A", and Christ will say of them, "This is what my grace did for poor, guilty, lost sinners."

When everything is said and done, Jesus will be the focus, but he will brighten us too, so that even our darkest corners will shine like the noonday sun! The question is, has anyone ever looked at you and commented on your sunny disposition? How about your spirituality? Did you know that your appearance can be to the praise of God? Spending time with him is what makes that happen. Think about "snowbirds" spending months where winter is unknown. Returning to their northern climes, the usual comment is, "Don't you look great!" Why are they so radiant? Because the sun has been shining on them! So how about reflecting Christ in the same way?

For this to occur, we must be in the presence of God's Son over a period of time. The closer we get him, the more we will see our need. However, we can't even imagine the enormity of the Cross. For that, remember that Christ left the Courts of Heaven where there is neither death nor decay to die at the hands of sinners, the very agents that produced these horrible things to begin with! To see the enormity of *that*, we need to know who we are, who Jesus is, and what we have done to his world.

Taste of Home

Only one life, 'twill soon be past, only what's done for Christ will last.

My mother-in-law, a godly saint, lived in a nursing home for years. When asked about loneliness, she would always reply, "Never lonely, never bored", to which our children would respond, "Never sad, mad, or bad". How very different from the atheist strolling through the woods, admiring everything that the "*evolutionary accident*" produced. Lonely and detached, he mutters to himself, "Why do I feel like I've missed out on Christmas? Could it be that nobody cares?"

What a shame to see the world only through evolutionary eyes. Darwin, Sagan, and Gould all had their moments of fame, but they were more interested in the god whom they had created than the God who created them – more attracted to *their* way than *the* way. Like all humanity, they will be judged by God's standard. Is God an ogre, then? Not at all! "The ordinances of the Lord are sure and altogether righteous. They are more precious than gold, than much pure gold; they are sweeter than honey, than honey from the comb. [...] In keeping them there is great reward" (Ps. 19:10-12).

God is the God of promises, and there are thousands of them in the Bible. Seeing how he cares for seemingly insignificant creatures, I know he cares for me. What could be better than having the *God of the Universe* caring for us? But eternal life is not just a matter of going to heaven some day. Already now we can have a foretaste of it! Yes, there things I would like to see and do before I pass on, but here on Earth we have only a *taste of home*. "For we know in part and we prophesy in part, but when perfection comes, the imperfect disappears." Now we see but a poor reflection as in a mirror, but then we shall see face to face (1 Co. 13:9-12).

As to whether or not Adam might have splintered his thumb while dressing the Garden, I can only guess. However, following the Fall there is no record that he did anything but complain. Job lamented, "Man born of woman is of few days and full of trouble. He springs up like a flower and withers away; like a fleeting shadow, he does not endure" (Job 14: 1, 2). Like Job, we know all too well that our days are numbered, since God has set limits we cannot exceed. Thousands (even millions) of our cells are dying daily, so it will be only a short time until someone will look down on us and say, "Doesn't he (or she) look natural?" At that moment, we will be sold on God's incomprehensibility, immutability, and eternality!

God is loving, as he is frequently portrayed, but the wages of sin are still "death". Who would have expected the Twin Towers to fall? Klebold and Harris, Columbine and Cassie: these have entered our culture and will be with us for a long time. The question is not whether you and yours are safe or in control, but are you **ready**? You may be a homemaker or a truck-driver – a caretaker, a carpenter, or a computer-whiz. You may not see yourself as a big-time player in the game of life, but your uniqueness is not in yourself, and life is not a game. The gift within you is precious, so guard it well. In this world of six billion people, 145,000 will pass into eternity every day, and each of us is but a breath away from the Creator.

On a lighter note, someone once said: "To live above with saints we love, oh that will be such glory! But to live below with folks we know, well that's a different story!" Yet how else will people get a glimpse of God unless they see him in *us*? Isn't that what imaging is all about? Harmony with others is the hallmark of God's people, and it makes our testimony credible.

Moreover, when the Spirit shines into darkened hearts, things begin to happen! Andrew Reed (1787-1862), a London pastor, founded six hospitals. When his son set out to write his father's biography, Andrew responded, "I was born yesterday; I shall die tomorrow; I must not spend today in telling what I have done, but in doing what I may for Him who has done so much for me." The message is that we must get on with it! A bumper sticker says it well: One person can make a difference – Jesus did!

The debates over origins will go on until the end of time, but remember this:

- Creation was a one time event, a singularity.
- We must see evolutionary propaganda for what it is: propaganda, not truth.
- Man's knowledge is primarily deductive, and severely limited; God's is inductive, innate, and boundless. God never searches his hard-drive for information, nor does his computer crash. King David said, "Such knowledge is too wonderful for me, too lofty for me to attain" (Ps. 139:6).
- Seeing isn't always believing, but believing can be seeing. The facts will be proven by "rightly dividing the Word of Truth" (meaning a *straight cut*, as in 2 Ti. 2:15, KJV).
- Creation is the foundation for all other doctrines. If God lacked the power to create supernaturally, he will never have the power to raise us again.
- God is a God of infinite detail, especially in creation.
- Without the fall of a *perfect* creation, Christ's death would have been the most senseless act in history.
- The future of Planet Earth isn't nearly as important as the future of its inhabitants.
- Wheat and tares (weeds) will grow together until the harvest, which is why Jesus spoke in parables.
- People like fences, but God wants them down when they become barriers to the truth.
- Christians can trash evolutionary scenarios with a few incendiary comments, but rather than rising up foaming at the mouth, we must be completely humble and gentle, patient, bearing with one another in love, making every effort to keep the unity of the Spirit through the bond of peace (Eph. 1:1-4).
- Knowledge puffs up, but love builds up (1 Co. 8:1). Arguments for the sake of argument are thus of little value. Rather than a barrage of "opinion" there is a gentle, effective way for the Spirit to work in hearts. "The wisdom from heaven is first of all pure; then peace-loving, considerate, full of mercy and good fruit, impartial and sincere. [and] Peacemakers sowing in peace raise a harvest of righteousness" (Jas. 3:17-18).

Whether seeing creation literally or not, there will be a literal heaven and a literal hell, so I pray that my words will incline some toward heaven. For those on that path, to each of us grace has been given as Christ apportioned it, but we must speak truthfully, for we are all members of one body (Eph. 4: 7, 25).

Having reached the end of this book, I'm reminded of my clay pot-ness. Yet, poor though I am in God's sight, he has set eternity in my heart. I matter so much to him that he is concerned when I stumble, when I stop, and when I stray. In return, I must tell others that God matters to me. With his Word in my heart and his world before my eyes, knowing that he calls me to win souls (not arguments), may his grace reach out to you through these pages. And may we, together with all believers, experience the joy of the banquet, for our Savior will be there!

May the God of Creation, the God of the Cross, and the God of history give you knowledge, wisdom, and understanding. If you trust him, your name is already in his book, for before creating you he determined to save you – and he will manage your circumstances as well. "And this is my prayer: that your love may abound more and more in knowledge and depth of insight, so that you may be able to discern what is best and may be pure and blameless until the day of Christ, filled with the fruit of righteousness that comes through Jesus Christ – to the glory and praise of God" (Phl. 1:9-10).

Father: In the presence of all that you have created, help me to be still and know that you are God. In the quiet of this day, may nothing hold back the praise of my lips. Reclaim what is yours and let me be a wise steward of all that you have entrusted to my care – true to your Word, your world, and your will, no matter the cost. Help me to trust you, saying with the living creatures around your throne, "Holy, holy, holy is the Lord God Almighty, who was, and is, and is to come!" May the words of my mouth and the meditations of my heart be acceptable in your sight, oh Lord, my Rock and my Redeemer.

O Lord my God, when I in awesome wonder
consider all the worlds thy hands have made
I see the stars, I hear the rolling thunder,
thy power throughout the universe displayed:

But when I think that God, his Son not sparing,
sent him to die, I scarce can take it in,
that on the cross my burden gladly bearing
he bled and died to take away my sin:

Then sings my soul, my Savior God to thee:
how great thou art, how great thou art!
Then sings my soul, my Savior God to thee:
how great thou art, how great thou art!

(Stuart K. Hine, 1949)

Epilogue

Most people love their pets! Imagine saying to yourself, "I'd like a closer relationship with my pet beagle, so why not become a dog?" Were such a transformation actually possible, it would produce an unbreakable bond!

Did you know that Christ Jesus became human for believers? Out of his boundless love, he became one of us! But his becoming human is incomparable with your becoming an animal! Why? Because Jesus crossed the gulf between God and man, a chasm so immense that it dwarfs the separation between any of his creatures. He also gave his life so that we might be with him eternally!

To grasp the enormity of that, think about Christ's blood! Look also BEYOND intelligent design to him who bridged the gap. Then, let him take over your life, to the praise of his glory!

WA